MW01710839

Cosmology of the Divine Form

A Bible History of the Occult

Matthew T. Nimegeers

Matthew Nimegeers
3-61 Woodland Dr.
Hay River, NT X0E-0R8
mnimegeers@northwestel.net
TO ORDER 1-301-631-9073

PublishAmerica
Baltimore

First printing

ISBN: 1-4241-2178-7
PUBLISHED BY PUBLISHAMERICA, LLLP
www.publishamerica.com
Baltimore

Printed in the United States of America

Dedicated to my Mother and my Father who encouraged me in my interest in religion and history

Contents

NB: Words and phrases followed by an asterisk* in the text are explained in the Glossary of terms at the end of the book.

All Biblical quotations are taken from The Holy Bible Old and New Testaments In The King James Version
(Thomas Nelson INC, Nashville, USA 1972 ed.)

Introduction

The initial research and discovery that went into *Cosmology of the Divine Form*, rather than being written as the result of some formal plan or idea, was based primarily on the systematic study of Bible scripture originating with sound and fundamental Bible principles. As with any creative endeavor, the sequence of formulating a written work involves arranging and rearranging material to better accommodate one's process of understanding towards the writer's motivation and purpose. From this standpoint, in what might be similar to the methods of other authors, this introduction was written last. Concurrently, since *Cosmology of the Divine Form* is essentially based on a drastically new perspective of Bible history, the personal observations of such a retrospective should be helpful in explaining how the discovery of this new look at history came about.

As was stated earlier, the journey into this discovery, ironically, was not originally identified for its historical significance. Thus, if anything can be learned from the experience of performing this Bible research, the primary lesson would be that the Bible is firstly a theological book with its historical content based entirely on unlocking certain fundamental theological principles. It is within the context of revealing these mysteries that a new historical perspective comes about. The backbone of this history rests on the cause and effect relationship of these Bible principles, which, when framed together, shows forth an ancient cosmology that essentially explains mankind's destiny. This is the reasoning behind this treatise's chosen title, *The Cosmology of the Divine Form.*

While much of this treatise is based on spiritual insights, the bulk of this work is aimed at sorting through age-old superstitions, and is based, as far as possible on dispelling certain myths. The surprising new fact-finding direction that subsequently arises more than makes up for the stripping away of imaginations that have long thwarted an accurate understanding of scripture. Despite the revelation of many facts, a true faith in God's existence and interaction in the world of men is not extinguished; rather the reality of God's miraculous word is authenticated time and time again. Further to this experience, *Cosmology of the Divine Form* takes the reader on a round trip journey, investigating the language, geography, archeology, and ancient customs of a people that were frequently divided in their approach to God's divine wisdom.

Without further adieu, despite the far reaching implications of the initial chapter, to which the theology behind the resurrection is thoroughly explored, *Cosmology of the Divine Form* explains the opposition of a divisive spirituality known to exist from the dawn of creation, where the escalating details of subtle facts clearly exposes this controversy for all to see. Though this treatise, remarkably, was written by an individual with no real academic credentials to his credit, the combined detail of insights and facts is all the more reason to believe in God's ability to reveal scripture in the form and the time of his choosing.

In modern times theologians have been unduly influenced by society's historical and scientific applications for the formulating of their theological constructs. This has resulted in a linear based understanding of God's word that was never intended. *Cosmology of the Divine Form* is an account of my personal attempt to probe certain mysteries based on the absolute logic of God's spoken word. By exploring certain Biblical precepts in prescribed sequence the reader will be encouraged to transcend the limits that this linear perspective has imposed. It is my intention that such an investigation will inspire further speculation into Bible history with it's rightful application in mind and that the original values and beliefs of the early church will be expounded. I challenge the willing reader to remain open as boundless historical and Biblical issues are investigated.

This treatise however is not for the light-hearted, but for those with a desire to probe the deeper Bible mysteries while keeping an open mind. It includes a definitive look at prophecy in the context of Christian thought as well as an investigation into the nature of the antichrist and the false prophet.

I

The Truth About the Resurrection

It is often said that the true cornerstone of the Christian faith is one's belief in the death and resurrection* of Jesus Christ. According to Bible history; Jesus was put to death by crucifixion on the cross of Calvary. Later, after his body was placed in a tomb where it stayed for three days, it is traditionally held that Jesus was raised from the dead by a miraculous transformation. The foundational teachings of the Christian church are perhaps best defined by these events. Though scripture clearly supports this claim, beyond the face-value miracle of the resurrection the significance that the resurrection poses in relation to the preceding thousands of years of spiritual thought often goes overlooked for its theological value. When it comes to the fundamental belief of the resurrection, the true connection with the preexisting framework of Old Testament theology is rarely identified or explored.

In truth, the intrinsic theological value of the resurrection is as elaborate and grandiose a design as creation itself and must not be overlooked for its theological worth. Even the disciples themselves were not persuaded or fully indoctrinated till after Jesus of Nazareth had died and was resurrected. It was in the midst of the revelation of Christ's resurrection that all power and authority was finally activated on behalf of Christ's followers so that the legacy of the Christ's death and resurrection could continue. In the gospel of John, when Jesus says, "I am the way the truth and the life, no one comes to the father except through me," one may conclude that Jesus and his teaching is the starting point when it comes to establishing a true relationship with God the Father. The logical beginning of this treatise, therefore, may be sought at its simplest, most compelling beginning, in the gospel that comes most highly recommended even to new Christians. "In the beginning was the word and the word was with God, and the word was God..." so begins the gospel of John.

The gospel according to John is unparalleled when it comes to its regard and Biblical teaching surrounding Christ's death and resurrection. This is because John's gospel provides one with teaching surrounding the subject of Christ's coming death and resurrection in Jesus' own words, spoken even before the events were to take place. The truth of the gospel presented here is perhaps the first instance where one's linear way of thinking is challenged.

John is recognized as being Christ's beloved disciple(1) and has been linked with John the Baptist and the John of the book of Revelations. Historians and other authorities on the subject link John the apostle as well as John the Baptist to a small religious movement on the plains of Megiddo in a place known as Qumran.(2) Poised to rival the theological virtues of the mainstream Temple, the Essences* may lay claim to teachings on the Kingdom of God,(3) and the notion of eternal life, a notion that was refuted by the mainstream. In fact despite the intervention of celebrated prophets the likes of Ezekiel and Daniel, historians claim that it is likely that the Sadducees had true authority over this mainstream religion.(4) These are the same Sadducees who would deny, by their doctrine, that there ever was or ever would be a resurrection of any kind. It is with in such a context that we may begin to understand that the truths which are now so widely respected were at one time much more obscure, passed down by a mere remnant of God's people rather than the mainstream.

The Anointed Christ

Upon closer examination it may be seen that the rudiments of all Christian thought may be traced to earlier Bible principles and precepts laid out in the Old Testament. It is therefore necessary to examine the fundamental significance and meaning of the term 'Christ' as it is substantiated in scripture. The gospel of John includes Jesus' teachings on what it means to be the 'Christ'*. It is here that one will soon discover how the words 'resurrection' and 'Christ' have a definite and consistent correlation.

The word *Christ** means "the anointed one." The book of Leviticus in the Old Testament describes how the sacred articles that were anointed for God's service(5) had a divine purpose. The power of the anointing upon these select articles was supernatural and cannot be understated. To the holy people of Israel, God's anointed purposes were infallible and certain to be fulfilled. In other words, if a purpose truly originated from God, it was reasonably understood that it would eventually return to God for its fulfillment. With this principle in mind, the concept of eternal life is not difficult to grasp since for the office of the anointed Christ, dominion over death would be a prerequisite in fulfilling such a purpose. Accordingly, in ancient scripture the expectancy of the divine role of the coming Christ was of primary importance. The Christ or anointed one may well have been considered the fixed origin and source of all of God's anointed purposes as well as the point of convergence to which all predetermined purposes return. This notion will be explained further in later Chapters.

Jesus says at the beginning of his teaching,
John 3 vs. 13...
And no man hath ascended up to heaven but he that came down from heaven, even the Son of man which is in heaven.
14 And as Moses lifted up the serpent in the wilderness, even so must the Son of man be lifted up.

Jesus, through his own admonition demonstrates a more abstract form of expression in this revealing prophecy pertaining to his death resurrection and eventual ascension into heaven. This three-fold ministry is reiterated throughout the gospel of John in what may be perceived as a subtle more inconspicuous form. Each reference supports Jesus of Nazareth's claim to being the chosen Christ. Furthermore, faith in the death and resurrection of Christ is stated as a requirement for the salvation of any believer. (Romans 10 vs. 9)

Jesus, the Only Son of God

To render a deeper application of this realization, is to embark on a journey whereby gaining a new perspective on Christ's ministry is possible. Since the mind of Christ is ultimately divine, Jesus inevitably arrives at this mode of preaching. Jesus consistently demonstrates how his mind and subsequent words transcends time. The gospel is an invitation to partake in the same mind set as a necessary preparation to enter into eternal life with Christ. The ultimate revelation comes when all of God's word is explored through the looking glass of the resurrection and mysteries of both the Old and New Testament are consequently unraveled.

John 6 vs. 27

Labor not for meat which perisheth, but for that meat which endureth unto everlasting life, which the Son of man shall give unto you: for him hath God the father sealed.

32 Then Jesus said unto them, Verily, verily, I say unto you, Moses gave you not that bread from heaven; but my Father giveth you the true bread from heaven.

33 For the bread of God is he which cometh down from heaven, and giveth life unto the world.

35 And Jesus said unto them, I am the bread of life: he that cometh to me shall never hunger; and he that believes in me shall never thirst.

40 And this is the will of him that sent me, that every one which seeth the son and believeth on him, may have everlasting life: and I will raise him up on the last day.

If many of our present day theologians had heard Jesus claim that he was the Son of God, such a claim would most likely be dismissed as blasphemy. Upon closer examination the value to such a claim is no longer dismissed, but to the contrary, the personality of Jesus Christ is seen as poised to fulfill scripture in the next, most logical revelation, set with in an ancient framework of theological thought. Later in this treatise additional proof will be submitted that would suggest how even the prophets of old had gained universal awareness of this revelation. Originally, the gravity of such a belief with its far reaching implications may have challenged the faith of Jesus' followers, yet, what prevails is a endurably sound foundation in scripture firmly grounded in the spiritual tradition of the day.

Thus, the theological connotations of Jesus' statement as being the Son of God* had definite theological value when one considers what was meant when the statement was first made.

Matthew 16 vs. 15

He saith unto them, But whom say ye that I am?

16 And Simon Peter answered and said, Thou art the Christ, the Son of the living God.
17 And Jesus answered and said unto him, Blessed art thou, Simon Bar-jo'na: for flesh and blood hath not revealed it unto thee, but my Father which is in heaven.
18 And I say also unto thee, That thou art Peter, and upon this rock I will build my church; and the gates of hell shall not prevail against it.
19 And I will give unto thee the keys of the kingdom of heaven: and whatsoever thou shalt bind on earth shall be bound in heaven: and whatsoever thou shalt loose on earth shall be loosed in heaven.
20 Then charged he his disciples that they should tell no man that he was Jesus the Christ.
21 From that time forth began Jesus to shew unto his disciples, how that he must go unto Jerusalem, and suffer many things of the elders and chief priests and scribes, and be killed, and be raised again the third day.

Jesus clearly felt that Peter's ability to identify him as being the Son of God came as a result of a God-given revelation. Upon further scrutiny, it is noteworthy that Jesus also states the importance of remaining inconspicuous and how certain events must transpire in the near future for this to come to pass. What Jesus was subtly implying was that the realization of the revelation of his son-ship rested on his success in carrying out his mission to its ultimate fulfillment...his death and resurrection. This theory is further supported since, when Peter denounces Jesus' prediction of his death and resurrection, Peter, who was called blessed by Jesus in previous passages, is at once degraded to Satan.

Matthew 16 vs. 22

Then Peter took him, and began to rebuke him, saying, be it far from thee, Lord: this shall not be unto thee.

23 But he turned, and said unto Peter, Get thee behind me, Satan: thou art an offence unto me: for thou savourest not the things that be of God, but those that be of men.

The possibility of an intended connection between the son-ship of Jesus and his resurrection should be identified in order for other mysteries to be revealed. From this point onward this treatise will investigate the likelihood that the belief in Jesus as God's son is based on the unique transformation that occurred at the time of his resurrection. Understanding the nature of this transformation, as will soon be addressed, is the key to unlocking boundless mysteries. Such a transformation, by its inherent nature, would seem to fit into the profile stipulated by the prophetic utterances and precepts of old. Even Jesus himself makes this connection while explaining how our ability to become children of God coincides with our ability to become children of the resurrection.

In the following passages Jesus is explaining to the Sadducees* how at the time of the coming resurrection the institution of marriage will become obsolete and for those individuals worthy of this resurrection they will attain a new nature as children of God.

Luke 20 vs. 34

And Jesus answering said unto them, The children of this world marry, and are given in marriage:

35 But they which shall be accounted worthy to obtain that world, and the resurrection from the dead, neither marry, nor are given in marriage:

36 Neither can they die any more: for they are equal unto the angels; and are children of God, being children of the resurrection.

Saul, later known as Paul the Apostle, was reputed to submit to the Sanhedrin* and was counted among the Pharisaical teaching class. (Acts 9 vs. 1) Paul, who would have been well versed in the religious teachings of the times explains his take on the new indoctrination he has received as described in the opening lines of his letter to the Romans.

Romans 1 vs. 1

Paul, a servant of Jesus Christ, called to be an apostle, separated unto the gospel of God,

2 (Which he had promised afore by his prophets in the holy scriptures,)

3 Concerning his Son Jesus Christ our Lord, which was made of the seed of David according to the flesh;

4 And declared to be the Son of God with power, according to the spirit of holiness, by the resurrection from the dead:

Citing various sources of scripture adds to the reality of the doctrinal connection between Christ's resurrection and his son-ship. Further, upon closer observation various scriptures seem to endeavor to explain the connection that Christ's son-ship* has in relation to the resurrection and how this revelation inevitably completes scripture. The ease in which all other precepts, insights and revelations in scripture may be jointly fit together as a result of this belief lends credence to this theory.

An explanation of how this understanding is effectively engaged may be examined further in Paul's exposition of Jesus Christ's resurrection and transformation.

Colossians 1 vs. 13
Who hath delivered us from the power of darkness, and hath translated us into the kingdom of his dear Son:
14 In whom we have redemption through his blood, even the forgiveness of sins:
15 Who is the image of the invisible God, the firstborn of every creature:
16 For by him were all things created, that are in heaven, and that are in earth, visible and invisible, whether they be thrones, or dominions, or principalities, or powers: all things were created by him and for him:
17 And he is before all things, and by him all things consist.
18 And he is the head of the body, the church: who is the beginning, the firstborn from the dead; that in all things he might have the preeminence.

The word preeminence* denotes Christ's place of priority in time, as well as authority, where he (meaning Christ) is engaged in this reality as the first-born from the dead. One may therefore surmise that a physical transformation occurred at the point of the resurrection that enabled Christ in his new glorified body to transcend time because of his new nature. In this primordial existence Christ Jesus became the substance and guiding feature of all things that were created. Christ's personality was then fastened as a permanent 'fixture' of inspiration to the holy prophets down through the ages as a reminder of his coming in the flesh.

When a credible connection between Christ's son-hip and resurrection is finally made, one is likely to come away with a teaching that is far reaching in it's implications, the breadth of which was poised to be explored further by Christ's disciples later on in the New Testament. Christ's teachings and consequent revelation was set to trigger a chain reaction sending a shock wave of epic proportions through the established religious authority of the day. Christ's doctrine implied a method of salvation that no longer depended on race or nationality, a realization, which the Sanhedrin found most troublesome. Thus, since Christ's resurrection power was recognized as a credible challenge to the Sadducees doctrinal footing, the Sanhedrin found it expedient to disengage the situation as quickly as possible.

John 11 vs. 47
Then gathered the chief priests and the Pharisees a council, and said, what do we? For this man doeth many miracles.
48 If we let him thus alone, all men will believe on him: and the Romans shall come and take away both our place and nation.
49 And one of them named Ca'ia-phas, being the high priest that same year, said unto them ye know nothing at all,
50 Nor consider that it is expedient for us, that one man should die for the people, and that the whole nation perish not.
51 And this spake he not of himself: but being high priest that year, he prophesied that Jesus should die for that nation;
52 And not for that nation only, but that also he should gather together in one the children of God that were scattered abroad.

This scripture, as it points to the motivation behind Christ's eventual crucifixion, clearly suggests that Jesus had credibility with the Sanhedrin. The unsettling turn of events set to follow invites speculation concerning the possible origin of the cosmological forces at work. The Sanhedrin was perhaps even more appalled by the realization that this unique revelation was implacably not devised by the wisdom of man, rather, it was suggestive of God's wisdom and handiwork.

St. Peter's Revelation and Testimony

When the revelation of Christ's son-ship is first identified and Simon Peter is poised to engage in this knowledge, Jesus gives Simon (Peter) his new name. Peter which means "the rock" is an appropriate name since it substantiates the many prophetic references pertaining to the rock of revelation written in Old Testament scripture. Identifying with scripture in this way reinforces the tremendous spiritual authority and privilege offered to Peter by Jesus. Along with this revelation Peter was promised authority with in Christ's Church.

Matthew 16 vs. 15
He saith unto them, But whom say ye that I am?
16 And Simon Peter answered and said, Thou art the Christ, the Son of the living God.
17 And Jesus answered and said unto him, Blessed art thou, Simon Bar-jo'na: for flesh and blood hath not revealed it unto thee, but my Father which is in heaven.

18 And I say also unto thee, That thou art Peter, and upon this rock I will build my church; and the gates of hell shall not prevail against it.
19 And I will give unto thee the keys of the kingdom of heaven: and whatsoever thou shalt bind on earth shall be bound in heaven: and whatsoever thou shalt loose on earth shall be loosed in heaven.
20 Then charged he his disciples that they should tell no man that he was Jesus the Christ.
21 From that time forth began Jesus to shew unto his disciples, how that he must go unto Jerusalem, and suffer many things of the elders and chief priests and scribes, and be killed, and be raised again the third day.

From this passage of scripture it may be deduced that St. Peter was chosen as the custodian of this revelation (the revelation of Christ's son-ship,) a designation that came with obvious authority. With the implications of such an appointment, it is considerable that Peter's subsequent words and testimony would support his claim to this custodianship. Scripture attributed to St. Peter is, therefore, a logical point of research regarding this deduction. Finally, if Peter did have license over teaching this revelation, then the existence of some form of generativity* does bare further investigation.

The accurate exploration of these questions and possibilities will consolidate the argument that a secret revelation and knowledge based on the resurrection does indeed exist. Accordingly, Peter's formal Jewish beliefs were in a position to be either contradicted or reinforced. Thus, both Old and New Testament concepts may be aptly and soundly explored in this context.

A Truly Prophetic Revelation

One documented fact, an aspect of Peter's testimony, is that the knowledge of Christ and his resurrection from the dead is essential in the realm of all prophecy. In fact, according to scripture, it is implied that all prophets, dating back to King David and beyond, shared a common working knowledge and belief in Christ and his resurrection. This privileged knowledge holds with it many mysteries and is identified as the token proof and prerequisite stipulated for all legitimate prophecy. The obvious importance of the message of Christ's resurrection in the ministry of the gospel is further proof of this theory. This prophetic link, detailed in the following scripture, seems to stand as an invitation to the willing reader to delve deeper into this revelation. It contains the incentive to reach out to a much deeper world where this resurrection knowledge is much more fundamental than previously thought.

Acts 2 vs. 29
Men and brethren, let me freely speak unto you of the patriarch David, that he is both dead and buried, and his sepulcher is with us unto this day.
30 Therefore being a prophet, and knowing that God had sworn with an oath to him, that of the fruit of his loins, according to the flesh, he would raise up the Christ to sit on his throne;
31 He seeing this before spake of the resurrection of Christ, that his soul was not left in hell, neither his flesh did see corruption.
32 This Jesus hath God raised up, whereof we all are witnesses.

According to Peter, King David, though primarily known as a political leader, was counted among the prophets because of his understanding of the revealing nature of Christ's resurrection. King David is also known for his intensely personal relationship with God as we see expressed in the Psalms. Here, David documents his experience and invitation to pass over to another spiritual domain.

Psalm 118 vs17
I shall not die, but live, and declare the works of the Lord.
18 The Lord hath chastened me sore: but he hath not given me over unto death.
19 Open to me the gates of righteousness: I will go into them, and I will praise the Lord:
20 This gate of the Lord, into which the righteous shall enter.
21 I will praise thee: for thou hast heard me, and art become my salvation.
22 The stone which the builders refused is become the head stone of the corner.
23 This is the Lord's doing; it is marvelous in our eyes.

Understanding the nature of Christ's resurrection is a necessary step in the transformation of one's mind and soul as a preparation for eternal life and subsequent salvation. Since the thinking of mankind is traditionally limited, primarily to a linear perspective, this type of revelation is reasonable evidence of God's wisdom and a working example of the mind of Christ. The token proof of this mentality is delineated when the various details of scripture, from a variety of literary sources, are unlocked and deciphered.

1 Peter 7
That the trial of your faith, being much more precious than of gold that perisheth, though it be tried with fire, might be found unto praise and honour and glory at the appearing of Jesus Christ:
8 Whom having not seen, ye love; in whom, though now ye see him not, yet believing, ye rejoice with joy unspeakable and full of glory:
9 Receiving the end of your faith, even the salvation of your souls.
10 Of which salvation the prophets have enquired and searched diligently, who prophesied of the grace that should come unto you:
11 Searching what, or what manner of time the Spirit of Christ which was in them did signify, when it testified beforehand the sufferings of Christ and the glory that should follow.

The preceding scripture is clearly in support of the claim that the prophets, after diligently searching, had encountered the same saving knowledge and understanding of Christ's suffering and the resurrection glory that would follow as is currently being proven. The manner of time in question, as was previously explained, identifies the fulfillment achieved in the resurrection; a transformation that ultimately transcended all time by the 'glory' of a new heavenly nature.

In the second chapter of Peter's first epistle Peter's epithet is clearly expounded in Old Testament scripture as a testimonial that is based on individual revelation rather than on the whims and doctrines of men. As Jesus explains in his own words, "He whom the Son sets free is free indeed," (Jn.8 vs. 36) when he promised his disciples, "And you shall know the truth and the truth shall set you free." (Jn. 8 vs. 32) Described here as a doctrine that is despised and rejected of men, this sound and peaceable revelation knowledge, jointly fit together in God's truth, promises to out do those restrictive linear-based teachings that have no real substance.

1 Peter 2 vs. 3
If so be ye have tasted that the Lord is gracious.
4 To whom coming, as unto a living stone, disallowed indeed of men, but chosen of God, and precious.
5 Ye also, as lively stones, are built up a spiritual house, an holy priesthood, to offer up spiritual sacrifices, acceptable to God by Jesus Christ.
6 Wherefore also it is contained in the scripture, Behold, I lay in Sion a chief corner stone, elect, precious: and he that believeth on him shall not be confounded.

Two essential truths are substantiated in these scriptures; first a stipulation for all believers to engage in the anointing* of God by way of a holy priesthood. Indisputably in this context, holy priesthood denotes the power of God's anointing in the Holy Spirit to protect and sanctify all believers. Traditionally, in the priesthood it was required to give sacrifice on a rock not cut by human hands, (Ex 20 vs. 24-26) hence the symbolic reference to the rock of revelation put in place by God's wisdom alone and those spiritual sacrifices deemed acceptable to God by Jesus Christ.

Secondly, by citing Old Testament scripture, a credible connection is established emphasizing the monumental and fundamental nature of the cornerstone revelation to which all other revelations are fitly joined. The Old Testament scripture quoted here echoes the promise given by Jesus when he ensured "there is nothing covered that shall not be revealed." (Matt 10 vs. 26)

Isaiah 28 vs. 9

Whom shall he teach knowledge? And whom shall he make to understand doctrine? Then that are weaned from the milk, and drawn from the breast.

11 For with stammering lips and another tongue will he speak to this people.

12 To whom he said, this is the rest wherewith ye may cause the weary to rest; and this is the refreshing: yet they would not hear.

13 But the word of the Lord was unto them precept upon precept, precept upon precept; line upon line, line upon line; here a little, and there a little; that they might go, and fall backward, and be broken, and snared and taken.

14 Wherefore hear the word of the Lord, ye scornful men, that rule this people which is in Jerusalem.

15 Because ye have said, We have made a covenant with death, and with hell are we at agreement; when the overflowing scourge shall pass through, it shall not come unto us: for we have made lies our refuge, and under falsehood have we hid ourselves;

16 Therefore thus saith the Lord God, Behold, I lay in Zion for a foundation a stone, a tried stone, a precious corner stone, a sure foundation; he that believeth shall not make haste.

17 Judgment also will I lay to the line, and righteousness to the plummet: and the hail shall sweep away the refuge of lies, and the waters shall overflow the hiding place.

Thus scripture clearly specifies the break with conventional knowledge from those teachings that were base on a line upon line, and precept upon precept teaching method. Certainly they could not compete with the anointed power of God's word and the revealing that came as a result of the resurrection power and glory of God's own son.

The nature of Christ is to fully complete our salvation in him. In terms of the prophetic, it has always been understood that the prophets of God were fully anointed with God's purpose and protection. With in this context, therefore, it may be understood that Christianity itself is ultimately a prophetic movement, based on the sanctification* and protection it lays claim to. In the New Testament this anointing and sanctification is acknowledged far more for it's redemptive qualities since it's protective powers proved to be especially fundamental in light of the apocalyptic climate of the day.

In this context salvation includes the following two criteria. First, in the transforming power the gospel has over our minds; a preparation that has been identified earlier in this treatise; secondly, by the supernatural nature of God's anointing and protective powers. (This notion holds weight when one considers the more ancient definition of the word prophet* which was applied to those individuals who were protected by God in a special way.(6)) Since our relationship with Christ rightly takes center stage, this prophetic element often goes unrealized by the majority of believers. Christ's true mandate on the other hand, has always been to teach us all things spiritual, leaving no stone unturned. Understandably, the anointing of the Holy Spirit carries with it a connection that is intensely personal since it is the spirit of Christ which drives us into all truth. (1 John 2 vs. 27) Along with this teaching comes the invitation to pass over certain thresholds by overcoming the constraints that human knowledge has imposed in order to press on to the divine mind of Christ. Peter's experience and invitation into this realm was of no exception as will soon be discovered.

Peter had the benefit of walking by Jesus' side. The invitation Jesus gives to engage in this revelation is a unique expression of this intimacy. In the sixteenth chapter of the gospel of Mathew, Peter, for the first time, is inclined to announce that Jesus is the Christ, the Son of the living God. It was just six days later when Peter and two other disciples were brought up to a high mountain in order to bare witness to this reality in the full. Once again, the connection Christ's son-ship has with his resurrection, although subtle, remains evident in this passage.

Matthew 17
And after six days Jesus taketh Peter, James, and John his brother, and bringeth them up into an high mountain apart.
2 And was transfigured before them: and his face did shine as the sun, and his raiment was white as the light.
3 And, behold, there appeared unto them Moses and Elijah talking with him.
4 Then answered Peter, and said unto Jesus, Lord, it is good for us to be here: if thou wilt, let us make here three tabernacles; one for thee, and one for Moses, and one for Elijah.
5 While he yet spake, behold, a bright cloud overshadowed them: and behold a voice out of the cloud, which said, This is my beloved Son, in whom I am well pleased; hear ye him.
6 And when the disciples heard it, they fell on their face, and were sore afraid.
7 And Jesus came and touched them, and said, Arise, and be not afraid.
8 And when they came down from the mountain, Jesus charged them, saying, Tell the vision to no man, until the Son of man be risen again from the dead.

The fulfillment of Christ's resurrection from the dead is once again stipulated in connection with Christ's son-ship and subsequent glory. This passage is an obvious example of the resurrection power of Jesus Christ in the face of select witnesses. The mountain top setting, along with the mentioning of Moses and Elijah, is reminiscent of previous biblical encounters on the mountaintop of mount Horeb where this excellent glory was previously witnessed. (Ex 33 vs. 22, 1 Kings 19 vs. 11) The impression left by this encounter would have had the opportunity to take on further connotations later on in scripture.

A Prophetic "Rite of Passage"

Peter must have realized that those with a true and faithful calling would continue to diligently search the scriptures in the hope of fully engaging in God's eternal word. Peter's God- given authority, along with his own first-hand revelation put him in a credible position to validate a true encounter with this truth (The revelation of Christ's son-ship) on behalf of those individuals. It is within this context that an encrypted rite of passage is discovered, subtly placed in order to bless those who are poised to receive its graces. It implies a prophetic line of succession along with prophetic instruction…That such an engagement should be entreated with the utmost respect.

2 Peter 1 vs.16

For we have not followed cunningly devised fables, when we made known unto you the power and coming of our Lord Jesus Christ, but were eyewitnesses of his majesty.

17 For he received from God the Father honor and glory, when there came such a voice to him from the excellent glory, This is my beloved Son in whom I am well pleased.

18 And this voice which came from heaven we heard, when we were with him in the holy mount.

19 We have also a more sure word of prophecy: whereunto ye do well that ye take heed, as unto a light that shineth in a dark place, until the day dawn, and the day star arise in your hearts:

20 Knowing this first that no prophesy of scripture is of any private interpretation.

21 For the prophecy came not in old time by the will of man: but men of God spake as they were moved by the Holy Ghost.

This passage, which makes reference to the word of prophecy* or resurrection whereby true sanctification may be secured, is followed by a clear warning pertaining to those who would knowingly abuse the privileges of God by denying our Lord and savior and the sacrifice made for the sins of mankind. For the first time Peter identifies the existence of those individuals who knew the truth of the resurrection and yet, by abusing God's privileges they merely turned away from Christ in order to oppose the ministry of this truth. The implications of this force of anti-Christ* will be explored further in the next chapter.

2 Peter 2 vs. 1

But there were false prophets also among the people, even as there shall be false teachers among you, who privily shall bring in damnable heresies, even denying the Lord that bought them, and bring upon themselves swift destruction.

2 And many shall follow their pernicious ways; by reason of whom the way of truth shall be evil spoken of.

3 And through covetousness shall they with feigned words make merchandise of you: whose judgment now of a long time lingereth not, and their damnation slumbereth not.

With the identification of this a rite of passage, the existence of a prophetic line of succession may be reasonably supposed. Its existence would be traceable to the beginning of the New Testament, beginning with Jesus himself, and supported by the whole of the Gospel. In truth, prophetic teachings did not end with the coming of Christ; rather, as was explained previously, certain aspects of prophecy had suddenly taken on new emphasis.

In the following scripture Jesus clearly acknowledges this succession of prophecy as well as the rewards associated with it.

Matthew 10 vs. 40

He that receiveth you receiveth me, and he that receiveth me receiveth him who sent me.

41 He that receiveth a prophet in the name of a prophet shall receive a prophet's reward; and he that receiveth a righteous man shall receive a righteous man's reward.

In considering the anointing* of God, certain absolutes prevail. Those who search the scripture will soon discover a series of Bible-related terminologies that have a consistent correlation in scripture. Collectively this terminology seems to envelope the various attributes of Christ and the identifying features associated with his calling. Prophecy* denotes God's anointing, while God's anointing in turn implies sanctification* and sanctification embodies the passage from death to life. The full realization of these attributes is only entreated to the believer through the revelation of Christ's son-ship, which is through his resurrection. Salvation comes as we are chosen by God to take part in this resurrection.

The Seal of God

The symbol and prelude to the attainment of our resurrected bodies is referred to as the seal of God*. A seal traditionally includes an identifying feature or symbol of special significance used to authenticate authorship and to seal up the written contents of a letter or some other correspondence. Such a seal is naturally only put in place by the author and contains the sealed or private information intended for a specific audience.(7)

This designation, as bestowed by God's living word, begins with the revelation that was put in place by God alone and is ultimately fulfilled in the calling of his only son Jesus Christ through his resurrected body. For the believer, following this initial revelation, a procession of God's oracles is opened up, providing a valid proof and illustration of God's seal being set in place. In other words, the revelation of Christ's son-ship, as it is secured through the resurrection, is a reasonable sign that God's seal has been set upon our minds. The initial depiction of when this seal is first documented remains consistent with the succession of prophecy mentioned previously.

John 3 vs. 27

John answered and said, A man can receive nothing, except it be given him from heaven.

28 Ye yourself bear me witness, that I said, I am not the Christ, but that I am sent before him.

29 He that hath the bride is the bridegroom: but the friend of the bridegroom, which standeth and heareth him, rejoiceth greatly because of the bridegroom's voice:this my joy therefore is fulfilled.

30 He must increase, but I must decrease.

31 He that cometh from above is above all: he that is of the earth is earthly, and speaketh of the earth: he that cometh from heaven is above all.

32 And what he hath seen and heard, that he testifieth; and no man receiveth his testimony.

33 He that hath received his testimony hath set to his seal that God is true.

34 For he whom God hath sent speaketh the words of God: for God giveth not the Spirit by measure unto him.

35 The Father loves the Son, and hath given all things into his hand.

36 He that believeth on the Son hath everlasting life: and he that believeth not the Son shall not see life; but the wrath of God abideth on him.

God's supernatural seal validates the absoluteness of this completed salvation plan for our lives. Likewise, as we delve deeper into the oracles of God, this absolute indestructible nature of God's word is suddenly more apparent. Thus, as the distinction of this incorruptible nature is made known, the individual is met with a growing expectation and reliance on the word's eternal nature.

Christ himself, the forerunner to this salvation plan, was the first to bare God's seal.

John 6 vs. 27
Labor not for the meat which perisheth, but for that meat which endureth unto everlasting life, which the Son of man shall give unto you; for him hath God the Father sealed.

God's seal was initially set in place as a preparation for Christ's death and resurrection. Those found worthy to touch on the mystery of Christ's son-ship and resurrection are therefore set at liberty to tap into those mysteries pertaining to Christ's eternal nature. These mysteries, as we will soon explore, are just beyond the limitations imposed on us by death's eventual sting. By reason of God's seal set in place the invitation is made to attain to the same nature as our glorified Christ.

2 Corinthians 1 vs. 20
For all the promises of God in him are yea, and in him Amen, unto the glory of God by us.
21 Now he which stablisheth us with you in Christ, and hath anointed us, is God;
Who hath also sealed us, and given the earnest of the Spirit in our hearts.

Beyond Death's Barrier

The next, most reasonable step of faith is to believe emphatically in the power and promise of God's seal; the resurrection and transformation into Christ's own glorified nature. Relative to Bible scripture, if we have this belief we will surely entertain the notion that, in certain instances, God has already exercised his power over death*, and that death was, and is, no longer an end for those under his dominion. If this is true what evidence and understanding, if any, could be identified in God's own word to show us that this glorified nature and subsequent preeminence has already been in effect?

Is it credible that God's power has already been at work in this area, in one form or another, among his chosen prophets? Sources regarding this question bare a remarkable resemblance and consistency in a variety of Biblical sources and at seemingly random points in history. This evidence may draw two conclusions. First, as was discussed earlier, one may conclude that Bible scripture converges on the same founding principle, the principle of Christ's son-ship, a knowledge revealed to inspired teachers and prophets alike down through the ages. Secondly, that God's word is truly authentic lending itself to a consistency that has surpassed man's wisdom since the beginning of time.

The following excerpt is taken from the book of Job, a book of the Bible that some experts say is the oldest,(8) yet it bares a remarkable consistency with the principles that have been brought forward thus far.

Job 38 vs. 1

THEN the Lord answered Job out of the whirlwind, and said,

2 Who is this that darkeneth counsel by words without knowledge?

3 Gird up now thy loins like a man: for I will demand of thee, and answer thou me.

4 Where wast thou when I laid the foundations of the earth? declare, if thou hast understanding.

5 Who hath laid the measures thereof, if thou knowest? or who hath stretched the line upon it?

6 Whereupon are the foundations thereof fastened? or who laid the corner stone thereof;

7 When the morning stars sang together, and all the sons of God shouted for joy?

It is noteworthy that many of the key components written in this treatise are reflected here in God's own words. This particular reference to the Sons of God must, therefore, be given the same consideration for the definitive application as revealed in the son-ship of Jesus Christ. This leads us to the logical conclusion that the mind of God knows and sees the end from the very beginning.

Jesus Christ reiterates this statement in the following passage:

Luke 20 vs. 34

And Jesus answering said unto them, The children of this world marry, and are given in marriage:

35 But they which shall be accounted worthy to obtain that world, and the resurrection from the dead, neither marry nor are given in marriage:

36 Neither can they die any more: for they are equal unto the angels; and are the children of God, being children of the resurrection.

37 Now that the dead are raised, even Moses shewed at the bush, when he calleth the Lord the God of Abraham, and the God of Isaac, and the God of Jacob.

38 For he is not a God of the dead, but of the living for all live unto him.

In so many instances God's power and omnipotence is acknowledged but scarcely is it identified and understood. As Jesus himself points out, the true misconception preventing an accurate knowledge on behalf of the Pharisees and Sadducees was in their inability to understand the nature of God's power. The following excerpt is another account of the story of the Sadducees* taken from the gospel according to Matthew.

Matthew 22 vs. 28

Therefore in the resurrection whose wife shall she be of the seven? For they all had her.

29 Jesus answered and said unto them, Ye do err, not knowing the scriptures, nor the power of God.

30 For in the resurrection they neither marry, nor are given in marriage, but are as the angels of God in heaven.

Thus, the implications of this knowledge not only suggests that all of those who bare God's seal will be privileged to take part in the resurrection, but that such individuals shall transcend time in a spiritual existence and preeminence that resembles the nature of Christ himself. Once attained, this premise would seem to be exploitable for the abuse of God's power, yet, graciously, God's word converges on still other mysteries.

The Bible clearly documents the existence of those who, having once attained this enlightenment turned against God to go into perdition. This knowledge does not detract from the spiritual existence promised above, rather it provides reasonable proof for the very real existence of an anti-Christ* which has existed in one form or another down through the ages.

Many aspects of God's power may therefore be revealed, but not without the due diligence towards the moral virtues of our Lord and Christ. Christ himself explains while lending a very human connotation to Satan's fall from grace. In the following scripture Christ seems to persuade his disciples that there is, perhaps, a fate worse than death that his anointed need guard against.

Luke 10 vs. 17

And the seventy returned again with joy, saying, Lord, even the devils are subject unto us through thy name.

18 And he said unto them, I beheld Satan as lightening fall from heaven.

19 Behold, I give unto you power to tread on serpents and scorpions, and over all the power of the enemy: and nothing shall by any means hurt you.

20 Notwithstanding in this rejoice not that the spirits are subject unto you; but rather rejoice, because your names are written in heaven.

In the chapters that follow, the nature of the anti-Christ will be uncovered, followed by an exposition of a secret identity familiar to that of the anti-Christ. Although this involves many of the same principles previously expounded, a radical new view of history will be suggested. With the application of the principles presented here, numerous facts have also been compiled in support, which bear investigating.

II
Schism of the anti-Christ

In the previous chapter the existence of a key revelation in scripture (the revelation of Christ's son-ship)* was identified as common knowledge among God's chosen prophets. Although a degree of subtlety is reflected in scripture's portrayal, the very existence of this revelation seems remarkable for it's historical and theological value.

Subtleties in scripture also identify the existence of an opposition to this prophetic movement. From a historical perspective, the balance of power in the political and religious movements of the times did not remain static, rather, there were obvious points in Bible history where religious loyalties were exploited for political gain. If religious and political powers became volatile, even the most legitimate Biblical and historical scholars would have shown discretion while writing this history down. Under God's direction, the legacy of the true nature of this 'opposition' may well have been preserved and chronicled by these historians.

Theologically, the existence of an anti-Christ has obvious implications early on in scripture. References pertaining to the coming of an anti-Christ seem to run parallel to those references pertaining to the coming of our savior and Christ. (Such a context is not unwarranted since knowledge of Christ's son-ship and resurrection is required, followed by a deliberate turning away from Christ in order for this anti-Christ nature to be established.) Although this rebellious nature is opposite to Christ's in every respect, the personality of the anti-Christ consistently attempts to imitate and out-do God's plan. With regards to Christ's preeminence*and son-ship*, the true character of the anti-Christ* is revealed as this attempt to imitate and out-do God's plan is played- out.

When the works of darkness are gradually exposed a series of God inspired revelations are identified in scripture. With this, the righteous nature of Christ's kingdom is duly edified, along with God's boundless mercy. Lastly, if it were in the realm of possibility for the true nature, motive and personality of the antichrist to be exposed, this would be in fulfillment of Holy Scripture, which stipulates, "Every hidden work of darkness will be uncovered." (Matt. 10 vs. 26) Thus, with in the annals of history, the eventuality of uncovering a specific identity that meets the profile for identifying this antichrist personality is credible, considering the absolution of God's seal and the irrevocable nature of his word. The identity of such an individual would be ascertained based on his or her decision to turn away from God in rebellion despite the enormous privilege of God's anointing*and protection.

In the following scripture 'the rock of salvation'*that Moses himself describes foreshadows the coming of our Lord and Christ. Likewise, scripture's first inclination to identifying this anti-Christ nature is clearly documented in the existence of another rock, a rock that openly contends with the true will of God. This opposition is aimed at ensnaring and enslaving mankind by inciting this rebellious nature into practice.

Deuteronomy 32 vs. 9

For the Lord's portion is his people: Jacob is the lot of his inheritance

10 He found him in a desert land, and in the waste-howling wilderness: he led him about, he instructed him, and he kept him as the apple of his eye.

15 But Jeshurun waxed fat, and kicked: thou art waxen fat, thou art grown thick, thou art covered with fatness; then he forsook God which made him and lightly esteemed the Rock of his salvation.

16 They provoked him to jealousy with strange gods, with abominations provoked they him to anger.

17 They sacrificed unto devils, not to God; to gods whom they knew not, to new Gods that came newly up, whom your fathers feared not.

29 O that they were wise, that they understand this, that they would consider their latter end!

30 How should one chase a thousand, and two put ten thousand to flight, except their Rock had sold them and the Lord had shut them up?

31 For their rock is not as our Rock, even our enemies themselves being judges.

32 For their vine is of the vine of Sodom, and of the fields of Gomorrah: their grapes are grapes of gall, their clusters are bitter:
33 Their wine is the poison of dragons, and the cruel venom of asps.
34 Is not this laid up in store with me, and sealed up among my treasures?

Our understanding of this scripture is no longer confined to the linear perspective that history usually implies, rather, it's highly prophetic nature obviously points to some future tense attributed to a significant falling away. The preexistence of this ant-Christ' nature is also implied by the mentioning of another rock* who's intent is to poison mankind by sin. Both existences (that of the antichrist of the future, as well as the ancient- preexistent form) share a common identity. In the context of the revelation of Christ's son ship and his prophetic seal, access into those things that would normally be hidden or sealed by God are submitted for our interpretation. The release of this revelation, as always, is based on the eternal nature that one subscribes to through the testimony of Christ's son ship and resurrection.

When considering the story of Genesis, a substantial gain in understanding is put into effect in the realization that seemingly random points in history may in fact bare a significant spiritual connection. If all previous assertions are true, the creation story is obviously far less a myth than what many previously supposed. Accordingly, just as Christ and his resurrection generates a hope in the setting of God's seal, to the contrary, it is likely that the fruit of the tree of knowledge which is so often linked with man's disobedience, carried with it a shameful or stigmatizing effect. It is not unlikely that this stigmatizing effect also included a foreknowledge of the future exploits of the antichrist.

In this case the antichrist himself assumes a more original form as the serpent that beguiled Adam and Eve in the Garden of Eden.

Genesis 3 vs. 4

And the serpent said unto the woman, ye shall not surely die:

5 For God doth know that in the day ye eat thereof, then your eyes shall be opened, and ye shall be as gods, knowing good and evil.

6 And when the woman saw that the tree was good for food, and that it was pleasant to the eyes, and a tree to be desired to make one wise, she took of the fruit thereof, and did eat, and gave also unto her husband with her; and he did eat.

7 And the eyes of them both were opened, and they knew that they were naked; and they sewed fig leaves together, and made themselves aprons.

The knowledge of good and evil referenced here has special significance to a specific personality in scripture, as we will soon explore.

Types and Shadows* of the anti-Christ

Before a certain key personality can be implicated in the identity of the antichrist, the types and shadows that best suit this personality must also be examined. A type and shadow* may be defined as an ordinance of active duty towards God that by its nature comes to symbolize a future personality or moral character written about in scripture.

As has already been identified that a stigmatizing effect could well have been inflicted on Adam and Eve when they first disobeyed God. It is reasonable to suppose that this single act of disobedience had repercussions that lasted up until later generations. In the book of Genesis, as Cain and Abel offer us our first glimpse into the nature of the ordinance of sacrifice, two specific types of sacrifices are offered. One type of sacrifice would please God, the other would not. Hidden within these two types of sacrifices are two distinct personalities. One represents the nature of Christ, the other the nature of anti-Christ. As one of God's eternal ordinances the nature and meaning these different types of sacrifices does not change. Abel, at this point in scripture, offers a sacrifice from the firstlings of his flock. Traditionally, according to its Levitical significance, this type of offering was a sin offering*, symbolized by the death of an animal to atone for sin. (Lev. 4 vs. 3) This sin offering is symbolic of Christ's saving sacrifice on the cross. God respects Abel's sacrifice....

Cain, on the other hand, offered a sacrifice that would commonly accompany what was traditionally known as a peace offering*. (Lev. 3; 7 vs. 11-36) Such an offering would include a vow of thanksgiving based on the good fortune that God has bestowed. Accordingly, the peace offering, in it's levitical context, was considered more of a conditional gesture of thanksgiving representing free will, where as, the sin offering was more of a mandatory offering of atonement. (1) In this context, Cain's attempt to make 'peace' with God without rendering a sacrifice for sin reflects the more subtle nature of the antichrist.

Soon, after Cain offers his sacrifice, he succumbs to his jealousy and ill will leading to the murder of his brother Abel.

Genesis 4 vs. 8
And Cain talked with Abel his brother: and it came to pass, when they were in the field, that Cain rose up against Abel his brother and slew him.
9 And the Lord said unto Cain, Where is Abel thy brother? And he said, I know not: Am I my brother's keeper?
10 And he said, What hast thou done? the voice of thy brother's blood crieth unto me from the ground.

As an interesting footnote, the symbolism of these sacrifices is suddenly transferred to the personalities of Cain and Abel themselves. Abel's blood is a reminder of the sin offering he sacrificed, where as Cain's first malicious act of murder is consistent with the anti-Christ nature of his sacrifice. Christ himself implicates Satan as "...a murderer from the beginning" who, abode not in the truth". (Jn. 8 vs. 44) In this context Cain makes a worthy representative of this anti-Christ nature.

The Mark of the Anti-Christ

Sin itself has long carried with it a stigmatizing effect, perpetuating a shameful existence, cut off from the salvation we have in Christ. Further, a higher spirituality rests in the hope that God himself has identified us and called us as one of his own. The setting of God's seal fulfills this hope; a faithful sign of his choosing, yet for individuals lost in a world of sin, or exposed to certain evils, this hope seems to be all but cut-off.

Mankind's need to be recognized and identified by our heavenly father is innately supplanted into our created nature. Scriptural connotations exist throughout the Bible identifying this ideal need. Also reflected in scripture is the tendency for sin to lead to an unfulfilling life style where the seal of God is substituted with practices of self-loathing like self-mutilation and ritual blood letting.

The basic spiritual need fulfilled by God's supernatural seal may be identified in the demoniac who grew up opposite to Galilee on the shores of the Gaderenes. The young man in question, having extinguished the hope of this calling in himself, is overcome by a demonic presence was found in the tombs crying and wailing; an expression of a resurrection that he (The demon or unclean spirit) would never attain, and cutting his flesh as an expression of the seal of God that would never be placed. (Luke 8 vs. 26)

Another type or shadow* of this stigmatizing mark is seen shortly after

Cain slays his brother Abel. As a punishment for Cain's actions, God is forced to curse Cain by taking away his livelihood as a tiller of the ground. Cain responds showing he understands the extent of such a curse. Cain also knows that God will never put him through anything "more than he can bear" (1 Cor. 10 vs. 13), consequently, God sets a mark upon Cain to prevent further harm from coming to him.

Genesis 4 vs. 10

And he said, What hast thou done? the voice of thy brother's blood crieth unto me from the ground.

11 And now art thou cursed from the earth, which hath opened her mouth to receive thy brother's blood from thy hand;

12 When thou tillest the ground, it shall not henceforth yield unto thee her strength; a fugitive and a vagabond shalt thou be in the earth.

13 And Cain said unto the Lord, My punishment is greater than I can bear.

14 Behold, thou hast driven me out this day from the face of the earth; and from thy face shall I be hid; and I shall be a fugitive and a vagabond in the earth; and it shall come to pass that everyone that findeth me shall slay me.

15 And the Lord said unto him, Therefore whosoever slayeth Cain, vengeance shall be taken on him sevenfold. And the Lord set a mark upon Cain lest any finding him should kill him.

The mark of the anti-Christ* has a threefold motivation; firstly, representative of a grab for political power in order to secure supremacy in an existing form of government. The second is a monetary or economic motivation. Both of these motivations can be seen in examining the type of peace offering or free will offering offered by Cain in the events leading up to the stigmatizing mark that he himself received. Lastly the mark of the anti-Christ is used as a means of identification, however, unlike God's seal of favor and promise, the mark of the anti-Christ is bent on controlling and imprisoning it's barer to an unruly fate. God only allows receiving a mark of this nature because of our free will.

Defilement* is defined as sin's ability to separate us from God. Without Christ there is no offering or atonement for sin. Those who knowingly receive the mark of the anti-Christ will thereby submit themselves to the ultimate defilement, which is devoid of God's protection. These individuals will thus expose themselves to a systematic terrorizing and demonizing by God's enemies.

The Mystery of Lawlessness

The political motivations for the mark of the beast may be explored elsewhere in scripture as well. The traditional insignia of this mark is the number 666. In this historical context it may be seen that this number (666) is a sign used to distinguish the identity and original personality of the anti-Christ*. Historically it may even be possible to identify traces of an ancient civilization that fosters an age-old system of government based on the exploits of this individual. Although on the surface the political motivations of the past seem primitive in comparison, the essential drive and notable existence of this political force is evident up to the present day.

The true identity of the anti-Christ is implied by citations of the number (666) dispersed throughout the book of 1 Chronicles. The Bible speaks of the existence of a man with six fingers and toes on his hands and feet who were vanquished by David's brother in battle. As was stated earlier, these references to 666 were strategically placed for the identity in question to be subtly revealed. Following this scripture another major clue to the existence and political influence of this individual is shown when the very first reference to Satan as a common name appears in scripture for the first time.(2) (1 Chronicles' 21 vs. 1)

1 Chronicles 20 vs. 6

And yet again there was war at Gath, where was a man of great stature, whose fingers and toes were four and twenty, six on each hand, and six on each foot: and he also was the son of the giant.

7 But when he defied Israel, Jonathan the son of Shimea David's brother slew him.

8 These were born unto the giant in Gath: and they fell by the hand of David, and by the hand of his servants.

1 Chronicles 21 vs. 1

AND Satan stood up against Israel, and provoked David to number Israel

2 And David said to Joab and to the rulers of the people, Go, number Israel from Beersheba even to Dan; and bring me the number that may know it.

3 And Joab answered, The Lord make his people an hundred times so many more than they be: but, my lord the King, are they not all my lord's servants? why then doth my lord require this thing? why will he be a cause of trespass to Israel?

This scripture describes how David was persuaded or moved by Satan to perform a census of the nation of Israel. From the perspective of David's trusted advisor this was considered an abominable request, since it was traditionally understood that God would multiply the nation of Israel to be "as the stars of heaven" (Genesis 15 vs. 4) and "as the dust of the earth". (Genesis 13 vs. 16) Nevertheless, eventually, Joab, David's trusted advisor carried out the order for the census to be conducted out of obedience to the King. Joab's protest is documented in scripture. (1 Chr. 21 vs. 3)

The turn of events that transpire as a result of this census is that God's displeasure is voiced, and the nation of Israel is given a choice of three punishments; famine, plague or sword. After weighing the three choices carefully, David chooses the Lord's pestilence stating, " Let me fall into the hands of the Lord for his mercy is very great." (1 Chr. 21 vs. 13) After the death of seventy thousand of his men the Lord requested that David build an alter on the threshing floor of Araunah the Jebusite. The Angel of the Lord then appeared on the threshing floor and the Lord finally relented. (1 Chr. 21 vs1 6, 25, 26) David consequently purchased this property for six hundred sheckles of gold, for what would become the future sight of the Temple of God.

The original usage of the term Satan was a formal reference to the anger of God. Typically, the word Satan appeared with a Hebrew article to depersonalize such a reference, but in the 21st chapter of 1 Chronicles, when David is first persuaded to take his census, the name appears without article showing it as a proper name. In the traditional Hebrew usage Satan referred to any kind of human or supernatural adversary or one who blocked the way in a determined fashion.(3) Satan, as a personality, stands traditionally in the role of an accuser of mankind as in a court of law.(4) The serpent in the Garden of Eden may be taken along with this definition to exemplify the cunning and subtle nature of this personality. Under careful scrutiny it becomes evident that the reference to Satan in this instance, conceals a specific identity that was influential enough to persuade David to take the census, yet required Biblical/historical references to this individual to be kept secret.

Solomon would have been as old as fifteen years of age and able to advise his father in his decision to conduct a census of the nation of Israel. What transpires early on in Solomon's reign suggests that Solomon was, at the very least, supportive of David's decision. Scripture clearly documents Joab's protest, (1 Chr. 21 vs. 3) and notes the fact that Joab deliberately excluded the tribes of Levi and Benjamin when the census was initially conducted.(1 Chr. 21 vs. 6) Audaciously, even after it was deemed an abomination in the sight of God and after Joab's refusal, (1 Chr. 27 vs. 24) Solomon continues the census of the tribe of Levi after he is inaugurated King. (1 Chr. 23 vs. 1-4)

After Solomon came to power, even though Joab had claimed sanctuary on holy ground and taken hold of the horns of the alter, Solomon ordered Joab's execution. (1 Ki. 2 vs. 28-32) Solomon's reasoning for this action is that Joab had shed innocent blood, namely Abner son of Ner, who was killed by Joab to avenge the death of his brother Asahel (2 Sam 3 vs. 27) and Amasa the son of Jether captain of the host of Judah, whose actions were bordering on treason. (2 Sam 17 vs. 25) Lastly, scripture states that Joab's first loyalty for the office of king was Adonijah and not Solomon, implying that a rift between Joab and Solomon and his policies would have existed. (1 Ki. 2 vs. 28)

Since knowledge of Christ's son ship and resurrection followed by a deliberate turning away' from Christ is necessary in order for this anarchist nature to be established, such an individual would be endowed with special wisdom from God. Likewise it is likely that the saints of the New Testament had insight into of the identity of the anti-Christ and to other privileged knowledge that would otherwise be sealed up if not for the revelation and resurrection of Jesus Christ. In 2nd Thessalonians, in what is traditionally understood as a reference to the future exploits of the ant-Christ, it becomes evident and feasible that a "mystery of lawlessness"* already at work would be responsible for a major defection from the truth. In this context this scripture could be implying that after significant erosion of doctrine that the answer to this 'mystery' would resurface. This scripture could therefore reasonably contain further 'hints' as to the identity of this personality.

2 Thessalonians 2 vs. 1

Now we beseech you, brethren, by the coming of our Lord Jesus Christ, and by our gathering together unto him,

2 That ye be not soon shaken in mind, or be troubled, neither by spirit, nor by word, nor by letter as from us, as that the day of Christ is at hand.

3 Let no man deceive you by any means: for that day shall not come, except there come a falling away first, and that man of sin be revealed, the son of perdition:

4 Who opposeth and exalteth himself above all that is called God, or that is worshipped; so that he as God sitteth in the temple of God, shewing himself that he is God.

5 Remember ye not, that, when I was yet with you, I told you these things?
6 And now ye know what withholdeth that he might be revealed in his time.
7 For the mystery of iniquity doth already work: only he who now letteth will let, until he be taken out of the way.
8 And then shall that Wicked be revealed, whom the Lord shall consume with the spirit of his mouth, and shall destroy with the brightness of his coming:
9 Even him, whose coming is after the working of Satan with all power and signs and lying wonders,
10 And with all deceivableness of unrighteousness in them that perish: because they received not the love of the truth, that they might be saved.
11 And for this cause God shall send them strong delusion, that they should believe a lie:
12 That they all might be damned who believed not the truth, but had pleasure in unrighteousness.

Solomon, credited with building the original temple of God, seems to answer to the profile stipulated for the anti-Christ thus far. The construction of the Temple itself is suggestive of Solomon's unprecedented personal influence over the religious authorities of the day. This explains how a group of spiritually elite given access to the Temple of God could secretly practice idol worship and exercise unholy rituals to inwardly exploit God's privilege for personal gain. (Ez. 8 vs. 12) Solomon, whose name means peace in the Hebrew dialect, was supernaturally endowed with wisdom. (1 Kings 3 vs. 9-12) Solomon is the first person in the Bible to be named as God's son (1 Chr. 28 vs. 6) and was anointed by God in the traditional sense. (1 Kings 1 vs. 39)

The Wisdom of Solomon

Wisdom is documented as Solomon's most famous attribute. His economic policies translated into legendary wealth. In the area of judgment he enjoyed a status of perceptive power that was unrivaled and never to be matched. (1 Ki. 3 vs. 12) Even to the present day Solomon's wisdom has continued to foster a 'cult' status on behalf of groups that claim to originate from his teachings and philosophies. To his credit Solomon's inspired wisdom is responsible for the authorship of at least three books of the Bible.

With all this wisdom many would find it difficult to imagine that Solomon ever used his influence in a way that was meant to deceive, yet under closer scrutiny his actions often reflect a tendency to fall short of God's intended path. This tendency to fall just short of God's perfect will eventually becomes Solomon's trade mark, as we will soon explore.

In the area of judgment many examples reflecting Solomon's wisdom may be cited. The following excerpt reveals Solomon's expressed desire to be endowed with wisdom, as he makes his petition known before God.

1 Kings 3 vs. 9

Give therefore thy servant an understanding heart to judge thy people, that I may discern between good and bad: for who is able to judge this thy so great a people?

10 And the speech pleased the Lord, that Solomon had asked this thing.

11 And God said unto him, Because thou hast asked this thing, and hast not asked for long life; neither hast asked for riches for thyself, nor hast asked the life of thine enemies: but hast asked for thyself to discern judgment;

12 Behold, I have done according to thy words: lo, I have given thee a wise and understanding heart; so that there was none like thee before thee neither after thee shall any arise like unto thee.

Solomon was indeed a judge who was well versed in the knowledge of good and evil. With such a statement given from the Lord, Solomon effectually became the hallmark and sum of all earthly wisdom and judgment. This wisdom with its supernatural appeal qualifies Solomon for a pre-eminent* status similar to that of Christ's. In the event of a falling away Solomon would be doomed to stand in the shadow of God's perfect will beset with the motivation to deceive mankind into sharing his fate. Ironically, scripture pertaining to the anti-Christ often makes reference to wisdom. In Genesis the serpent beguiles Eve to pick from the tree of the knowledge of good and evil suggesting that eating this fruit will make one wise. This is an obvious picture of the anti-Christ's beginning platitudes.

Genesis 3 vs. 4

And the serpent said unto the woman, ye shall not surely die:

5 For God doth know that in the day ye eat thereof, then your eyes shall be opened, and ye shall be as gods, knowing good and evil.

6 And when the woman saw that the tree was good for food, and that it was pleasant to the eyes, and a tree to be desired to make one wise,

she took of the fruit thereof, and did eat, and gave also unto her husband with her; and he did eat.

7 And the eyes of them both were opened, and they knew that they were naked; and they sewed fig leaves together, and made themselves aprons.

Else where in scripture the Bible speaks of swelling words of vanity bent on deceiving mankind. (2 Pet. 2 vs. 18) In the book of Romans Paul describes how those who were "professing to be wise had become fools." The following reference could easily be applied to Solomon's eventual passage into idol worship. This turning away although deliberate, was probably sparked as a result of Solomon's newfound ability to manipulate political powers through divination and witchcraft. Under Solomon's reign idol worship enjoyed an obvious resurgence, due in part to the promise of achieving an almost god-like status under Solomon's direction.

Romans 1 vs. 18

For the wrath of God is revealed from heaven against all ungodliness and unrighteousness of men who hold the truth in unrighteousness;

19 Because that which may be known of God is manifest in them; for God hath shewed it unto them.

20 For the invisible things of him from the creation of the world are clearly seen, being understood by the things that are made, even his eternal power and Godhead; so that they are without excuse:

21 Because that, when they knew God, they glorified him not as God, neither were thankful; but became vain in their imaginations, and their foolish heart was darkened.

22 Professing themselves to be wise; they became fools,

23 And changed the glory of the incoruptible God into an image made like to corruptible man, and to birds, and four footed beasts, and creeping things.

Gradually, political alliances were forged on the basis of Solomon's wisdom. Clearly, influential rulers who were swept away by Solomon's abilities were eager to pledge their allegiance and help in the hope of being included in the platform of Solomon's foreseeable power. Solomon's wisdom crossed many political borders and was not restricted to his own nationality. The ancient wisdom Solomon had acquired evidently had a cross-cultural appeal and served to strengthen old alliances. The tone of this suggested power base as it was unfolding was built on the ancient of ways defined by his spiritual ability to transcend all time. The building blocks of Babylon itself are theoretically traceable to this power base.

The following is a description of the events as they unfolded just prior to the construction of the temple.

1 Kings 4 vs. 29

And God gave Solomon wisdom and understanding exceeding much, and largeness of heart, even as the sand that is on the seashore.

30 And Solomon's wisdom excelled the wisdom of all the children of the east country, and all the wisdom of Egypt.

31 For he was wiser than all men; than Ethan the Ezrahite, and Heman, and Chalcol, and Darda, the son of Mahol: and his fame was in all the nations round about.

32 And he spake three thousand proverbs: and his songs were a thousand and five.

33 And he spake of trees, from the cedar tree that is in Lebanon even unto the hyssop that springeth out of the wall: he spake also of beasts, and of fowl, and of creeping things, and of fishes.

34 And there came of all people to hear the wisdom of Solomon, from all kings of the earth, which had heard of his wisdom.

Construction of the Temple Masonry

Solomon's wisdom eventually translated into political alliances. Surrounding nations scrambled to pay tribute to Solomon and his legendary wisdom. A broad base of support was exacted prior to the Temple's construction so that enormous amounts of silver and gold were accumulated. The construction of the Temple enabled Solomon to amass incredible wealth into his personal treasury as well. Solomon set precedent in that he made a practice of drinking only from vessels that were made of pure gold, (2 Chr. 9 vs. 20) a practice that was contrary to the lawful obligations of the King. (Deuteronomy 17 vs. 17) Eventually, the leadership of Israel took on all of the worldly standards of kingly rule.

Scripture may well imply that the Lord took great exception to these alliances. One may be dissuaded into thinking that God kept his silence, but to the contrary, there are many examples of the Lord voicing his displeasure. In discovering these passages it is necessary to recognize certain fundamental principles in the timing and way of God's response.

First, one must realize that the Lord answers in his timing and not man's. Well after physical death of a man occurs God is still able to tap into the eternal soul and nature of an individual. Unlike the words of men, God's word never loses it's value and objectivity. Scripture tells us that "one day is with the Lord as a thousand years, and a thousand years as one day," (2 Peter 3 vs. 8) so that his answers needn't be restricted to our knowledge of time.

Secondly, when it comes to alliances, the Lord will never equate one of his loyal subjects with those who are disloyal. In other words as scripture says, "Of whom a man is overcome, of the same is he brought in bondage." (2 Peter 2 vs. 19) Therefore when an unholy alliance is forged and the true standing of one of God's would-be subjects is identified, the Lord will undoubtedly cast such an individual as belonging to the nation where this unholy alliance was originally made. A degree of subtlety exists so that only those who diligently search the scriptures can identify this trend.

One such example of these fundamental principles may be discovered in the alliance that Solomon forged with the King of Tyre. As is often the case, originally there are no traces of wrong doing in such an alliance. Later with Solomon's passage into idolatry it is likely that those who remained loyal to Solomon would eventually follow him on the same destructive path.

1 Kings 5 vs. 1

AND Hiram king of Tyre sent his servants unto Solomon; for he had heard that they had anointed him king in the room of his father: for Hiram was ever a lover of David

12 And the Lord gave Solomon wisdom, as he promised him: and there was peace between Hiram and Solomon; and the two made a league together.

15 And Solomon had three-score and ten thousand that bare burdens, and fourscore thousand hewers in the mountains;

17 And the king commanded, and they brought great stones, costly stones, and hewed stones, to lay the foundation of the house.

18 And Solomon's builders and Hiram's builders did hew them, and the stonesquarers: so they prepared timber and stones to build the house.

In the following scripture the Lord makes his address to the prince of Tyrus. The content however, is beyond a doubt referring to Solomon and the consequences and outcomes of the unholy alliance that was forged.

Ezekiel 28 vs. 1

The word of the Lord came again unto me, saying,

2 Son of man, say unto the prince of Tyrus, Thus saith the Lord God;

Because thine heart is lifted up, and thou hast said, I am a God, I sit in the seat of God, in the midst of the seas; yet thou art a man, and not a God, though thou set thine heart as the heart of God;
3 Behold, thou art wiser than Daniel; there is no secret that they can hide from thee:
4 With thy wisdom and with thine understanding thou hast gotten thee riches, and thine heart is lifted up because of thy riches
5 By thy great wisdom and by thy traffick hast thou increased thy riches, and thine heart is lifted up because of thy riches:
6 Therefore thus saith the Lord God; Because thou hast set thine heart as the heart of God;
7 Behold, therefore I will bring strangers upon thee, the terrible of the nations: and they shall draw their swords against the beauty of thy wisdom, and they shall defile thy brightness.

A connotation of a hierarchy based on occult practices seems to emerge in the construction of the temple. In this context an ulterior motive in using foreign labor to build the temple comes as no surprise. From a historical standpoint cultic symbolic representations like the onyx stone gains in momentum when one considers the Biblical context of such references, as well as their use in building the Temple. (1 Chr. 29 vs. 2) As the scriptures provided continue to reveal images that are consistent with cultic behavior, foreign involvement becomes more apparent in the Temple's construction.

II Chronicles 2 vs. 17

And Solomon numbered all the strangers that were in the land of Israel, after the numbering wherewith David his father had numbered them; and they were found an hundred and fifty thousand and three thousand and six hundred.
18 And he set threescore and ten thousand of them to be bearers of burdens, and fourscore thousand to be hewers in the mountain, and three thousand and six hundred overseers to set the people at work.

Scripture describes a molten sea held up by the images of twelve oxen cast in bronze. The inside of the Temple was plated with gold with the images of cherubim overlaid with pure gold. The most unsettling image of all is the six steps leading up to a throne of ivory that was entirely overlaid with gold. (1 Chr. 9vs 17,18) Whether this throne was in place in the actual temple or not remains to be seen. What is known is that the president set by such a display may have had blasphemous impression on genuine God-fearing devotees.

Despite all foreign influence, evidence of the Lord's displeasure seems to mount towards Solomon and his supporters. God's own word mentions the audacity of that individual who presumptuously enthroned himself in the midst of the sea boasting of his God-like status. (2 Thessalonians 2 vs. 4, Ezekiel 28 vs. 2) Further, in the following scripture the connotation of precious stones mentioned bare distinct similarities to the exact jewels that were fastened in the breastplate of Israel's Levitical priests. The anointed cherub that covereth bares a similarity to the imagery that decorated Solomon's Temple.

Ezekial 28 vs. 12

Son of man, take up a lamentation upon the king of Tyrus, and say unto him, Thus saith the Lord God; Thou sealest up the sum, full of wisdom, and perfect in beauty.

13 Thou hast been in Eden the garden of God; every precious stone was thy covering, the sardius, topaz, and the diamond, the beryl, the onyx, and the jasper, the sapphire, the emerald, and the carbuncle, and gold: the workmanship of thy tabrets and of thy pipes was prepared in thee in the day that thou wast created

14 Thou art the anointed cherub that covereth; and I have set thee so; thou wast upon the holy mountain of God; thou hast walked up and down in the midst of the stones of fire.

15 Thou wast perfect in thy ways from the day that thou wast created, till iniquity was found in thee.

16 By the multitude of thy merchandise they have filled the midst of thee with violence, and thou hast sinned: therefore I will cast thee as profane out of the mountain of God: and I will destroy thee, O covering cherub, from the midst of the stones of fire

17 Thine heart was lifted up because of thy beauty, thou hast corrupted thy wisdom by reason of thy brightness: I will cast thee to the ground; I will lay thee before kings that they may behold thee.

Towards the end of this scripture the uncanny consistency with which scripture makes mention of an unsurpassable wisdom in connection with references to Satan and the anti-Christ has become commonplace. Wisdom is an obvious trademark of this satanic influence, however, even more infamous is the tendency for this satanic role to always fall short of God's true glory. The number 666 symbolizes this tendency.

The Number of the Beast

In the pages of scripture, a series of numerological insights are brought to light. Seven has long been equated with God's perfect judgment and the summit of God's creative capacity in which seven days were set aside for the creation of the Universe. (Gen 2 vs. 2) Six, on the other hand is quoted as being a human number which shows its inferiority in light of God's perfection. The fact that the book of 1st Chronicles has many references to the number six is not coincidental.

It may be that Solomon developed a morbid fascination in associating himself with this number or that historians secretly devised a way of identifying and preserving the true identity of the anti-Christ. Whatever the reason, certain clues arise suggesting that such references are probably deliberate. The stairway of six steps overlaid with gold leading to the ivory throne overlaid with pure gold might be overlooked if not for the reference to the Queen of Sheba's tribute of 666 talents of gold given to Solomon annually.

1 Kings 10 vs. 1

AND when the queen of Sheba heard of the fame of Solomon concerning the names of the Lord, she came to prove him with hard questions

2 And she came to Jerusalem with a very great train, with camels that bare spices, and very much gold, and precious stones: and when she was come to Solomon, she communed with him of all that was in her heart.

3 And Solomon told her all her questions: there was not any thing hid from the king, which he told her not.

14 Now the weight of gold that came to Solomon in one year was 666 talents of gold.

18 Moreover the king made a great throne of ivory, and overlaid it with the best gold.

19 The throne had six steps, and the top of the throne was round behind: and there were stays on either side on the place of the seat, and two lions stood beside the stays.

20 And twelve lions stood there on the one side and on the other upon the six steps: there was not the like made in any kingdom.

This final reference to the number of the beast from the book of Revelations seems to stand as a notice of the enemy's virtual defeat. The abuses of God's privilege and power though allowed temporarily as an expression of our free will not go unpunished, rather God uses Satan's rebellious nature for an opportunity to identify those who are truly responding to Christ's calling. In the following scripture the wisdom exercised by the anti-Christ is eternally undone and bares the eternal punishment of God's wrath.

Revelations 13 vs. 18

Here is wisdom, let him that hath understanding count the number of the beast: for it is the number of a man; and his number is 666.

Another sign of Solomon's infidelity is the vision that Ezekiel was given of a new Temple with several obvious differences to the former Temple. For example the ominous six steps that lead up to the ivory throne overlaid with gold, is replaced by the notion that the new Temple would contain several gates with stairs of seven steps. (Ezekiel 40 vs. 22, 26) The Lord himself voices his displeasure by addressing the vain attempts of former kings to fashion their royal stations as if they were comparable to his.

Ezekial 43 vs. 6

And I heard him speaking unto me out of the house; and the man stood by me.

7 And he said unto me. Son of man, the place of my throne, and the place of the soles of my feet, where I will dwell in the midst of the children of Israel forever, and my holy name, shall the house of Israel no more defile, neither they, nor their kings, by their whoredom, nor by the carcasses of their kings in their high places.

8 In their setting of their threshold by my thresholds, and their post by my posts, and the wall between me and them, they have even defiled my holy name by their abominations that they have committed: wherefore I have consumed them in my anger.

9 Now let them put away their whoredom, and the carcasses of their kings, far from me, and I will dwell in the midst of them forever.

In the next chapter we will examine at length, the nature of the occult practices that first infiltrated the nation of Israel and how God's final judgment is ultimately shaped and decided by this infidelity. The historical significance surrounding the true identity of the anti-Christ including personal testimonials of this revelation will be further explored, leading up to documented scientific and archeological discoveries that support the existence of occult practices in the early Temple period. Still other mysteries wait to be unraveled so that the legacy of God's word can fulfill its purpose in exposing the works of darkness.

III
Fallen Priesthood

Solomon's gradual moral decline was overshadowed by the abuse of certain irrevocable God-given privileges. In the place of certain keynote religious platforms that were established, it is evident that Solomon would serve as a type of satanic high priest who would gradually come to devise the standards for satanic worship and practice for his generation and for generations to come. Just as the provocation of Solomon's deplorable actions seems to reach a climax, the form and intention of God's judgment emerges in scripture to reflect the exact nature of these crimes. The nature and standard of God's punishment ultimately fits the crime for any and all individuals engrossed in this form of rebellion.

The initial craft of Solomon's moral character is to carefully test the limits of God's irrevocable word in the same way a child tends to instinctively test the limits imposed by any designated guardian. In this tendency Solomon's disobedience is subtle. From society's standpoint most of Solomon's behavior is seldom identified for it's truly sinful nature since the media is already preoccupied with the idealistic, rich, and powerful playboy image that Solomon has come to represent.

Promise Based On God's Irrevocable Word

Solomon is also careful to capitalize on every opportunity to identify himself with the power of God's unfailing word. Even when Solomon's behavior seems to transgress all the lawful obligations of kingly rule*, Solomon continues to pursue his every desire knowing full well that none of these transgressions could possibly exceed the bounds of God's supernatural promise.

In the case of Solomon's priesthood, it is achieved when Solomon effectively fulfills the prophecy concerning a new priestly order that was soon to arise. Even though Solomon's future exploits are not hidden from God, Solomon's secret desire for instatement to this priestly authority is unequivocally granted. The instatement of this priestly role is allowed at Solomon's expense so that the true vocation of God's anger and judgment can be adequately represented. Since Solomon is apt to receive this priestly authority, he ultimately takes on the role of symbolically representing the brunt of God's fiery judgment. This fallen representation is also allowed in order to secure a balance; Satan's traditional role as an accuser of the brethren is evenly set against Christ's priestly role as a mediator for the sins of mankind.

1 Samuel 2 vs. 34
And this shall be a sign unto thee, that shall come upon thy two sons, on Hophni and Phinehas; in one day they shall die both of them.
35 And I will raise me up a faithful priest, that shall do according to that which is in mine heart and my mind: and I will build him a sure house; and he shall walk before mine anointed forever.
36 And it shall come to pass, that every one that is left in thine house shall come and crouch to him for a piece of silver and a morsel of bread, and shall say, Put me, I pray thee, into one of the priests' offices, that I may eat a piece of bread.

Despite the tendency for Bible scholars to attribute the fulfillment of this prophecy to Zadok, statements in this scripture seems to point to Solomon. Scriptures mentioning of a sure house is suggestive of the building of the Temple. The mentioning of silver is an obvious reference to one of Solomon's well-known trademarks as will soon be explored. Lastly the following scripture evidently depicts Solomon as the only one who would have the authority to appoint the individual of his choosing to one of the priest's offices. Solomon's name is clearly stated as fulfilling the word of the Lord regarding this prophecy.

1 Kings 2 vs 27

So Solomon thrust out Abiathar from being priest unto the Lord; that he might fulfill the word of the Lord, which he spake concerning the house of Eli in Shiloh.

Perhaps the most unprecedented example of God's favor being set upon an individual is shown when God identifies Solomon as his own son. This is the specific statement that qualifies Solomon to take on the identity of the son of perdition. As Solomon's moral decay draws to its demolition, this son ship develops into the morbid allegory of a prodigal son that refuses to be redeemed. The eternal nature of this allegory becomes even more vivid when it is compared with Christ's many opposite symbolic representations.

1 Chronicles 22 vs. 7

And David said to Solomon, My son, as for me, it was in my mind to build a house unto the name of the Lord my God:

8 But the word of the Lord came to me saying, Thou hast shed blood abundantly, and hast made great wars: thou shalt not build an house unto my name, because thou hast shed much blood upon the earth in my sight.

9 Behold, a son shall be born to thee, who shall be a man of rest: and I will give him rest from all his enemies round about: for his name shall be Solomon, and I will give peace and quietness unto Israel in his days.

10 He shall build an house for my name; and he shall be my son, and I will be his father; and I will establish the throne of his kingdom over Israel forever.

The most encompassing symbol of Solomon's personality is revealed by the types and shadows* of sacrifice hinted at in the previous chapter. Solomon's name means peace in the original Hebrew tongue. In keeping with Levitical ordinances of sacrifice, the offering that Jesus Christ accomplishes for the sins of mankind runs parallel to the peace offering best represented by Solomon and the self will of all of those who follow after his rebellion. The implications of these types and shadows will be further explored later on in this chapter.

Lawful Obligations of the king

The lawful obligations of kingly rule were clearly spelled out in scripture in a way that was simple and direct. History proves beyond a reasonable doubt that Solomon was both intelligent and wise by any standard. It is therefore difficult to believe that his infringement of deuteronic law could be anything short of deliberate and self-serving. While these infractions may seem light in comparison to Solomon's future betrayal, it is clear that Solomon was testing the resolve of his growing political might and popularity. Since much of the royal privilege typical to foreign nations was still unprecedented in Israel, not only was Solomon's political supremacy exercised as a result of this agenda, but also it soon gave Solomon the ability to enjoy all the pleasures of the surrounding heathen nations without the fear of reprisal from insiders.

The acuity with which these lawful obligations* were disobeyed leaves little doubt as to Solomon's guilt in terms of his intentional violation. One comes away with the sneaking suspicion that most, if not all of these requirements were violated in one form or another. Since this treatise is meant to reflect the deeper spiritual implications of Solomon's more covert actions the assessment of Solomon's direct moral character will be dealt with here only on a limited basis.

Deuteronomy 17 vs. 14

When thou art come unto the land which the Lord thy God giveth thee, and shalt possess it, and shalt dwell therein, and shalt say, I will set a king over me, like as all the nations that are about me;

15 Thou shalt in any wise set him king over thee, whom the Lord thy God shall choose: one from among thy bretheren shalt thou set king over thee: thou mayest not set a stranger over thee, which is not thy brother.

16 But he shall not multiply horses to himself, nor cause the people to return to Egypt, to the end that he should multiply horses; forasmuch as the Lord hath said unto you ye shall henceforth return no more that way.

17 Neither shall he multiply wives to himself, that his heart turn not away: neither shall he greatly multiply to himself silver and gold.

18 And it shall be, when he sitteth upon the throne of his kingdom, that he shall write him a copy of this law in a book out of that which is before the preists the Levites:

19 And it shall be with him,and he shall read therein all the days of his

life: that he may learn to fear the Lord his God, to keep all the words of this law and these statues, to do them:
20 That his heart be not lifted up above his bretheren, and that he turn not aside from the commandment, to the right hand or to the left: to the end that he may prolong his days in his kingdom, he, and his children, in the midst of Israel.

Concerning the first lawful obligation, as stated, Solomon was not to go into Egypt to get horses. Despite scriptures clear and emphatic direction, early on in Solomon's reign this ethical requirement is bluntly violated. Though the following scripture is an obvious historical record of Solomon's violation, the Lord's disapproval with this course of action would not be voiced till centuries later as spoken through the prophet Ezekiel.

2 Chronicles 1 vs. 14 And Solomon gathered chariots and horsemen: and he had a thousand and four hundred chariots, and twelve thousand horsemen, which he placed in the chariot cities, and with the king at Jerusalem.
16 And Solomon had horses brought out of Egypt, and linen yarn: the king's merchants received the linen yarn at a price.
17 And they fetched up, and brought forth out of Egypt a chariot for six hundred shekels of silver, and an horse for an hundred and fifty: and so brought they out horses for all the kings of the Hittites, and for the kings of Syria, by their means.

Regarding Solomon's delinquent behavior, the Lord's response is clearly documented at various points in scripture. In the following excerpt, scripture declares the consequences of the king Solomon's deliberate neglect of these lawful obligations. The violation of this legal requirement leaves Israel with a dire consequence. Contextually it is true that this recourse takes place many years after Solomon's particular violation, however, one may reasonably conclude that because of the initial promise of his irrevocable word, the Lord waited for this consequence to be carried out.

Ezekiel 17 vs. 12
Say now to the rebellious house, Know ye not what these things mean? Tell them, Behold, the kings of Babylon is come to Jerusalem, and hath taken the king thereof, and led them with him to Babylon:
13 And hath taken of the king's seed, and made a covenant with him, and hath taken an oath of him: he hath also taken the mighty of the land:
14 That the kingdom might be base, that it might not lift itself up, but

that by keeping of his covenant it might stand.

15 But he rebelled against him in sending his ambassadors into Egypt, that they might give him horses and much people. Shall he prosper? shall he escape that doeth such things? Or shall he break the covenant, and be delivered?

16 As I live, saith the lord God, surely in the place where the king dwelleth that made him king, whose oath he despised, and whose covenant he brake, even with him in the midst of Babylon he shall die

Concerning King Solomon's remaining obligations many historical examples of these infractions did follow. Regarding the issue of not multiplying wives unto him, Solomon is recorded as multiplying as many as 700 wives, and princesses and three hundred concubines. (1 Kings 11 vs. 3) Incredibly, scripture states that Solomon had made silver and gold "as plenteous as stones" in the city of Jerusalem. (2 Chr. 1 vs15) Concerning the law that states how the king should keep a copy of these rules to be made accessible in a book, surprisingly, history suggests that this was done. Ironically, when this book of lawful obligations* was first found, history documents a very strong reaction to the notion of these infractions on the part of Solomon's predecessor.

II Kings 22 vs. 8

And Hilkiah the high priest said unto Shaphan the scribe, I have found the book of the law in the house of the Lord, And Hilkiah gave the book to Shaphan and he read it.

10 And Shaphan the scribe shewed the king saying, Hilkiah the priest hath delivered me a book. And Shaphan read it before the king.

11 And it came to pass, when the king heard the words of the book of the law, that he rent his clothes.

12 And the king commanded Hilkiah the priest, and Ahikam the son of Shaphan, and Achbor the son of Michaiah, and Shaphan the scribe, and Asahiah a servant of the king's saying,

13 Go ye, inquire of the Lord for me, and for the people, and for all Judah, concerning the words of this book that is found: for great is the wrath of the Lord that is kindled against us, because our fathers have not harkened unto the words of this book, to do according unto all that which is written concerning us.

Although one could safely argue that the book that was found was not the book that was specified in deuteronic law, it is undeniable that the future moral decay of the nation of Israel stems from Solomon's reign. In fact many of the occult artifacts that were uncovered and were discovered in the same period that this book was found shared a mutual association with the reign of Solomon. Although Solomon's emergence as a satanic high priest is far more covert, these obvious infractions seem to support this claim from a tip of the iceberg effect.

The Fire of Sacrifice

Solomon's slow decline into the occult was fueled by his unquenchable desire to achieve a God-like status. With his legendary wisdom, Solomon exhibited an accurate knowledge of the spirit's eternal nature. Solomon's prophetic gifting would have unlocked the mystery of immortality reflected in Christ's death and resurrection, and rendered an account of the sanctification of Christ's indestructible life. Unfortunately, it is certain by his falling away, that Solomon's thirst for power was not yet satisfied by these promises.

Solomon's subtle influence over Israel slowly ignited into a resurgence of idolatry based on the manipulation of these divine principles. Moved by his secret desire to become the true object of men's worship, Solomon emerged with a premonition of the first satanic ritual. Eventually this subversive nature touched on areas of Old Testament law that were destined to fall into disuse because of this irreverent approach. Undoubtedly Solomon's short-lived power translated into lavish ritual and imaginative incantations aimed at fulfilling his own selfish desires. The true ulterior motive to this rhetoric was to secure a satanic following by distracting mankind from following after Christ.

Although many aspects of Old Testament worship were soon rejected after this period, the best known example of a practice that the Lord eventually dismissed is that of ritual animal sacrifice. Solomon's peace offerings, which included the sacrifice of animals, eventually became too extravagant and insincere in practice and not reflecting the true heart of worship. Solomon was known to have had a strange understanding and affinity to animals. (1 Kings 5 vs. 33,34) Folklore suggests that Solomon's psychic connection was so strong that he could literally speak to animals and understand their reply. Experimentation in these occult practices allowed Solomon to explore the questions he had regarding the sanctification of animals. (ECL 3 vs. 21) Eventually the whole ritual of animal sacrifice began to harbor qualities of spiritual animism and demonic influence. When

Solomon began to openly practice the worship of idols, the sacrifice of animals continued on as an occult ritual, inciting divination to be practiced at an alarming rate. Unsurprisingly the church of Satan has not excused animal sacrifice as a form of worship up to the present day.

The Temple Dedication

At first glance Solomon's initiative in the building of the temple and his prayerful dedication seems sincere, even inspirational. It therefore seems unlikely that Solomon would ever pursue these unholy ambitions at this point in history. Solomon's prayers were even honored by God during the dedication of the temple when fire came down from heaven to consume the sacrifice. As God continues, as always, to honor the promises he made concerning Solomon, God's true feelings involving the ritual sacrifice and dedication of the Temple are waiting to emerge as a result of a more detailed investigation of scripture.

The following is an excerpt from one of King David's prayers where another example of the Lord's irrevocable promise is expounded.

Psalm 132 vs. 1

LORD remember David, and all his afflictions;

2 How he sware unto the Lord, and vowed unto the mighty God of Jacob;

3 Surely I will not come into the tabernacle of my house, nor go up into my bed;

4 I will not give sleep to mine eyes, or slumber to mine eyelids,

5 Until I find out a place for the Lord, an habitation for the mighty God of Jacob

10 For thy servant David's sake turn not away the face of thine anointed.

11 The Lord hath sworn in truth unto David, he will not turn from it; Of the fruit of thy body will I set upon thy throne.

12 If thy children will keep my covenant and my testimony that I shall teach them, their children shall also sit upon thy throne for evermore.

13 For the Lord hath chosen Zion; he hath desired it for his habitation.

The dedication of the Lord's Temple was clearly the most pivotal point in Solomon's reign as king. In order to be honored by God as one of his anointed servants Solomon had to word his intentions very carefully. It is after Solomon's historic prayer of dedication that the Lord's fire falls from heaven to consume the sacrifice, in an awesome display of God's power.

II Chronicles 6 vs. 40

Now, my God, let, I beseech thee, thine eyes be opened and let thine ears be attent unto the prayer that is made in this place.

41 Now therefore arise, O lord God, into thy resting place, thou and the ark of thy strength: let thy priests, O Lord God, be clothed with salvation, and let thy saints rejoice in goodness.

42 O Lord God, turn not away the face of thine anointed: remember the mercies of David thy servant.

7 vs1

NOW when Solomon had made an end of praying, the fire came down from heaven and consumed the burnt offering and the sacrifices, and the glory of the Lord filled the house.

Before excusing every avenue of Solomon's disobedience as a result of this supernatural occurrence, the promise of the Lord's irrevocable word should be taken into account. According to the word of the Lord, Solomon's prayer, as well as his statements regarding the former promises and covenants of God, is virtually flawless. Regarding the fire that fell from heaven, scripture has on occasion disclaimed such exhibitions as false signs and wonders. Two of Aaron's own sons were killed because they offered profane fire before the Lord. (Lev. 10 vs. 1,2) In the book of Revelations a mysterious succession of satanic authority is described. An individual with the authority to speak like a dragon and to exercise false signs and wonders even to "make fire come down from heaven on the earth" in the sight of men is specifically mentioned. When our limited linear perspective is stripped away, it becomes obvious that this reference could very well pertain to Solomon and his unholy priesthood.

Revelations 13 vs. 11

And I beheld another beast coming up out of the earth; and he had two horns like a lamb, and he spake as a dragon.

12 And he exerciseth all the power of the first beast before him, and causeth the earth and them which dwell therein to worship the first beast, whose deadly wound was healed.

13 And he doeth great wonders, so that he maketh fire come down from the earth in the sight of men,

14 And deceiveth them that dwell on the earth by the means of those miracles which he had power to do in the sight of the beast; saying to them that dwell on the earth, that they should make an image to the beast, which had the wound by a sword, and did live.

The wide range of interpretations and complex symbols in the book of Revelations will be further examined in later chapters. Though the meanings of these scriptures are subject to interpretation, though fire did fall from heaven to consume the sacrifice, the Lord remains curiously silent during the Temple dedication. In the verses that follow, the Lord sternly warns Solomon of the dire consequences if Solomon should ever turn away from him. (2 Chr. 7 vs. 17) The fact that Solomon eventually did turn away from God strengthens the argument that Solomon was engaged in the careful art of deception from the very beginning.

The Peace Offering

Pertaining to the sheer magnitude and ceremonial pomp of the Temple's first dedication, in order to fully understand the Lord's response it becomes necessary to reexamine the particular details of this proceeding including the nature of the sacrifice, and evident mood of the day. Even the accurate Levitical practice of this ceremony warrants investigation considering the burden of proof thus far instated. In investigation of the Lord's formal reply to this historic occasion it is likewise necessary to search the scriptures for the time and season of God's reply.

In the spirit of Solomon's usual approach it is not surprising that the offering used in the Temple dedication was, in fact, a peace offering*. In what could have been a more solemn occasion, as to the epic proportion of the peace offering, history shows that a grand feast was held that was similar in scale by all accounts. Strangely, nowhere in the historical account of the Temple's dedication is the sacrifice of a sin offering* ever mentioned.

1 Kings 8 vs. 62

And the king, and all Israel with him, offered sacrifice before the Lord.

63 And Solomon offered a sacrifice of peace offerings, which he offered unto the Lord, two and twenty thousand oxen, and an hundred and twenty thousand sheep. So the king and all the children of Israel dedicated the house of the Lord.

64 The same day did the king hallow the middle of the court that was before the house of the Lord: for there he offered burnt offerings, and meat offerings, and the fat of the peace offerings: because the brasen alter that was before the Lord was too little to receive the burnt offerings and meat offerings, and the fat of the peace offerings.

65 And at that time Solomon held a feast, and all Israel with him, a great

congregation, from the entering in of hamath unto the river of Egypt, before the Lord our God, seven days and seven days even fourteen days.

The specific Levitical practice regarding such a sacrifice also merits attention. It is true that a peace offering* is typically rendered in the swearing of a solemn oath, and that the priests retained the privilege of feasting on the burnt offering's remains. Accordingly, if Solomon's feast was based entirely on this ordinance of sacrifice the possibility that this meat was made available for feasting for the full fourteen days is in strict violation of this protocol. If this ritual was incorrectly followed deliberately or otherwise this could have made a very negative impression on the Lord. Not with standing, the ordinance of sacrifice takes on a very different connotation in scripture from this point onward.

Leviticus 19 vs. 4

Turn ye not unto idols, nor make to yourself molten gods; I am the Lord your God.

5 And if ye offer a sacrifice of peace offerings unto the Lord, ye shall offer it at your own will.

6 It shall be eaten the same day ye offer it, and on the morrow: and if ought remain until the third day, it shall be burnt in the fire.

7 And if it be eaten at all on the third day, it is abominable; it shall not be accepted.

8 Therefore everyone that eateth it shall bear his iniquity, because he hath profaned the hallowed thing of the Lord: and that soul shall be cut off from among his people.

In what would seem to be a reply, the Lord charges that the Temple's dedication was not in keeping with the true heart of sacrifice. The Lord is clearly more concerned with the sincere and contrite heart of true spiritual worship and less moved by ceremony and ritual. As for Solomon, the idea that he could impress God through his many sacrifices is a vain and presumptuous notion that meets with divine offense. The symbolic gesture of this peace offering and its failure to make a divine impression becomes a fitting motif when the form of God's judgment is finally expedited.

The following scripture draws on many of the artifacts left behind near the end of Solomon's reign. The shield made reference to could obviously pertain to Solomon's shields that were made for the house of the forest of Lebanon, mentioned here as the "house of the forest." (II Chron. 9 vs. 15,16) The Lord himself describes the landmarks specific to the sight of his holy Temple all of which would have been constructed in Solomon's time. God's word goes on to chastise its audience of listeners regarding the failure to consider the true nature of its chief architect.

Isaiah 22 vs. 6
And Elam bare the quiver with chariots of men and horsemen, and Kir uncovered the shield.
7 And it shall come to pass that thy choicest valleys shall be full of chariots, and the horses shall set themselves in array at the gate.
8 And he discovered the covering of Judah, and thou didst look in that day to the armour of the house of the forest.
9 Ye have seen also the breaches of the city of David, that they are many: and ye gathered together the waters of the lower pool.
10 And ye have numbered the houses of Jerusalem, and the houses have ye broken down to fortify the wall.
11 Ye made also a ditch between the two walls for the water of the old pool: but ye have not looked unto the maker thereof, neither had respect unto him that fashioned it long ago.
12 And in that day did the Lord God of hosts call to weeping, and to mourning, and to baldness and to girding with sackcloth:
13 And behold joy and gladness slaying oxen, and killing sheep, eating flesh, and drinking wine: let us eat and drink: for tomorrow we shall die.
14 And it was revealed in mine ears by the Lord of hosts, surely this iniquity shall not be purged from you till ye die, saith the Lord God of hosts.

The statement, "let us eat drink and be merry for tomorrow we shall die," is a famous quotation of the Bible that could well originate from Solomon himself. Solomon's wisdom, surprisingly, often takes on an existential view* whereby his readers are encouraged to live life to the full in the expectation that the pleasures of this life will not be enjoyed in the grave. (Eccl. 9 vs. 7-10) This mentality could well have originated from a more fatalistic personal belief held by Solomon. The catch-phrase quality of this statement would have made for excellent propaganda in the push for Solomon's religious and political agendas. Whatever the case this appeals, to the darker more selfish aspect of human nature, has certainly taken society by storm.

Amazingly even through the turmoil of this rebellion, the Lord expresses his readiness to forgive. In a declaration that closely parallel's Solomon's prayer for the temple dedication the Lord remonstrates with the nation of

Israel. As noted in the Lord's reply, Solomon would customarily spread his hands to heaven as he did in his prayer to dedicate the Temple. (1 Kings 8 vs. 22) In this famous passage of scripture the Lord offers to undue the harmful effects that Solomon's hidden agendas have reaped. More specifically, the Lord eventually offers mankind a bold new approach where the ordinance of sacrifice is about to take on a new form.

Isaiah 1 vs. 11

To what purpose is the multitude of your sacrifices unto me? Smith the Lord: I am full of the burnt offerings of rams, and the fat of fed beasts; and I delight not in the blood of bullocks, or lambs, or he goats.

12 When ye come to appear before me who hath required this at your hand to tread my courts?

13 Bring no more vain oblations; incense is an abomination unto me; the new moons and Sabbaths, the calling of the assemblies, I cannot away with; it is iniquity, even the solemn meeting.

15 And when ye spread forth your hands, I will hide mine eyes from you: yea, when ye make many prayers, I will not hear: your hands are full of blood.

17 Learn to do well; seek judgment, relieve the oppressed, judge the fatherless, plead for the widow.

18 Come now, and let us reason together, saith the Lord: though your sins be as scarlet, they shall be white as snow; though they be red like crimson, they shall be as wool.

Although the Lord effectually discourages ritual offerings it is evident that this ordinance continued to be practiced. Historical scholars support the belief that the succession of Solomon's priesthood was still in authority in the Temple up until the time of Christ's crucifixion. The Sadducees*, the priestly authority at time of Jesus death, are believed to have originated from Zadok and Solomon's priestly order.(1) This priesthood was clearly anti-christ from the standpoint of it's rejection of the principle belief in the resurrection. (Mark. 12 vs. 18) In fact, in the following centuries, there is a principle shift in theology that tends to deny the entire existence of the after life. (Acts 23 vs. 7) The essential medium of God's judgment is conveniently absent for all those who subscribe to this doctrine.

The Doctrine of Demons

The doctrine of demons* described in the Bible has recently become the subject of speculation regarding a common heresy that had emerged. (Tim. 4 vs. 1) The word demon bares a similar distinction to the ritual practice of idol worship described in the Old and New Testament.(2) It was perhaps the exploitation of this ancient ritual worship, blended with a new found spiritualism that facilitated the resurgence of idolatry in Solomon's time. An inquiry as to whether or not animals would ever receive a glorified nature similar to their human counter parts was eventually raised. The ritual sanctification of animals probably gained it's momentum from the understanding that if animals were ceremonially prepared and their place in the resurrection was thus secured then a spiritual release would exist in it's sacrifice. (Lev. 17 vs. 11) This spiritual entity would then find it's home in the idolatrous image of one's choosing. This explains the prophetic reference to the "god's that came newly up" described in deuteronic texts. (Deut. 32 vs. 17) (Eventually the Christian ritual of a prayer of thanksgiving was added to rectify this tendency, although such efforts were thwarted when the question of this sanctification resurfaced.) (1 Tim. 4 vs. 1)

This resurgence developed hand in hand with the more ancient belief that certain animals were originally deemed ceremonially unclean. (Lev. 11 vs. 20) Similarly, the release of unclean spirits was supposed when the ceremony of ritual cleansing was violated. This is the ceremonial spiritualism and witchcraft that was exploited by some in order to gain political advantage over their enemies. Unclean spirits were traditionally to blame for many sicknesses in Jesus time and were described as a very real spiritual force.

Thus, occult practices evolved from more ancient beliefs that fell into disuse. Religious icons traditionally repenting the Lord's divine deliverance, like the bronze serpent held by Moses in order to deliver Israel at the hand of poisonous vipers, was eventually destroyed because of its use in occult practices. This bronze serpent was soon worshipped as an idol and even given the name Nehushtan. (II Kings 18 vs. 4) The scapegoat traditionally released on the day of atonement took on a demonic connotation and was eventually used in a satanic form of worship. (Lev 16,17) Azazel, as this demonic spirit was called, was eventually associated with the satyrs that inhabited desolate waste lands and frequently took the form of a goat.(3) (Isa. 13 vs. 21) In most examples instances the object of occult worship usually retained some bestial qualities consistent with the rudiments of spiritual animism.

This bestial nature was eventually attributed to Satan himself as the rendering of divine punishment. Traditionally, scripture tells us that Satan has taken the form of many beasts including the serpent in the garden of Eden, (Gen 3 vs. 4) the dragon who was cast out of heaven (Rev 12 vs. 3) as well as many other beasts that have many other idolatrous connotations. The giving over to this bestial nature is purposed by God as a precursor to the nature of his divine judgment.

The Fire of God's Judgment

The ordinance of sacrifice is patterned after many aspects of God's judgment. Fire has long been seen as an instrument of God's wrath poised to consume the wicked with unquenchable fury on the great and terrible day of the Lord. (Isa. 66 vs. 15,16) It is also commonly attributed to a purging or rite of purification for those who are poised to withstand this fiery judgment. (Matt. 3 vs. 11) What ever the case, in the New Testament, the nature of this ordinance of sacrifice is soon indoctrinated into the minds of the faithful by way of a spiritual preparation and sanctification*, or, for those engaged in rebellion by way of being cast into the eternal lake of fire.

The myth of dualism has at times infiltrated Christian thought in the area of God's judgment. Although the apocalyptic notion of our accountability before God is accurate, the fire of God's judgment is primarily laid up for Satan and his false prophets. (Rev 20 vs. 10) Those who choose to remain in the shelter of God's spiritual protection are likely to remain unharmed. Still, devoted Christians are sequestered to "present their bodies a living sacrifice holy acceptable to God." (Romans 12 vs. 1)

With this revelation in mind, Solomon himself appears as a type of sacrifice in his affiliation with the beast that is cast into the lake of fire. Prophecy surrounding this divine retribution is equally compelling in the area of this satanic priesthood. This satanic presence is frequently discovered in the context of God's judgment. In the following scripture a hidden tabernacle of satanic significance is uncovered along with this religious authority where the corrupt nature of this priesthood is practiced.

Job 20 vs. 19

Because he hath oppressed and forsaken the poor; because he hath violently taken away an house which he builder not;

20 Surely he shall not feel quietness in his belly, he shall not save of that which he desired.
21 There shall none of his meat be left; therefore shall no man look for his goods.
22 In the fullness of his sufficiency he shall be in straits; every hand of the wicked shall come upon him.
23 When he is about to fill his belly, God shall cast the fury of his wrath upon him, and shall rain it upon him, while he is eating.
24 He shall flee from the iron weapon, and the boe of steel shall strike him through.
25 It is drawn, and cometh out of the body; yea, the glittering sword cometh out of his gall: terrors are about him.
26 All darkness shall be hid in his secret places: a fire not blown shall consume him; it shall go ill with him that is left in his tabernacle.
27 Then heaven shall reveal his iniquity; and the earth shall rise up against him.
28 The increase of his house shall depart, and his goods shall flow away in the day of his wrath.
29 This is the portion of a wicked man from God and the heritage appointed unto him by god.

Scripture makes clear reference to the act of "violently taking away a house which he builded not." This could well refer to Solomon's informal construction of the Lord's Temple and its eventual slip into idolatry. (Other prophetic statements pertaining to the demise of this anti-Christ figure, as attributed to Solomon, will be thoroughly dealt with in a separate chapter.) The religious reference to this hidden tabernacle suggests that all those who are covertly engaged in association with this occult force will suffer Solomon's sacrificial fate. The sum of this sacrifice will include all the evil imaginations and abominable practices since time began. With this understanding the stronghold of fear and superstition of Satan's existence is somewhat diffused. Despite the medias attempt to portray this satanic influence as a pop-culture phenomenon, this clarification gives one the assurance that Satan's association with these evil imaginations is purely incidental. According to the word of the Lord the fact that "all darkness shall be hid in his secret places" is entirely the result of God's eternal judgment.

Idol Worship

To conclude this investigation into the topic of Solomon's fallen priesthood the testimonial of a key witness in Solomon's practice of idolatry will be briefly examined. Every indication suggests that this individual witnessed the gradual fall of the Temple's spiritual worship as it occurred very early on in Solomon's reign. The witness in question expresses an obvious reluctance in implicating Solomon, due in part to the overwhelming burden of grief and frustration over this discovery.

Research suggests that Asaph*, as he was called, was probably a Levite priest, and chief minister of music along with his sons during the early Temple period. (4) The following excerpt is taken from Asaph's first psalm in a series of ten. Asaph's testament to the occurrences in the Temple is conspicuously placed just after David's final psalm, which sings the praises of his son Solomon.

Psalm 73

TRULY God is good to Israel, even to such as are of a clean heart.

2 But as for me my feet were almost gone; my steps had well nigh slipped.

3 For I was envious at the foolish, when I saw the prosperity of the wicked.

4 For there are no bands in their death; but their strength is firm

5 They are not in trouble as other men; neither are they plagued like other men

6 Therefore pride compasseth them about as a chain; violence covereth them as a garment.

7 Their eyes stand out with fatness; they have more than heart could wish.

8 They are corrupt, and speak wickedly concerning oppression: they speak loftily.

9 They set their mouth against the heavens, and their tongue walketh through the earth.

10 Therefore his people return hither; and waters of a full cup are wrung out to them.

11 And they say, How doth God know? and is there knowledge in the most High?

12 Behold, these are the ungodly, who prosper in the world; they increase in riches.

In this portion of Asaph's testimonial, the presence of an anti-Christ is clearly implied. The fact that he is speaking of an individual that has "no bands in death" and that "they are not in trouble as other men" makes

Solomon highly suspect as to it's subjectivity. Solomon clearly had the privilege of God's protection and anointing that reaches beyond the grave. Perhaps even more specifically, Solomon was not "in trouble as other men" since God granted him peace from his enemies according to his irrevocable word. (I Chr. 22 vs. 9) This portion of scripture also outlines Asaph's reaction to the tone of Solomon's many speeches. Although widely accepted today, by traditional standards and beliefs, Asaph may have taken great exception to these so-called teachings.

The next portion of this scripture reflects on the deep sorrow and frustration that Asaph would have wrestled with upon discovering Solomon's infidelity. Perhaps Asaph's most challenging burden would lie in the fact that his discovery regarding Solomon's deception was destined to remain a secret, at least for the time being. In the following passage Asaph expresses his dilemma and consequent reluctance in speaking out against the Lord's anointed servant and the generation of the Lord's own children. With the full weight of this knowledge in mind Asaph finds solace in the knowledge and understanding that God's judgment would soon be administered.

Psalm 73 vs. 13

Verily I have cleansed my heart in vain, and washed my hands in innocency.

14 For all the day long have I been plagued, and chastened every morning.
15 If I say, I will speak thus; behold, I should offend against the generation of thy children.
16 When I thought to know this, it was too painful for me;
17 Until I went into the sanctuary of God; then understood I their end.
18 Surely thou didst set them in slippery places; thou casted them down into destruction.
19 How are they brought into desolation, as in a moment! they are utterly consumed with terrors.
20 As a dream when one awaketh; so, O lord, when thou awakest, thou shalt despise their image.
21 Thus my heart was grieved, and I was pricked in my reins.
22 So foolish was I, and ignorant: I was as a beast before thee.
23 Nevertheless I am continually with thee: thou hast holden me by my right hand

Beyond Asaph's initial emotional reaction is the stark realization of Solomon's deception. Perhaps reminders of Solomon's subtle personality came back to haunt Asaph in an epiphany of Solomon's true identity. The tone the psalmist presents reflects the initial shock of this satanic nature being suddenly uncovered, as well as the psalmist's moment of clarity when the startling nature of God's judgment was first understood. As the psalmist puts it plainly to the Lord, "I was like a beast before thee." The fact that understanding finally came when the sanctuary was visited makes the notion that idolatry was being practiced as highly suspect.

Psalm 73 vs. 23

Nevertheless I am continually with thee: thou hast holden me by thy right hand.

24 Thou shalt guide me with thy counsel, and afterward receive me to glory.

25 Whom have I in heaven but thee? and there is none upon earth that I desire beside thee.

26 My flesh and my heart faileth: but God is the strength of my heart, and my portion forever.

27 For, lo, they that are far from thee shall perish: thou hast destroyed all them that go a whoring from thee.

28 But it is good for me to draw near to God: I have put my trust in the Lord God, that I may declare all thy works.

The psalmist ends on a positive note by expressing his hopes of being received into glory. Though the weight of this burden had made his heart fail, Asaph continues to pledge his undying faith and loyalty to God.

In the next chapter Solomon's idolatry will be explored at great length, along with substantial archeological evidence of the existence of pagan temples in and around the sight of the Temple mount during the early Temple period. The specific implications of how Solomon's behavior was influenced by this worship will be examined along with the religious significance regarding the deities that had special personal value to Solomon. Finally, geographical hot spots will be explored that have an additional bearing on the nature of God's final judgment.

IV
Solomon's Idol Worship

Regarding the subject of Solomon's idolatry, evidence suggests that Bible scholars took a conservative approach to revealing the extent of the abominations of idolatry that were practiced. Supplementary accounts have proven time and again that the practice of idolatry not only existed, but also actually flourished in and around the period of the early Temple. As Solomon's evasive spiritual maneuvering continued, idolatry would play a key role in preserving the essential values that sustained his regime.

Central to his most fundamental values and beliefs was the issue of prosperity. The practice of this idolatry would have enabled Solomon to take a self-serving approach to worship that was virtually nonexistent in his own traditional belief system. Unlike the Jewish faith, heathen nations were generally lacking in the foundational principles of reciprocity that were eventually supported by the teachings of Christ. Solomon's motivation for this self-serving propaganda had three essential components; firstly for exploiting God's power directly for selfish gain, including political power, religious authority, wealth, and pleasure, secondly, in a more maniacal sense, to preserve and sustain the protective powers that was innate to his survival. Lastly, Solomon's idolatrous practices fed into an anti-Christ mentality that kept his true identity from being revealed. Thus, Solomon's deceptive powers were preserved for many generations to come.

The enclave of Solomon's political motivation was primarily established out of a desire to achieve a God-like status of his own. Discovering that this was not likely in his present lifetime, Solomon set his sights on maintaining control by a system of government that would only reveal his self proclaimed divinity within the upper echelons of his organization. With the world's economic base firmly in toe, Solomon used his political and religious alliances to formulate an occult platform that would gather a universal appeal. In this way, human nature being what it is, Solomon's influence and deception served its purpose in gaining a substantial base of support.

Baal Worship

The prevalent sociological belief is that civilization as a whole is rooted in the primary shift from a hunter-gatherer existence to an agricultural based model.(1) According to Maslow's hierarchy of needs*, the more basic need of the provision of a consistent food supply is far more primal than the more advanced directive of spiritual self actualization*.(2) Baal worship represents the zenith of this agricultural existence as it developed in Mesopotamia' s fertile crescent, and because of this process, it is understandable how foreign deities appealed to the more basic elementary needs of humanity.

The God of Israel's consideration of moral issues as a primary focus, on the other hand, supports the existence of a God of authentic power and origin. For the true remnant of God's people a turn towards foreign gods represented a degradation of humanity's moral virtue. The prophets believed that only the continuation of authentic worship would truly facilitate mankind's fundamental growth and promised transformation into the divine glory of Christ. It is for this very reason that idolatry is considered such a treasonable moral offence in God's sight.

Baal, on the other hand is recognized primarily as a fertility God, who was worshiped with the hope that certain needs would eventually be requited. Baal along with his consorts presents a very basic example of this self-serving tendency of worship. Even the primary meaning of the name Baal means "possessor," however Baal was known to have many names and titles exclusive to the needs identified in each individual community.(3) Baal-hermon, meaning God of good fortune was named after the northern border of the half tribe of Manasseh, where the Lord eventually destroyed it's inhabitants because of their fall into idolatry. (1 Chr. 5 vs. 25) Baal-hamon meaning lord of abundant wealth was mentioned in The Song of Solomon as a place where a very fertile garden existed that reportedly belonged to Solomon. (Cant 8 vs. 11) Baalzebub, a derivative of the name Baal meaning "lord of the flies" (the god of Ekron) was later coined as the name for the prince of demons, (2 Kings 1 vs. 1-17) 4 (Mk 3 vs. 22) an appropriate name for an idol that will never be favored by the Lord's resurrection.

The following scripture lends one such example entailing the degrading practice of idol worship and it's shameful consequences.

Psalm 106 vs. 17

The earth opened and swallowed up Dathan and covered the company of Abiram

18 And a fire was kindled in their company; the flame burned up the wicked.

19 They made a calf in Horeb, and worshipped the molten image.

20 Thus they changed their glory into the similitude of an ox that eateth grass.

The worship of Baal was most commonly practiced by Israel's historical nemesis, the Canaanites, although the cross-cultural appeal was central to many nations. Ceremonial fertility rituals eventually encompassed a wide range of applications including the accumulation of wealth, sexual passions and reproduction, agricultural provision and good fortune. Almost certainly, the recurring theme to this worship is the basic fulfillment of personal needs and wants.

Although Bible history does not directly implicate Solomon in the worship of Baal, evidence suggests that Solomon converged on the specific aspects of this idolatry at full force. For Solomon, the ideology behind this form of worship was often effective when it came to recruiting proselytes. Since Solomon made for the perfect model of worldly success, this invited a gradual advancement through the ranks of his corporate pyramid, allowing for an appropriate level of disclosure at each station. Eventually this form of corporate government became internal to most worldly organizations. Perhaps the most limiting aspect of this spiritual trap is the popular assumption that godliness may be measured by one's personal gain. Solomon, as evidence will suggest, reportedly endorsed this popular belief. In the New Testament, when this doctrinal footing eventually resurfaced it was quickly dismissed as heresy by Jesus' followers.

1 Timothy 6 vs. 3
If any man teach otherwise, and consent not to wholesome words, even the words of our Lord Jesus Christ, and to the doctrine, which is according to godliness;
4 He is proud, knowing nothing, but doting about questions and strifes of words, where of cometh envy, strife, railings, evil surmisings.
5 Perverse disputings of men of corrupt minds, and destitute of the truth, supposing that gain is godliness: from such withdraw thyself.
6 But godliness with contentment is great gain.

Although Satan is not mentioned in this scriptural reference, satanic attributes are certainly implied. The teaching that these traits are subject to is clearly in conflict with Christ's teachings regarding his kingdom. Christ's spiritual freedom makes the bondage of this ego-ridden mentality all the more apparent. The tendency for this teaching of the anti-Christ to provoke its victims to covetousness perpetuates the snare of the enemy to be set on a global scale.

The Onset of Idolatry

Out of the many nations represented by Solomon's idolatry some included peoples that Israel failed to drive out upon God's instruction, (Duet 23 vs. 3-6) (1 Ki. 11 vs. 1, 5, 7) as well as those that were drawn by those unholy alliances mentioned previously. Some of the gods Solomon worshiped were universally known and accepted; still others had a more intimate personal connotation for Solomon. Whatever the case, Solomon's well known plunge into idolatry is the foundational premise of this treatise. While other evidence Solomon's rebellion is somewhat circumstantial Solomon's practice of idolatry seems to be a historical certainty.

The actual historical account of Solomon's idolatry is based on the persuasion of his many wives. This evidence is drawn out of the history of ill repute associated with the taking of foreign wives. Jacob was clearly dissuaded by his father from taking any foreign wife especially if the woman was a Canaanite. (Gen. 28 vs. 1) Centuries after Solomon's demise, foreign marriages were utterly condemned since it was understood that marriage was a form of covenant, where covenant's with the Lord's political exiles was adamantly condemned. (Ex 23 vs. 32) In the second temple period foreign marriages were even annulled on a massive basis in remembrance of

Solomon's transgressions. (Ezra 10 vs. 11) (Neh. 13 vs. 26)

Solomon's polygamy was practiced on such a scale that a spiritual connotation to his erotic tendencies existed far beyond a reasonable doubt. In the Bible idolatry is often compared to unfaithfulness in marriage since it is an example of the violation of a God given covenant. Solomon's experience in the occult had a strong basis on Solomon's polygamy alone. The strange customs and superstitions Solomon would have encountered with many of his foreign wives had all the earmarks of a coven of witches. In fact Ashtoreth, one of Solomon's idols listed here went on to be one of the principle deities later recognized in the practice of witchcraft.

1 Kings 11 vs. 1

BUT King Solomon loved many strange women, together with the daughter of Pharaoh, women of the Moabites, Ammonites, Edomites, Zidonians and Hittitites.

2 Of the nations concerning which the Lord said ye shall not go in to them, neither shall they come in to you: for surely they will turn away your heart after their gods: Solomon clave unto these in love.

3 And he had seven hundred wives, princesses, and three hundred concubines: and his wives turned away his heart.

4 For it came to pass, when Solomon was old, that his wives turned away his heart after other gods: and his heart was not perfect with the Lord his God, as was the heart of David his father.

5 For Solomon went after Ashtoreth the goddess of the Zidonians, and after Milcom the abomination of the Amorites.

6 And Solomon did evil in the sight of the Lord, and went not after the Lord, as did David his father.

7 Then did Solomon build an high place for chemosh, the abomination of Moab, in the hill that is before Jerusalem, and for Molech, the abomination of the children of Ammon.

8 And likewise did he for all his strange wives, which burnt incense and sacrificed unto their gods.

The Queen of Heaven (Ashtoreth)

The first idol listed in Solomon's list of abominations was known as Ashtoreth the goddess of Canaan and Phoenicia.(5) This idolatry bares a credible link with Solomon's alliance with Hiram the King of Tyre mentioned earlier as Tyre was traditionally identified as a Phoenician sea port. (1 Ki. 5 vs.

12) Conveniently for Solomon, Ashtoreth also strengthened his position with the indigenous peoples of Canaan since Ashtoreth was a commonly known consort to Baal, another Canaanite fertility god. (6) (mentioned previously)

The connection Ashotoreth has in terms of Solomon's polygamy is strangely appropriate. Ashtoreth is usually regarded as the goddess of love and sensual pleasure, particularly in the Babylonian tradition under the name Ishtar, but maintains a strong tie to it's traditional roots as a fertility goddess. (7) Another epithet common in Hebrew tradition is Ashtoreth-karnaim meaning Ashtoreth of the two horns where Ashtoreth is depicted by two sheep horns projecting out of the head.(8) (Rev 13 vs. 11) The Canaanite fertility goddess, also called Ashtaroth is most likely a misvocalization instituted in the Hebrew language substituting the word boset meaning "shame." (9) Immoral sexual rites were a common form of ritual worship, another obvious snare to Solomon's would- be disciples. Ishtar, who was commonly depicted as riding on a beast, (10) is probably the same as the image depicted in the book of Revelations as the whore of Babylon who is straightly charged with the moral corruption of the civilized world.

Rev. 17 vs. 1

AND there came one of the seven angels which had seven vials, and talked with me saying unto me, Come hither; I will shew unto thee the judgment of the great whore that sitteth upon many waters:

2 With whom the kings of the earth have committed fornication and their inhabitants of the earth have been made drunk with the wine of her fornication.

3 So he carried me away in the spirit into the wilderness: and I saw a woman sit upon a scarlet colored beast, full of names of blasphemy, having seven heads and ten horns

8 The beast that thou sawest was, and is not; and shall ascend out of the bottomless pit, and go into perdition: and they that dwell on the earth shall wonder whose names were not written in the book of life from the foundations of the world when they behold the beast that was, and is not, and yet is.

15 Then he said to me, "The waters which you saw, where the harlot sits, are peoples, multitudes, nations, and tongues.

Historically, Ashtoreth could have come to exemplify human nature's tendency to be corrupted by erotic sensual desires and pleasures. The many waters that the Bible speaks of symbolizes a primordial existence that acts as the true spiritual source of the world's present physical reality. Once having been born to these flesh bodies humanity is exposed to a new spiritual influence that is as sure as any other force of nature. Ashtoreth shows her immoral contempt for humanity by unleashing this obscene spirit indiscriminately upon mankind. (This theory denotes the existence of a spiritual dimension that all of humanity is akin to, as will be further explored in later chapters.)

Ashtoreth could have emerged as a cosmological force based on Solomon's invested power. Evidence will emerge to suggest that this was entirely possible. Centuries later the practice of this idolatry has clearly grown exponentially. Anathoth, the town where the prophet Jeremiah was reared was known to be given over to this particular form of worship. Eventually Ashtoreth is given the title of "queen of heaven" and is worshipped openly in Israel. (Jer.44 vs. 18) This title of queen is a curious one because it refers to a human form of political office. A similar title is curiously used for another idol that was worshipped by Solomon.

The King of Shame (Molech)

Molech, the pagan deity openly worshipped by the Ammonites, (1 Ki. 11 vs. 7) had a special attraction for Solomon. In the Bible's traditional reference to this deity, Melek, the Hebrew word for king, was substituted for the Ammonite word molech. Next, in a step similar to the misvocalization of Ashtoreth, the consonants of melek were merged with the vowels boshet; the Hebrews word for shame.(11) Thus, the Hebrew word for Molech, is best translated "the king of shame." Since the political connotation suggested by this name is exclusively Hebrew, it is possible that king Solomon himself is secretly implicated by Bible historians as the true object of worship in this form of idolatry.

The Ammonites were easily persuaded to take part in this abominable form of worship. Though the nation of Israel was ordered of the Lord not to enter into peaceful relations with Ammonites (Deut. 23 vs. 3-6), crushing military defeats, along with centuries of occupation and oppression made the Ammonites especially vulnerable to Solomon's political manipulation. (2 S. 10; 1 Ch. 14) The political vacuum that existed would soon be filled as a result of a radical change in policy, which included the joining of political alliances forged on the basis of Solomon's many marriages. With Solomon's incredible wealth and influence he was eventually accredited among the Ammonites as a divine presence worthy of the name Molech.

Milcom, God of the Amorites

Another factor that suggests that Solomon was the true object of worship in the name of Molech, is the fact that two names referring to the same god are mentioned together. Milcom the god of the Amorites, the second deity mentioned on Solomon's short list of abominations, bares only a slight jurisdictional difference with Molech the god of the Ammonites who is mentioned last.(12) Similar to Molech, Milcom means ruler in the ancient Hebrew tongue staying true to the political connotation in the name Molech. For all intensive purposes these gods are one and the same. This implies that the worship of Molech could have taken on some unique new characteristic. Perhaps Bible scholars encountered this new ritual form of worship and decided that it warranted it's own distinct reference.

In keeping with the name Molech, which means the king, it is noteworthy how at separate and random points in scripture, the Lord refers specifically to a king who is identified as the true brunt of his fiery judgment. The subject of Israel's kingship draws on a long history of enmity that existed between the Lord and the nation of Israel. Historically, it was Israel's choice to establish a kingship despite attempts to dissuade such a practice on the part of Samuel the prophet. Ironically, the initial desire to be ruled by a king came as the result of Israel's covetousness towards political reign of the king of the Ammonites. (1 Sam.12 vs. 12) The prophet Samuel specifically warns the nation of Israel that the new direction they are taking requires true loyalty towards God or, Samuel warns, "ye shall be consumed, both ye and your king." (1 Sam. 12 vs. 25)

Later, with a remarkable consistency, scripture renders an account of God's anger building towards an unspecified king denoted by the word Satan (Hebrew; meaning the anger of God) in various points in scripture.

The following is one example of such a reference.

Hosea 13 vs. 9

O Israel, thou hast destroyed thyself; but in me is thine help.

10 I will be thy king: where is any other that may save thee in all thy cities? And thy judges of whom thou saidst, Give me a king and princes?

11 I gave thee a king in mine anger, and took him away in my wrath.

12 The iniquity of Ephraim is bound up; his sin is hid.

13 The sorrows of a travailing woman shall come upon him: he is an unwise son for he should not stay long in the place of the breaking forth of children.

14 I will ransom them from the power of the grave; I will redeem them from death: O death, I will be thy plagues; O grave, I will be thy destruction; repentance shall be hid from mine eyes.
15 Though he be fruitful among his brethren, an east wind shall come up from the wilderness, and his spring shall become dry and his fountain shall be dried up: he shall spoil the treasure of all pleasant vessels.

The reference to the king who was known to be taken away in wrath, makes Solomon highly suspect considering the many other questionable practices reflected in Solomon's falling away. The reference to the unwise son is an obvious jeering of Solomon's foolish slip into idolatry. The spoiling of his many pleasant vessels is reminiscent of Solomon's drinking goblets that were all made of pure gold.(2 Chr. 9 vs. 20) The Lord himself assures that this king will not stay long "in the place of breaking forth of children," pertaining to the supernatural covering of the Lord's anointing which will inevitably be lifted at the dawn of the next earth age. Scripture states that at this time the graves will be opened and many will rise again, some to the resurrection of the righteous and some to the resurrection of condemnation. (John 5 vs. 29) God's fiery judgment will then be released as the beast and the false prophet are thrown into the eternal lake of fire. (Rev. 19 vs. 20)

Chemosh and the High Places

The onset of ritual idol worship was likely first initiated at the ceremonial high places that accumulated in and around Jerusalem on the outskirts of the designated places of worship.(13) Traditionally it was held that legitimate places of worship would be chosen and designated by God. (Deut 26 vs. 2,3) As the practice of worshipping God outside of this jurisdiction developed, idol worship increased proportionately. Settings of breath-taking esthetic beauty were likely to attract sizable followings. As considerable time passed and these places of worship were gradually taken over for idolatrous practices, a mystic and secretive quality began to ensue. Nature soon took on a central role in this type of worship. Asherah poles, for example, were tree idols that originally represented the goddess Asherah. The trunk of the tree was believed to house the spirit, and therefore was ceremonially worshiped.(14) This type of nature worship could well have been a forerunner of nature cults like the Druids who saw trees as essential in their ritual practice.

This subtle deviation eventually took the nation of Israel by storm because of the corrupt nature of this practice. While the following scripture notes that this tendency was initially well intended, it also points out that the worship at high places was clearly discouraged.

I Kings 3 vs. 2

Only the people sacrificed in high places, because there was no house built unto the name of the Lord, until those days.

3 And Solomon loved the Lord walking in the statutes of David his father: only he sacrificed and burnt incense in high places.

4 And the king went to Gibeon to sacrifice there; for that was a great high place: a thousand burnt offerings did Solomon offer upon that alter.

Out of the those listed in Solomon's fall into idolatry, Chemosh, the abomination of Moab, is the final deity mentioned in Solomon's list. High places for the idol Chemosh were among the ritual places of worship where secretive occult practices and immoral acts played out at an alarming rate.(15) Chemosh along with Molech were known to include the abominable practice of human sacrifice in their ritual form of worship. (II Kings 3 vs. 27) Human sacrifice by fire was a practice that was straightly condemned by God in the worship of Molech because this worship was frequently used to profane the Lord's holy name. (Lev 18 vs. 21) The abominable practice of human sacrifice was so despised by the Lord that the nature of God's fiery judgment was ultimately affected on the basis of this practice.

Historically it seems possible that Solomon himself eventually engaged in the practice of human sacrifice. While human faculties of perception often fail when it comes to identifying the actual perpetrators of these offences, the Lord knows every secret sin and will bring every deed before his righteous throne of judgment. (Romans 2 vs. 5,6) Accordingly, while documented cases of human sacrifice exist, (2 Kings 16 vs. 3) (2 Kings 21 vs. 6) God's word implies that the practice did in fact occur earlier than what Bible historians traditionally suggest.

Tophet and the Lake of Fire

Tophet is a well-known high place cited in scripture where the abominable and shameful practice of human sacrifice was known to occur. Not unlike the high places that were mentioned previously Tophet existed in a location just outside of Jerusalem but not far from the site of the original Temple in the valley of Hinnom.(16) In this most unholy site the children of Israel were forced to pass through the fire to Molech as burnt offerings. This particular setting of ritual human sacrifice reveals Satan's growing contempt for God and humanity as a result of this sinister plot.

Leviticus 18 vs. 20

Moreover thou shalt not lie carnally with thy neighbor's wife, to defile thyself with her.

21 And thou shalt not let any of thy seed pass through the fire to Molech, neither shalt thou profane the name of thy God, I am the Lord.

In the following scripture the circumstantial evidence presented leaves little doubt as to Solomon's initial involvement in setting up this abominable high place to Molech. By describing these abominable practices in plain terms the Lord reveals the intentional nature of these actions. Unsatisfied with proclaiming his divinity to his more intimate follower, Solomon soon aimed his maniacal tendencies towards somehow proving his divine supremacy once and for all. In this harrowing account scripture even describes how steps were taken to deliberately provoke the Lord to jealousy by setting up idols in and around Jerusalem. Scripture goes on to describe how an idol was even set up in the house that was called by the Lord's holy name.

Jeremiah 7 vs. 29

Cut off thine hair, O Jerusalem, and cast it away, and take up a lamentation on high places; for the Lord hath rejected and frosaken the generation of his wrath.

30 For the children of Judah have done evil in my sight, saith the Lord: they have set their abominations in the house which is called by my name, to pollute it.

31 And they have built the high places of Tophet, which is in the valley of Hinnom, to burn their sons and their daughters in the fire: which I commanded them not neither came it into my heart.

32 Therefore behold, the days come saith the Lord, that it shall no more be called Tophet, nor the valley of the son of Hinnom, but the valley of slaughter: for they shall burry in Tophet till there be no place.

The actual existence of a place of eternal torture, fire and brimstone is included in the ancient folklore and mythology of a variety of cultures and traditions worldwide. In fact, God's judgment is so deeply seeded in the human psyche that the knowledge of an after life is known, almost instinctively, as either a place of eternal reward or a place of eternal condemnation. The wickedness of Tophet begins to take on a similar spiritual connotation as the primary source of the Lord's eternal judgment is first encountered. Under closer scrutiny scripture seems to identify Tophet as the actual focal point of this eternal punishment whereby the practice of human sacrifice and related crimes against humanity are given their just recompense.

Isaiah 30 vs. 30

And the Lord shall cause his glorious voice to be heard, and shall shew the lightening down of his arm, with the indignation of his anger, and with the flame of a devouring fire, with scattering and tempest, and hailstones.

31 For through the voice of the Lord shall the Assyrians be beaten down, which smote with a rod.

32 And in every place where the grounded staff shall pass, which the Lord shall lay upon him, it shall be with tabrets and harps: and in battles of shaking will he fight with it.

33 For Tophet is ordained of old; yea, for the king, it is prepared; he hath made it deep and large: the pile thereof is fire and much wood; the breadth of the Lord, like a stream of brimstone, doth kindle it.

This account of God's judgment bares a remarkable consistency in implicating Solomon as the anonymous king previously discussed. Thus, the course of God's judgment emerges as a just punishment to all those who would choose to knowingly rebel against his perfect will. If Solomon did in fact have human sacrifice included on the list of his many crimes, God's judgment is appropriate in requiting these wrong intentions back to its sender.

In a primordial sense Tophet could well be the location designated for God's eternal judgment. Bible scholars suggest a likely connection between Tophet and the eternal lake of fire where Satan and the false prophet will be fittingly cast at the end of the current earth age. The false prophet encompasses all those individuals who refuse to acknowledge the Lordship of creation's one true savior Jesus Christ. In this sense every false prophet* is anti-Christ by nature. The name aptly used for these eternal fires is Gehenna, which was derived from the Hebrew name for the valley of Hinnom, the confirmed geographical location of the high place of Tophet. (17)

Revelations 20 vs. 6

Blessed and holy is he that hath part in the first resurrection: on such the second death hath no power, but they shall be priests of God and of Christ, and shall reign with him a thousand years.

10 And the devil that deceived them was cast into the lake of fire and brimstone, where the beast and the false prophet are, and shall be tormented day and night forever and ever.

As was described in the previous chapter, Satan is ultimately cast as a type of sacrifice bent entirely on his stubborn self-will. In the words of Samuel one of the Lord's loyal prophets; "Behold to obey is better than sacrifice, and to heed the fat of rams. For rebellion is as the sin of witchcraft, and stubbornness is as iniquity and idolatry." (1 Sam 15 vs. 22)

The one question that could be raised that would effectually exonerate Solomon from the fate of this fiery judgment is the notion of his repentance before God. Though this possibility is thoroughly explored by many Bible scholars it is entirely impossible. Solomon remained king up until the time of his death (1 Kings 12 vs. 43) and would have had ample time to make a royal edict to have his high places removed. Historically it is known that no such edict was ever made since Solomon's high places clearly existed until the reign of King Josiah (II Kings 23 vs. 13) when these high places were finally systematically defiled*.

The Provocation*

The most intriguing example of the abominations arrayed against the Lord is brought to light by the Lord's own omnipotent all-seeing and all-knowing mind. Never has God's word so explicitly revealed such a carnal exhibition of insult and mayhem personally committed against the Lord in order to make him go far from his holy Temple. In the prophet Ezekiel's burdensome vision (Ez. 8), the Lord himself takes us on a journey through space and time to reveal the true extent of the abominable crimes committed against him. The Lord's exposition uncovers the intrigue of secret rooms as well as the more obvious spectacle of satanic rituals exercised in this unholy attack. This account will also be supplemented by the deposition of archeological evidence supplied by infrared imaging that plainly proves that these things probably took place in and around the early temple period.

The Image of Jealousy

Surprisingly, as was suggested by the eyewitness account provided at the end of the third chapter, the practice of open idol worship was evidently practiced at some point within the Lord's Temple. The setting up of this idol in the Lord's temple is perhaps the most blatantly offensive act in all of Bible history. In Ezekiel's analysis of this atrocity, similar language is used that would suggest that this idol bares a credible connection with abomination of desolation, the offensive image that is set to be uncovered when God's judgment is finally set in motion.

Matthew 24 vs. 15

When ye therefore shall see the abomination of desolation spoken of by Daniel the prophet, stand in the holy place, (who so readeth, let him understand:)

16 Then let them which be in Judea flee into the mountains:

17 Let him which is on the housetop not come down to take any thing out of his house;

18 Neither let him which is in the field return back to take his clothes.

Bible scholars make the mistake of commonly assuming that this scripture refers to an abomination that is yet to occur, when in fact it could well refer to the archeological uncovering of the image that provokes to jealousy that is set to be uncovered at some point in the near future.

Ezekiel 8 vs. 1

AND it came to pass in the sixth year, in the sixth month, in the fifth day of the month, as I sat in mine house, and the elders of Judah sat before me, that the hand of the Lord God fell there upon me.

3 And he put forth the form of an hand, and took me by a lock of mine head; and the spirit lifted me up between the earth and the heaven, and brought me in the visions of God to Jerusalem, to the door of the inner gate that looketh toward the north; where was the seat of the image of jealousy, which provoketh to jealousy.

4 And, behold, the glory of the God of Israel was there, according to the vision that I saw in the plain.

5 Then said he unto me, Son of man, lift up thine eyes now the way toward the north. So I lifted up mine eyes the way toward the north, and behold northward at the gate of the alter this image of jealousy in the entry.

6 He said furthermore unto me, Son of man, seest thou what they do? even the great abominations that the house of Israel committeth here that I should go far off from my sanctuary? but turn thee yet again, and thou shalt see greater abominations.

Archeological evidence supports the existence of an idolatrous high place represented by traces of an imperfectly pentagonal structure found in the foundation stones under the Golden Dome.(18) Phoenicia, Israel's political ally during Solomon's time has a similar pentagonal structure in the sea port archaeological site of Strato's tower in Caesarea. Archaeological evidence supports that the Phoenician king, Abd Ashtart, built this tower. Both the names, Strato's Tower, and Abd Ashtart, preserve the name of the goddess, Ashtoreth.(19) Although in the Chalcolithic Period* finding pentagonal structures in architecture was extremely rare, the ancient symbols of an octagon and a pentagon traditionally known to represent the goddess Ashtoreth are found at this sight. (20) Since these pentagonal structures were found in both instances just to the north of the inhabited area, one may reasonably deduce that both structures served as idolatrous high places during the early temple period. (21)

Although the political climate of the day does not make excavation of these sites soon likely, in the archaeological world it is generally understood that idolatrous artifacts would probably be found in abundance in area of the early temple. The possibility that a graven image may soon be uncovered here, at the very least, does merit an awareness of such a discovery.

The Secret Room

Based on the previous eyewitness account the existence of a covert cultic form of worship inside the actual temple is even more likely. In the following account, the ritual animistic practices in worship seem to be well supported by the imagery presented here. Archaeological evidence seems to suggest a very ancient existence of a secret room where this form of worship would be a likely practice. The mystic new-age appeal that the Temple has come to serve has triggered an onslaught of religious hopefuls who continue to imagine the presence of some cultic enlightenment hidden within the temple's ancient walls. From the Lord's standpoint, on the other hand, this practice was held as an entirely loathsome disgrace.

Ezekiel 8 vs. 7 And he brought me to the door of the court; and when I looked, behold a hole in the wall.

8 Then said he unto me, Son of man dig now in the wall: and when I had digged in the wall, behold a door.

9 And he said unto me, Go in and behold the wicked abominations that they do here.

10 So I went in and saw; and behold every form of creeping things and abominable beasts and all the idols of the house of Israel, portrayed upon the wall round about.

12 Then said he unto me, Son of man, hast thou seen what the ancients of the house of Israel do in the dark, every man in the chambers of his imagery? For they say, The Lord seeth us not; the Lord hath forsaken the earth

13 He said unto me, Turn thee yet again, and thou shalt see greater abominations that they do.

The well known existence of an ancient cave exists within the bedrock of the Golden dome.(22) In a similar outcropping the existence of a pentagonal shape may be clearly found with infrared imaging with it's geometrical shape facing east-west. Further in from this outcropping the definition of an ancient stair well may be clearly seen in the bedrock that is believed to predate the Dome of the rock.(23) Some archaeologists believe that this cave may even have been used as an ancient burial site, a theory that will be further explored in later chapters.(24) The notion that the sacred ground of the Lord's holy temple would be defiled by the existence of a burial site is in clear violation of all accepted ritual practices known to exist in Israel. (Lev.26 vs. 30) The pentagonal shape as it shows up on infrared scanners, is a well-known symbol in occult worship, making this a likely haven for idolatrous practices.

Facing the East

In consideration to the final insult mentioned in this final offence against the Lord in this particular list, the abominable practice of turning away from the Temple in prayer is a very serious affront to God. It therefore comes as no surprise that infrared imaging reveals how the ritual high places and hidden rooms that were sighted were facing east-west. (See above) Traditionally it was well known that true devotees would only face towards the temple when they prayed. In this account what was held as a long-standing tradition is abruptly violated.

Ezekiel 8 vs. 16

And he brought me into the inner court of the Lord's house, and behold, at the door of the temple of the Lord, between the porch and the altar, were about five and twenty men with their backs toward the temple of the Lord, and their faces toward the east; and they worshipped the sun toward the east.

17 Then he said unto me, Hast thou seen this, O son of man? Is it a light thing to the house of Judah that they commit the abominations which they commit here? for they have filled the land with violence, and have returned to provoke me to anger: and lo, they put the branch to their nose.

18 Therefore will I also deal in fury: mine eyes shall not spare, neither will I have pity: and though they cry in mine ears with a loud voice, yet will I not hear them.

The central argument that the setting up of the abomination of desolation will occur when the Temple is rebuilt is somewhat misleading. These deliberate attacks on the Lord's sovereignty came as an effort to defile* the Lord's holy Temple. Although the Lord allowed this abomination to occur because of mankind's free will, his perfect will dictates that the Temple will ultimately be rebuilt in a location that is free from all defilement.

The following scripture repeats the full account of this form of idolatry and summarizes the essence of the abominable practices examined thus far.

Jeremiah 32 vs. 32

Because of all the evil of the children of Israel and of the children of Judah, which they have done to provoke me to anger, they, their kings, their princes, their priests, and their prophets, and the men of Judah, and the inhabitants of Jerusalem.

33 And they have turned unto me the back, and not the face: though I taught them, rising up early and teaching them, yet they have not hearkened to receive instruction.

34 But they set their abominations in my house, which is called by my name, to defile it.

35 And they built the high places of Baal, which are in the valley of the
son of hinnom, to cause their sons and their daughters to pass through
the fire unto Molech: which I commanded them not, neither came it
into my mind, that they should do this abomination, to cause Judah to sin

Weeping for Tammuz

At first, this subtle practice of weeping for Tammuz carries little significance aside from the fact that this practice is a recognized form of idolatry that was evidently practiced within the Lord's holy Temple itself. The male god Tammuz, believed to be the husband and brother to Ashtoreth the goddess of fertility, (25) was a Sumerian vegetation deity who was ceremonially worship as the seasons changed. In the winter it was customarily to mourn the death of the deity whereas the coming of spring represented a regeneration and rebirth.(26) This classic imagery is skillfully represented in Solomon's well-known "Song of Songs" as will soon be examined. How be it, under the circumstances that are laid out, Solomon's involvement in these actions comes as no surprise.

Ezekiel 8 vs. 14

Then he brought me to the door of the gate of the Lord's house which was toward the north; and behold, there sat women weeping for Tammuz.

In the following chapter a most unconventional look at The Song of Solomon will reveal the probability that this revered book of the Bible is actually not what it appears. The illicit sexual imagery that has come to be widely accepted will be reexamined along with the striking similarities that 'The Song of Songs' bares when it comes to Canaanite fertility rituals. Most significantly of all, the documentation of an unusual incantation will be explored that seems to substantiate the eerie possibility of Solomon's involvement in triggering the sinful fall of mankind in the garden of Eden.

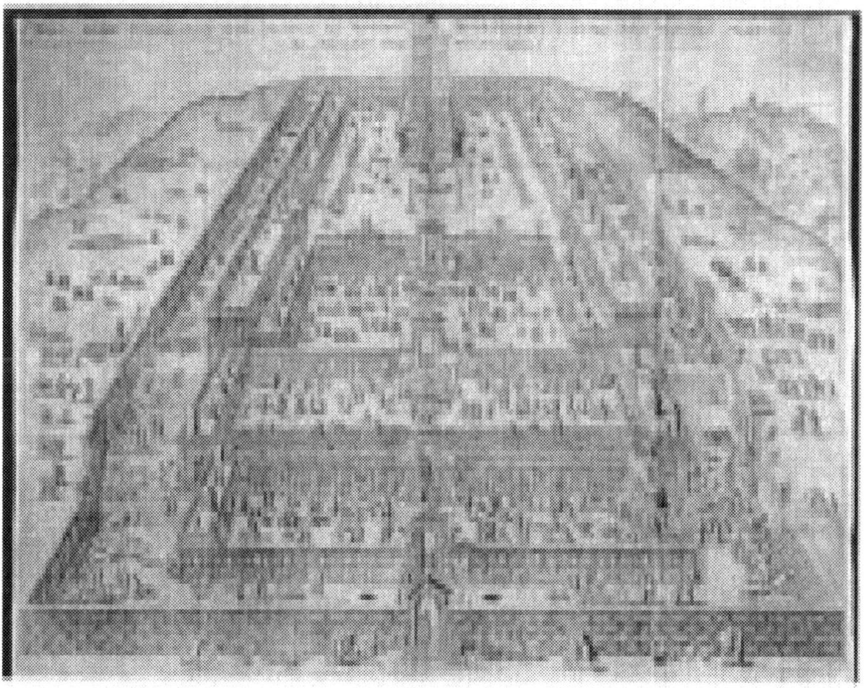

Depiction of original layout & construction of Soloman's Temple

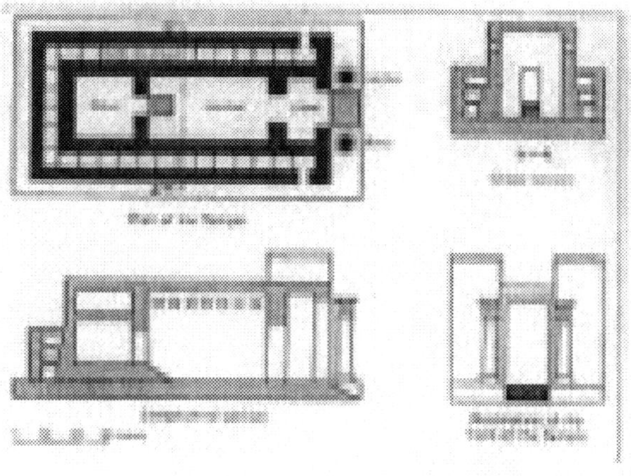

Hills outside of Jerusalem near Engedi featuring a popular garden habitat

Image of Ishtar

High place to Molech

V
The Song of Solomon

At first glance The Song of Solomon appears to be no more than a flamboyant romp of melodrama and pageantry set against a backdrop of visual imagery and sensual eroticism. Set amidst a garden landscape, on a superficial level, the story describes a romantic engagement involving King Solomon and his shulamite lover. At a deeper level, scripture seems to support the fact that the characters involved are based on real people, and that the psychological overtones could well be based on very real feelings and motivations. In the context of our current investigation into the personality of Solomon certain incentives are brought to light that seem to drastically alter any previous attempt at interpreting this source of scripture.

True to any literary source is the sense that the writer is drawing on underlying themes that are based firmly in reality and rooted in very real feelings and emotions. Far from any specific malicious intent, The Song of Solomon paints an intimate portrait of Solomon's private life, his sexual deviations and fantasies, as well as his obvious tendency to fall short of the expectations of his peers. Unlike more popular interpretations, it is arguable that the true motivation behind The Song of Solomon is based entirely on self-centered and self-serving intentions. All the key elements that have been incorporated in this treatise are represented here in one form or another, but the substance of this scripture proceeds in a very relaxed tone of personal sentiment.

At the same token, the spiritual connotations to this work are very real, incorporating many of the insights mentioned previously. The explanation that will follow stays true to the initial premise that Solomon's true spiritual fascination gravitated more to occult ritual and practice. In fact, Solomon's wisdom plays a defining role in the entire make up of this literary work. In rendering a true interpretation the argument will be put forward, that, much like a delinquent child, Solomon is well aware of his deviant behavior but continues to draw on the deeper spiritual truths and nuances, which he is accustomed to. The Song of Solomon best represents the reality of Solomon's immediate surroundings as well the attitudes and practices which are based on his self preservation. The true spiritual irony is that, while this writing still draws upon Solomon's God given anointing, however squandered that anointing may seem, the Song of Solomon still serves to expose Solomon's deviant behavior on a deeper more intimate level.

The Vineyard

Similar to most works of literature, the setting in this writing is a crucial element to it's understanding. Common to Solomon's ritual high places was the abundant provision of his many stately gardens and vineyards. Consistent with the more central theme of fertility, these gardens likely hosted many Canaanite fertility rites that bare a striking similarity to the poetic formula presented in the Song of Solomon.(1) In neighboring countries picturesque garden habitats like the hanging gardens of Babylon soon became popular. Overtones reflecting on the theological value of the Garden of Eden would also have had an influential impact on how this story was written. Before introducing the essential role of each particular character, it is important to establish a credible link with the key personalities as they are actually represented in Old Testament scripture. Solomon, for example, is denoted by a particular effigy that perhaps less well known, yet is prevalent in this literary work.

Although Solomon's common name is mentioned on more than one occasion, Solomon was also given another name, which is used extensively throughout The Song of Solomon. It is from this particular name that the endearing term "my beloved" is coined. The name Jedidiah, (yediyd meaning beloved in the ancient Hebrew,) was a name given to Solomon by the prophet

Nathan shortly after his birth and is characterized by the Hebrew word yediyd.(2)

2 Samuel 12 vs. 24

And David comforted Bathsheba his wife, and went in unto her, and lay with her: and she bare a son, and he called his name Solomon: and the Lord loved him.

25 And he sent by the hand of Nathan the prophet; and he called his name Jedidiah, because of the Lord.

With this subtle truth in mind, the symbolic virtue of Solomon's vineyard may now be expounded. At a broader scope of interpretation Solomon's vineyard could obviously be a fair representation of Solomon's political endeavors. In the first chapter of The Song of Solomon, a character emerges who through his own admonition, has created civil unrest as the result of the initial neglect of his powers. Although this implied statement's rings true, it proceeds with a purely patronizing tone that will be examined shortly for it's historical value. What is clear at present is that this character is none other than Solomon himself describing, in retrospect, the events surrounding his first few days as king.

Canticles. 1 vs. 5

I am black, but comely, O ye daughters of Jerusalem, as the tents of Kedar, as the curtains of Solomon.

6 Look not upon me, because I am black, because the sun hath looked upon me: my mother's children were angry with me; they made me the keeper of the vineyards; but mine own vineyard have I not kept.

The shockingly subversive tone to this statement is brought to light when one examines the initial days of Solomon's reign as king. Although an even more shocking revelation is contained by these events, the initial premise explains why the reference to my mother's children is addressed. The civil unrest is indicated when Solomon's character declares the displeasure of his mother's sons just as the neglect of his power is indicated when Solomon states, "my own vineyard I have not tended."

Despite Adonijah's eventual willingness to succumb to his brother Solomon's rule as king, Adonijah had one final request that was addressed on behalf of his mother, Bathsheba. Abishag the Shunimmite (another character represented in The Song of Solomon) was requested to be taken as a wife by Adonijah. Outlandishly, at the mere request, Solomon had Adonijah executed. Not only could this be considered murder, but it also violates the third commandment of honoring thy father and thy mother. (Ex 20 vs12,13)

1 Kings 2 vs19

Bathsheba, therefore went unto King Solomon, to speak unto him for Adonijah. And the king rose up to meet her, and bowed himself unto her, and sat down on his throne, and caused a seat to be set for the king's mother; and she sat on his right hand.

20 Then she said, I desire one small petition of thee: I pray thee, say me not nay, And the king said unto his her, Ask on, my mother: for I will not say thee nay.

21 And she said, Let Abishag the Shunammite be given to Adonijah thy brother to wife.

22 And King Solomon answered and said unto his mother, And why dost thou ask Abishag the Shunammite for Adonijah? Ask for him the kingdom also: for he is mine elder brother; even for him, and for Abaithar the priest, and for Joab the son of Zeruiah.

23 Then King Solomon sware by the Lord saying, God do so to me and more also, if Adonijah have not spoken this word against his own life.

Thus the reference to "my mother's children" could also serve as a patronizing dig addressed to the shulamite maiden (the Shunammite) for ever having been remotely involved with his brother Adonijah.

Solomon's lover immediately recants by inquiring on the location of his flocks and posing the subtle threat of following after the flocks of his companions. Solomon's reply nonchalantly tells the maiden to feel free to seek out the flocks beside the shepherd's tent.

Cant. 1 vs. 7

Tell me, O thou whom my soul loveth, where thou feedest, where thou makest thy flock to rest at noon: for why should I be as one that turneth aside by the flocks of thy companions?

8 If thou know not, O thou fairest among women, go thy way forth by the footsteps of the flock, and feed thy kids beside the shepherds' tents.

9 I have compared thee, O my love, to a company of horses in Pharaoh's chariots.

In this passage Solomon is likened unto a shepherd. This could well be a reference to Solomon's self acclaimed religious authority, but when the maiden subtly threatens to seek out the flocks of his companions, Solomon refers her to the shepherd's tent, a possible symbolic reference to the Lord's Temple and the abominable outcrop of idolatrous high places that were set up in the vicinity. Solomon's crude comparison of the maiden to Pharaoh's horses is a personal reminder of how he can break God's rules and allegedly get away with it. (Deut. 17 vs. 16) In other words, Solomon suggests that there is no point in undermining his authority.

Toward the end of the first chapter, The Song of Solomon turns to a more erotic tone. The flare of costly scented oils like spikenard and myrrh are mentioned to set a more sensual mood. Finally the maiden states outright how Solomon the king "shall lay all night betwixt" her breasts. A very sexual tendency begins to emerge with innuendos intended by "the beams" of cedar and "rafters" of fir where Solomon is clearly making a claim regarding his superior "manhood."

Cant. 1 vs. 13
A bundle of myrrh is my well beloved unto me; he shall lie all night betwixt my breasts.
14 My beloved is unto me as a cluster of camhire in the vineyard of Engedi.
15 Behold thou art fair, my love; behold thou art fair; thou hast doves eyes.
16 Behold, thou art fair my beloved, yea, pleasant; also our bed is green.
17 The beams of our house are cedar, and our rafters of fir.

In the initial assessment of these images, one would expect that the Lord would eventually voice some form of objection if Solomon's, Song of Songs were indeed deemed to be pretentious and false. The following scripture is a brief account of the Lord's response to the outlandish portrayal contained within the pages of The Song of Solomon. The reference to Solomon's name, Jedidiah, which in the original Hebrew means beloved gives reasonable, heed to the argument that the Lord is addressing his displeasure towards this heretical work.

The Lord's Reply

The Lord evidently finds an answer to Solomon's Song as he voices his displeasure concerning Solomon and his vineyard. In this surprising passage the Lord uses the name Jedidiah specifically to address his former affections to Solomon. (2) In what could be one of the most direct reference to Solomon's abominations, the Lord proceeds with an air of discretion in revealing his displeasure. The Lord is even careful to continue on in the flowery style of language first displayed in The Song of Solomon.

Isaiah 5 vs. 1

NOW will I sing to my well beloved a song of my beloved touching his vineyard. My well-beloved hath a vineyard in a very fruitful hill:

2 And he fenced it, and gathered out the stones thereof, and planted it with the choicest vine, and built a tower in the midst of it, and also made a winepress therein: and he looked that it should bring forth grapes, and it brought forth wild grapes.

3 And now, O inhabitants of Jerusalem, and men of Judah, judge, I pray you betwixt me and my vineyard.

4 What could have been done more to my vineyard, that I have not done in it? Wherefore, when I looked that it should bring forth grapes, brought it forth wild grapes?

5 And now go to: I will tell you what I will do to my vineyard: I will take away the hedge thereof, and it shall be eaten up: and break down the wall thereof, and it shall be trodden down:

6 And I will lay it waste; it shall not be pruned, nor digged; but there shall come up briers and thorns; I will also command the clouds that they rain no rain upon it.

7 For the vineyard of the Lord of Hosts is the house of Israel, and the men of Judah his pleasant plant: and he looked for judgment, but behold oppression; for righteousness, but behold a cry.

14 Therefore hell hath enlarged herself and opened her mouth without measure and their glory and their multitude and their pomp and he that rejoice shall descend into it.

15 And the mean man shall be brought down, and the mighty man shall be humbled, and the eyes of the lofty shall be humbled:

16 But the Lord of hosts shall be exalted in judgment, and God that is holy shall be sanctified in righteousness.

Many similarities with Solomon's vineyard exist between the vineyard described in these verses from the prophet Isaiah and the book of The Song of Solomon. The exact symbolic representations demonstrated in The Song of Solomon are arguably represented here. Solomon's many vineyards are obviously purposed to symbolize his incredible wealth and prosperity, while still other features of his vineyard aptly represent various aspects of his kingdom and even the Lord's temple itself. The tower in the midst of the vineyard could well be a reference to the similarities of Strato's tower the abominable symbol of the goddess Ashtoreth and the indelible impression it left on the Temple grounds. (See Chpt IV (19)) This potential imagery is underscored by the Lord's fierce anger as it is expressed towards the end of these selected verses. In terms of the Lord's judgment, the hedge of God's anointing* and protection is about to be torn down.

Chapter II

The second chapter starts with the declaration of Solomon's superior nature stating; "I am the rose of Sharon." From here of The Song of Solomon finally begins to tap into the primordial existence of God's supernatural anointing.

Cant. 2 vs. 1

I AM the rose of Sharon, and the lily of the valley.

2 As the lily among thorns, so is my love among the daughters.

3 As the apple tree among the trees of the wood, so is my beloved among the sons. I sat down under his shadow with great delight, and his fruit was sweet to my taste.

4 He brought me to the banqueting house, and his banner over me was love.

5 Stay me with flagons. comfort me with apples: for I am sick of love.

6 His left hand is under my head, and his right hand doth embrace me.

7 I charge you, O ye daughters of Jerusalem, by the roes, and by the hinds of the field, that ye stir not up, nor awake my love, till he please.

This passage is clearly a reference to the tree of the knowledge of good and evil. The maiden sings Solomon's praises as the son who clearly has the most to offer over all the sons of God, comparable to an apple tree among a forest full of ordinary trees. The reference to the apple tree (a symbol of the tree of the knowledge of good and evil) reveals the maiden's willingness to taste of the sweetness of this fruit even if it is to Solomon's detriment. This is based on Solomon's own fatalistic view that his eventual stroll down the road to perdition is unavoidable. Because Solomon believes he is the only human being who could ever be perfect in judgment, he expects that his perceptive powers will eventually lead him to a virtual show down with God. Solomon's prognostication is based on the belief that since he is doomed to lose this battle with the Lord, his punishment of being transformed into the serpent figure in the Garden of Eden is inevitable. Solomon is resolved to this fate the same way he is resolved to the immoral love he is bound to with the maiden.

In this case Solomon's love is his curse since it takes on so many immoral and idolatrous forms. When Solomon says "I charge you, O ye daughters of Jerusalem, by the roes, and by the hinds of the field, that ye stir not up nor awake my love, till he please," he is persuading his lovers not to provoke the Lord to pour out this fate before it is time. The object of Solomon's affection will be explained more thoroughly in the ongoing analysis of The Song of Solomon.

The maiden responds enthusiastically to the prospect of Solomon's answer to this calling. The reference to Solomon's voice is made as the maiden's most prized commodity since it is so cunningly spun in the art of persuading Adam and Eve to pick the fruit from the tree of the knowledge of good and evil. The book of Revelations recalls how the antichrist would "be given power to give life unto the beast, that the image of the beast should speak." (Rev 13 vs15) The reference to the roe is meant to encourage Solomon to make haste to fulfill his destiny as the deceiver of the world. In the following verse Solomon is reminded of the promise that he made to include the maiden in this unholy incantation.

Cant. 2 vs. 8

The voice of my beloved! behold, behold, he cometh leaping upon the mountains, skipping upon the hills.

9 My beloved is like a roe or a young hart: behold, he standeth behind our wall, he looketh forth at the windows, shewing himself through the lattice.

10 My beloved spake, and said unto me, Rise up my love, my fair one and come away.

As was stated earlier, the he Solomon commonly refers to could well be the Lord. Solomon, despite his every attempt, is still unable to expel the Lord from the sacred site that bares God's name. In this particular reference one can also imagine Solomon shut in inside one of his idolatrous high places or perhaps in a secret room, hidden behind a wall, where his female cohorts frequently remind Solomon of this inability.

Seasonal Overtones

In the remaining verses of the second chapter, the more seasonal overtones presented seem to be consistent with the ceremonial worship of

Tammuz.(3) Since Tammuz is traditionally held to be the brother and husband of Ashtoreth, it becomes notable how Solomon's relationship with his maiden slowly begins to emulate this unholy union. The seasons change from winter to spring represents the new birth and fertility that is frequently celebrated in the regeneration of Tammuz.4 Even with this seemingly endless cycle of death and regeneration, the maiden warns Solomon that the "fig tree is putting forth her green buds," a symbol that is often used in the dawning of the next earth age.

Mention is soon made to "the clefts of the rock" a reference that is consistent with the rock of revelation concerning Christ's son-ship and anointing. At this point in history, although known by the prophets, this place in the clefts of the rock remains a secret and enigmatic place. The mentioning of the secret stair case seems to suggest the existence an actual hidden place of idolatrous worship already proven to have existed. (See Chpt IV (23)) Although this anointing is the true credit of Solomon's power, the maiden carefully reminds Solomon that others will have exposure to this vine, including the little foxes, who are blamed for stealing the vine's grapes. This is a clear reference to those individuals who are poised to engage in the true gift of prophecy and set to inadvertently uncover Solomon's shame.

Cant. 2 vs. 12

The flowers appear on the earth; the time of the singing of birds is come, and the voice of the turtle is heard in our land;

13 The fig tree putteth forth her green figs, and the vines with the tender grape give a good smell. Arise, my love, my fair one, and come away.

14 O my dove, that art in the clefts of the rock, in the secret places of the stairs, let me see thy countenance is comely

15 Take us the foxes, the little foxes, that spoil the vines: for our vines have tender grapes.

Finally, with a sense of renewed vigor and fervor, the maiden reminds Solomon of his bestial nature as one who is set to "feedeth among the lilies" and urges Solomon to "be like the young hart" in pursuing his untimely fate. The "shadows that flee away" refers to Solomon's practice of spiritual animism that will soon be brought to an end with the expulsion of these demonizing sprits from the Lord's Temple.

Cant. 2 vs. 16 My beloved is mine, and he feedeth among the lilies.

17 Until the day break, and the shadows flee away, turn my beloved, and be thou like a roe or a young hart upon the mountains of Bether.

The Shulamite

The shulamite is perhaps the most enigmatic character in the Song of Solomon. Bible scholars agree, for the most part, that this character is based on an actual person. Abishag the Shunammite, had a long and illustrious history with the Israel's royal family. When David was approaching old age his servants took it upon themselves to seek out a fair damsel from all the coasts of Israel to be a nurse mate for King David. Although Abishag, the Shunammite, was chosen for her beauty, her principle duty was to lay with David in his old age in order to keep him warm. (1 Kings 1 vs. 3) Scripture clearly notes that David was ministered to and cherished by his nurse mate Abishag, but no sexual relations were entered in to. After David's death, Abishag the Shunammite, long famed for her inspiring beauty, was noticed by David's eldest son Adonijah. Solomon's mother eventually approached Solomon to request that Abishag the Shunammite be given to Adonijah in marriage. Incredibly, Solomon loses his composure and in a jealous rage has Adonijah executed. (1 Ki. 2 vs. 24,25) From this point it is traditionally believed that Solomon takes Abishag the Shunammite as his own wife.

From a more definitive standpoint it is generally accepted that the name selomoh could have been the feminine form of a name or title that was carefully appointed by Solomon. Some even theorize that this name is an epithet of the goddess Ashtoreth. (Assyrian name Ishtar) (5) It is also noteworthy that the name and relationship of this appointed name bares only a slight difference from the actual name Solomon. (Meaning peace)

Chapter III

For the first time, beginning in this third chapter, The Song of Solomon takes on a rather incestuous tone. This could be an immoral distortion of Solomon's own device based on two possible applications. Firstly this distortion could be an incestuous fantasy that is played out by Solomon based on the Shunammite's former relationship with his father, David. (1 Ki. 1 vs. 3) Although a sexual relationship did not ensue between David and Abishag the Shunammite, Solomon could have added this analogy on the premise of fueling his own twisted perversion. The second application of this incestuous tone may prove that The Song of Solomon imitating the formula of most Canaanite fertility rituals where a symbolic ritual mating could be implied between Tammuz (Sumerian deity of vegetation) and Ashtoreth.(6)

(Canaanite fertility goddess) The cosmological features of this relationship could have been exploited in the same twisted fancy based on the goddess Ashtoreth's title as both sister and spouse to Tammuz. This shameful connotation seems to be deliberately added in order to underscore the existence of an unholy quality, which exists within the relationship between Solomon and the maiden.

Thematically, the dialogue between Solomon and the maiden continues on the same note that it left off on towards the end of the second chapter with Solomon slightly on the retreat and the maiden encouraging him onward. Consistent with the imagery of the budding fig tree, the maiden now takes a patronizing tone. She explains how for a time she was unable to find Solomon, and that when the watchmen found her that go about the city; she asked them if they had seen him. This seems to be a subtle poke at Solomon's fear previously implied. Ultimately, the maiden is suggesting that the watchmen are blind and that Solomon's true identity is secure.

Cant. 3 vs. 1 By night on my bed I sought him whom my soul loveth: I sought him, but I found him not.

2 I will rise now, and go about the city in the streets, and in the broad ways I will seek him whom my soul loveth: I sought him, but I found him not.

3 The watchmen that go about the city found me: to whom I said, Saw ye him whom my soul loveth?

4 It was but a little that I passed from them, but I found him whom my soul loveth: I held him and would not let him go, until I had brought him into my mother's house, and into the chamber of her that conceived me.

The maiden's mother is also implicated in this incestuous triangle, as will be further explored. The reference to this mother reflects on the primordial nature of Ashtoreth and her implied role as a cosmological force. As was previously discussed Ashtoreth could well be implicated as the whore of Babylon spoken of in the book of Revelations. (Rev 17 vs. 8) In this sense the mother figure serves an implied type of mother of creation and the true gateway for Solomon's return. Ashtoreth is quite possibly hailed by Solomon as an eschatological force instrumental in the cycle of his death and rebirth as the serpent in the Garden of Eden.

Cant. 3 vs. 5

I charge you O ye daughter of Jerusalem, by the roes, and the hinds of the

field, that ye stir not up, nor awake my love, till he please.
6 Who is this that cometh out of the wilderness like pillars of smoke, perfumed with myrrh and frankincense, with all powders of the merchants?
7 Behold his bed, which is Solomon's; threescore valiant men are about it, of the valiant of Israel.
8 They all hold swords, being experts in war: every man hath his sword upon his thigh because of fear in the night.

Again, this plot continues, as Solomon charges that maiden stir not up or agitates this eternal consequence into reality. The maiden makes a sarcastic attempt at comforting Solomon by speaking of the valiant men who are experts in war, though her initial reaction to these men is clearly made to provoke Solomon by jealousy into fulfilling his implied purpose. Likewise does the maiden make an example of their courage and how "every man hath his sword upon his thigh because of fear in the night."

Cant. 3 vs. 9

King Solomon made himself a chariot of the wood of Lebanon.
10 He made the pillars thereof of silver, the bottom thereof of gold, the covering of it of purple, the midst thereof being paved with love, for the daughters of Jerusalem.
11 Go forth, O ye daughters of Zion and behold king Solomon with the crown wherewith his mother crowned him in the day of his espousals, and the day of the gladness of his heart.

As the third chapter draws to a close, the maiden continues her persuasion. By alluding to Solomon's chariot, the maiden is pointing out that Solomon has all the means to get to where he is going. The maiden could well be probing Solomon's demeanor for a possible sign of regret regarding "the day of his espousals." This could refer to the day when Solomon had his brother Adonijah executed in order to gain her hand. The maiden is clearly baiting Solomon to resolve the issue of his loyalty once and for all.

Chapter IV

The fourth chapter of The Song of Solomon is Solomon's response to the maiden's manipulation showing that Solomon is evidently falling for her remarks. Solomon suddenly bursts into a monologue of flattery bent on appeasing his maiden lover. Based on this statuesque physical description, it becomes apparent that Solomon could well be describing the effigy of one of his idols, as in the stately appearance of the tower of the armory used in this description. The doves eyes commonly referred to is just one example in a long list of bestial characteristics used in this description.

A more sexual tone becomes apparent as Solomon speaks of his lover's breasts. In this context "the mountain of myrrh' and "the hill of frankincense" straightly bares a sexually explicit connotation the incestuous overtones continue as Solomon begins to address his maiden lover as "my sister and my spouse." The chapter continues on with this vivid imagery in its description of the maidens lips, which "drop like honey comb" and "the orchards with many pleasant fruits."

Cant. 4 vs. 4

Thy neck is like the tower of David builded for an armory, whereon there hang a thousand bucklers, all shields of mighty men.

5 Thy two breasts are like two young roes that are twins, which feed among the lilies.

6 Until the daybreak, and the shadows flee away, I will get me to the mountain of myrrh, and to the hill of frankincense.

7 Thou art all fair, my love; there is no spot in thee.

8 Come with me from Lebanon my spouse, with me from Lebanon: look from the top of Shenir and Hermon, from the lion's dens, from the mountains of the leopards.

9 Thou hast ravished my heart, my sister, my spouse; thou hast ravished my heart with one of thine eyes, with one chain of thy neck.

10 How fair is thy love, my sister, my spouse! how much better is thy love than wine! and the smell of thine ointments than all spices!

11 Thy lips, O my spouse, drop as the honeycomb: honey and milk are under my tongue; and the smell of thy garments is like the smell of Lebanon.

The Primordial Waters

By the conclusion of the fourth chapter Solomon redeems himself in the eyes of his maiden lover. Solomon makes a bold reference to the primordial waters that will soon overtake him, baring a resemblance to "the great whore who sitteth upon many waters." Solomon compares his love to a "spring shut up" and a "fountain sealed," denoting that the details of his demise are settled so that as he reenters the waters of this primordial existence his house is set in order. Solomon's rebirth as the serpent in the Garden of Eden will allow him to "come into his garden, and eat his pleasant fruits."

Cant. 4 vs. 12

A garden enclosed is my sister, my spouse; a spring shut up, a fountain sealed.

13 Thy plants are an orchard of pomegranates, with pleasant fruits; camphire, with spikenard,

14 Spikenard and saffron; calamus and cinnamon, with all trees of frankincense; myrrh and aloes, with all the chief spices:

15 A fountain of gardens, a well of living waters, and streams from Lebanon.

16 Awake, O north wind; and come, thou south; blow upon my garden, that the spices thereof may flow out. Let my beloved come into his garden, and eat his pleasant fruits.

The waters of the fountain are significant in a geological sense since Jerusalem is known to be in close proximity to the river Gihon. The grounds of the early temple were known to be subject to mystical springs of living water that held miraculous healing properties (7) (John 5 vs. 2), yet because of Solomon's more selfish preoccupations this resource never met with it's full potential. The possibility that Solomon was hording this secret for his own selfish rejuvenation will be thoroughly examined in a separate chapter. The following scripture is quoted from the previous chapter as a further illustration of God's judgment.

Hosea 13 vs. 11

I gave thee a king in mine anger, and took him away in my wrath.

15 Though he be fruitful among his brethren, an east wind of the Lord shall come, the wind of the Lord shall come up from the wilderness, and his springs shall become dry, and his fountain shall be dried up: he shall spoil the treasure of all his pleasant vessels.

Chapter V

The fifth chapter is filled with numerous allusions to the type of idol worship that would have gone on during the early Temple period. True worship is subject to the belief that ceremonial worship must remain pure and undefiled. It is this belief that would have been influential in Solomon's choice to worship his idols more covertly in order to preserve his abominable high places for future generations. The effort was made to remain ceremonial pure so that the disqualification and ineffectiveness associated with spiritual defilement might be avoided, in the event that such defilement would render one's efforts in worship and sacrifice useless.(8) This ongoing challenge is alluded to in this chapter in the description of the images that would have been worshipped in and around the period of the early temple.

These particular descriptions were useful to Solomon on many different levels. Firstly, written visual imagery supplied the reader with a clear record as to the use of ancient symbols and the basic visual make up of these idols. For all intents and purposes a written historical blue print was preserved for future generations for all those endeavoring to follow after this idolatrous worship. Solomon by his wisdom evidently knew that the popularity of these idols would enjoy resurgence at different points in history. Secondly, the existence of this record gave the remnant of Solomon's followers a rallying point in the event of prolonged historical opposition, where by a shift towards a textual tradition would slowly replace the practice of erecting idols. Lastly, in the event that the subtle nature existing in this book could covertly survive, the perverse nature of its writings would pose as a perpetual snare to God's faithful devotees because of its illicit sexual connotation.

In what is perhaps the most surprising depiction of all, the secret site of this worship is symbolized by the image of female anatomy as "the hole of a door," or a room where Solomon was conveniently locked away. During this time the watchmen of the city confront the maiden when a hidden high place of worship was discovered. The basic value of self preservation takes even more of a central theme as the watchmen of the city are flatly accused of attempting to uncover the hidden presence of one of these high places as is symbolized by the veil that was removed from the face of the shulamite maiden.

Cant. 5 vs. 2

I sleep, but my heart waketh: it is the voice of my beloved that knocketh saying, Open to me, my sister, my love, my dove, my undefiled: for my head is filled with dew, and my locks with the drops of the night.

3 I have put off my coat: how shall I put it on? I have washed my feet: how shall I defile them?

4 My beloved put in his hand by the hole of the door, and my bowels were moved for him.

5 I rose up to open to my beloved: and my hands dropped with myrrh, and my fingers with sweet smelling myrrh, upon the handles of the lock.

6 I opened to my beloved: but my beloved had withdrawn himself, and

was gone: my soul failed when he spake: I sought him, but I could not find him; I called him but he gave me no answer.
7 The watchmen that went about the city found me, they smote me, they wounded me; the keepers of the walls took away my veil from me.
8 I charge you, daughters of Jerusalem, if ye find my beloved, that ye tell him that I am sick of love.

Toward the end of the fifth chapter the analogy of two Solomons is implied in what could well be a reference to the existence of the idolatrous high place devoted to Molech (meaning the shameful king.) Solomon asks rhetorically, "what is thy beloved more than another beloved?" (Recall that Solomon was given the name Jedidiah.) As this chapter closes, one is left with the distinct impression that an idolatrous image of some kind is indeed being described.

Cant 5 vs. 9
What is thy beloved more than another beloved, O thou fairest among women? what is thy beloved more than another beloved that thou dost so charge us?
10 My beloved is white and ruddy, the chiefest among ten thousand.
11 His head is as the most fine gold, his locks are bushy, and black as a raven.
12 His eyes are as the eyes of doves by the rivers of waters washed with milk, and fitly set.
13 His cheeks are as a bed of spices, as sweet flowers: his lips like lilies, dropping sweet smelling myrrh.
14 His hands are as gold rings set with the beryl: his belly is as bright ivory overlaid with sapphires.
15 His legs are as pillars of marble, set upon sockets of fine gold: his countenance is as Lebanon, excellent as the cedars.
16 His mouth is most sweet: yea, he is altogether lovely. This is my beloved, and this is my friend, O daughters of Jerusalem.

Chapter VI

The sixth chapter continues on in the function of preserving a written historical record of this idol's appearance. In fact, this verbal record bares a striking resemblance to a statue of Artemis (fig.1a.) (9) recovered at Ephesus which fused Greek with near eastern cults.(10) This reaffirms the cross-cultural appeal that was spread as a result of Solomon's scheming. Bible scholars believe that Artemis was a goddess of fertility who was specifically modeled after the goddess Ashtoreth from early Mesopotamian history.(11)

The symbolism preserved in this record will now be more closely examined along with an insight into of the values that these symbols were based on.

In Ashtoreth's historical representation a double role emerges. Not only is this deity the goddess of sensual pleasure and fertility, but she is also a representative of war and military might especially within the Assyrian tradition.(12) Ashtoreth is consequently described by Solomon as "terrible as an army with two banners." (Cant 6 vs. 4)

The flock of goats that is spoken of is clearly represented in the statue of Artemis that was recovered from Ephesus. In the photograph depicting this image, goats can clearly be seen carved into the hair ascending in rows of two on either side of the head. (See fig 1.a) (13) Symbolically goats often became associated with satanic ritual and practice since the goat that was traditionally used in the Day of Atonement eventually became regularly associated with forms of religious idolatry. (Lev 16,17) The frequent mentioning of deer or roes is consistent with the fact that deer are considered the sacred animal of the goddess Artemis possibly represented by the figures seen bilaterally to the image of Artemis. 14 (fig. 1b)

Cant. 6 vs. 5

Turn away thine eyes from me, for they have overcome me: thy hair is a flock of goats that appear from Gilead.

6 Thy teeth are as a flock of sheep which go up from the washing, whereof every one beareth twins, and there is not one barren among them.

7 As a piece of pomegranate are thy temples within thy locks.

8 There are threescore queens, and fourscore concubines, and virgins without number.

9 My dove, my undefiled is but one: she is the only one of her mother, she is the choice one of her that bare her, and blessed her, The daughters saw her, and blessed her; yea, the queens and the concubines, and they praised her.

At the last few verses of this passage Solomon, in a sounding off of religious ecstasy, clearly sings praises to the creation of this image as he describes how the idol came to be worshipped by his harem of wives. The dual role implied in Ashtoreth's character, is conjectured to be representative of the evening and morning stars, the former being identified with sexual passion and the latter with war.(15) For this reason, Ashtoreth is identified as more of an androgynous figure at times depicted as wearing a beard.(16) Towards the end of the sixth chapter Solomon asks, "Who is she that looketh forth as the morning fair as the sun, and terrible as an army with banners?" (Cant 6 vs. 10)

In the final verses of the sixth chapter the one and only mention of the shulamite comes into play, whose incestuous connotations mentioned previously, are soon to be revealed.

Cant. 6 vs. 13

Return, return, O Shulamite; return, return, that we may look upon thee. What will ye see in the Shulamite? As it were the company of two armies.

Chapter VII

The seventh chapter continues on in what would seem to be an obvious blue- print for the image of the goddess Artemis, based on the artifact that was found in Ephesus. The description of this idol becomes even more blatant as Solomon clearly states "the work of the hands of a cunning workman". The 'breasts' of the image have a twofold representation. The 'two' " breasts that are like two young roes that are twins" describes the fact that this image actually has many breasts with an initial layer of 'six' seen depicted on image from Ephesus. (Fig 1.a) 13 The distinct reality of this image is reinforced when the idols breasts are likened to "a cluster of grapes", thus, the fact that the breasts that are being described are not one, but many is clearly supported.

Second to the actual visual image, is the symbolic representation of the breasts suggested by the metaphor of the two young roes with in the realm of fertility worship and belief these breasts generally represent the prosperity consistently associated with worship of this type.

Cant. 7 vs. 1

HOW beautiful are thy feet with shoes, O prince's daughter! The joints of thy thighs are like jewels, the work of the hands of a cunning workman.

2 Thy navel is like a round goblet, which wanteth not liquor: thy belly is like an heap of wheat set about with lilies.

3 Thy two breasts are like two young roes that are twins.

4 Thy neck is as a tower of ivory; thine eyes like the fish pools in Heshbon, by the gate of Bathrabbim: thy nose is as the tower of Lebanon which looketh towards Damascus.

5 Thine head upon thee is like Carmel, and the hair of thine head is purple; the king is held in the galleries.

6 How fair and how pleasant art thou, O love, for delights!

7 This stature is like to a palm tree, and thy breasts to a cluster of grapes.

In one last obscene gesture, the chapter ends with what appears to be a symbolic display of Solomon breast-feeding. Represented by 'the clusters of grapes', which are likened to "the best wine that goeth down sweetly for my beloved." This image could very well represent Solomon's final affirmation of loyalty and devotion to this deity. The purely sexual tone is not disregarded by these representations. The chapter ends with a reference to the mandrakes a root indigenous to the Middle East, which is said to be a known aphrodisiac, (a word which preserves the name Aphrodite, the goddess of love, identified with Ashtoreth in Hellenistic times). The name love apple or devil's apple was appropriately attributed to the mandrake and it's use.(17)

Cant. 7 vs. 8

I said, I will go up to the palm tree, I will take hold of the boughs thereof: now also thy breasts shall be as clusters of the vine, and the smell of thy nose like apples;

9 And the roof of thy mouth like the best wine for my beloved that goeth down sweetly, causing the lips of those that are asleep to speak.

10 I am my beloved's, and his desire is towards me.

11 Come, my beloved, let us go forth into the field: let us lodge in the villages.

12 Let us get up early to the vineyards; let us see if the vine flourish, whether the tender grape appear, and the pomegranates bud forth: there will I give thee my loves.

13 The mandrakes give a smell, and at our gates are all manner of pleasant fruits, new and old, which I have laid up for thee, O my beloved.

Chapter VIII

In the eighth and final chapter of The Song of Solomon this dramatic portrayal is brought to a climax of utter disgrace as the song's various points of conflict are brought to a shameful resolution. The issue of Solomon being implicated in the incestuous triangle is clearly exposed and Solomon is finally sequestered to pass through the primordial waters where his fateful transformation into the serpent of the Garden of Eden awaits him.

Prior to his departure the shulamite maiden notices two silhouetted figures emerging from the wilderness as though summoned out of a mystic oracle. The maiden clearly describes the apple tree where she raised and gave birth to this serpent figure as it was drawn out of the primordial waters.

Cant. 8 vs. 1

O THAT thou wert as my brother, that sucked the breasts of my mother! When I should find thee without, I would kiss thee: yea, I should not be despised.

2 I would lead thee, and bring thee into my mother's house who would instruct me: I would cause thee to drink of spiced wine of the juice of my pomegranate.
3 His left hand should be under my head, and his right hand should embrace me.
4 I charge you, O daughters of Jerusalem, that ye stir not up, nor awake my love until he please.
5 Who is this that cometh up from the wilderness, leaning upon her beloved? I raised thee up under the apple tree: there thy mother brought thee forth: there she brought thee forth that bare thee.

Solomon, realizing that his fate now awaits him, prefers to accredit his transformation into the serpent figure to his maiden lover who is likely a representation of none other than the goddess Ashtoreth herself. In a final request Solomon suggests that this transition should be set upon her as a seal of remembrance that will transcend the limits of time and space. As a pledge of undying loyalty Solomon promises that the waters of time will not quench the love of this unholy bond.

Cant. 8 vs. 6

Set me as a seal upon thine heart, as a seal upon thine arm: for love is strong as death: jealousy is cruel as the grave: the coals thereof are coals of fire, which hath a most vehement flame.

7 Many waters cannot quench love, neither can the floods drown it: if a man would give all the substance of his house for love, it would utterly be contemned.

In a final question posed by the shulamite maiden the issue of what should be done with the sister who has no breasts is raised. This reference is a mockery posed towards the principles and precepts laid out in the preaching and the teaching of the gospel of the kingdom of God, whereby Jesus teaches his followers to "store up their treasures in heaven." This teaching of an existing afterlife where deeds will be either rewarded or punished is among the most rudimentary teachings of Christ. (Matthew 6 vs. 19-21) The sister who has no breasts ultimately symbolizes the true daughter of Zion and church of Christ who Solomon considers unfruitful from his worldly standpoint.

Solomon's answer is equally patronizing whereby he suggests that this teaching, which is according to godliness can be hidden away by the promise of worldly prosperity. In this case a pretentious show of wealth, symbolized by a palace of silver, was to be constructed in order to keep this doctrine safely concealed. One may recall that silver was counted as nothing in the days of Solomon, (2 Chr. 9 vs. 20) as it was plenteous as stones. (2 Chr. 1 vs. 15) The reference to Baal-hamon (lord of abundant wealth in the original Hebrew) has obvious idolatrous connotations in this context.

Cant. 8 vs. 8

We have a little sister and she hath no breasts: what shall we do for our sister in the day when she shall be spoken for?

9 If she be a wall, we will build upon her a palace of silver: and if she be a door, we will enclose her with boards of cedar.

10 I am a wall, and my breasts like Towers: then was I in his eyes as one that found favour.

11 Solomon had a vineyard at Baal-hamon: he let out the vineyard unto keepers; every one for the fruit thereof was to bring a thousand pieces of silver.

12 My vineyard, which is mine, is before me: thou, O Solomon, must have a thousand, and those that keep the fruit thereof two hundred.

In the final two verses of The Song of Solomon, the maiden holds Solomon to her request of being allowed to hear and bare witness to the unholy exchange that is about to unfold in the Garden of Eden.

Cant. 8 vs. 13

Thou that dwellest in the gardens, the companions hearken to thy voice: cause me to hear it.

14 Make haste, my beloved, and be thou like to a roe or to a young hart upon the mountains of spice.

New Testament References to the Vineyard

Jesus made reference to the vineyard in his many parables attributed to the kingdom of God. From the subject matter surrounding these parables it would appear that Jesus had an understanding consistent with many of the ideas presented in this treatise. When the chief priests of the Temple first approached him in order to question his authority Jesus interjects by telling the parable of the vineyard and the two sons.

Matthew 21 vs. 28

But what think ye? A certain man had two sons; and he came to the first,

and said, Son go work today in my vineyard.
29 He answered and said I will not: but afterward he repented, and went.
30 And he came to the second, and said likewise, And he answered and said, I go sir: and went not.
31 Whether of them did the will of his father? They say unto him, The first, Jesus saith unto them, Verily I say unto you, That the publicans and the harlots go into the kingdom of God before you.

The mention of the two sons could clearly be a subtle reference to Solomon who in the end, chose not to do the will of his heavenly father. Historians believe that at this time the Temple was under the authority of the Sadducees* the religious sect that was said to have descended from Solomon's rule.(18) Perhaps Jesus could discern their involvement in the occult deception that was so prevalently unleashed upon the world.

In a second reference Jesus tells the parable of a vineyard that was lent out to a certain husbandman. In this particular parable Jesus clearly predicts his death as a result of his established reform to this vineyard. In this reference the images depicted are strikingly similar to both the vineyard described in The Song of Solomon as well as the vineyard mentioned in the book of Isaiah where the men of Judah clearly symbolize the pleasant plants that are to be held accountable for the state of the vineyard. (Isaiah 5 vs. 7) Jesus clearly maneuvers himself as a credible authority for divine judgment by the end of the telling of this parable. Accordingly, it is documented that the priests and Pharisees clearly believed that Jesus was referring to them in this speech. (Matthew 21 vs. 45,46)

MATTHEW 21 vs. 33

Hear another parable: There was a certain householder, which planted a vineyard, and hedged it round about, and digged a winepress in it, and built a tower, and let it out to a husbandmen, and went into a far country:
34 And when the time of the fruit drew near, he sent his servants to the husbandmen that they might receive the fruits of it.
35 And the husbandmen took his servants, and beat one, and killed another, and stoned another.
36 Again, he sent other servants more than the first: and they did unto them likewise.
37 But last of all he sent unto them his son, saying, They will reverence my son.
38 But when the husbandmen saw the son, they said among themselves,

this is the heir; come let us kill him, and let us seize his inheritance.
39 And they caught him, and cast him out of the vineyard and slew him.

Within the images of Bible history and prophecy, there is perhaps none more vivid than the winepress of the wrath of God, where the clusters of grapes of the vine of the earth are finally harvested. (Rev 14 vs. 18) At this time God's judgment will be thoroughly rendered against the ungodly whom through their "swelling words of vanity, they allure through the lusts of the flesh, through much wantonness." (II Peter 2 vs. 18) In this account, along with former analogies, we see a consistent correspondence of symbolic representation between Solomon's alleged actions and the chosen form of God's eternal punishment.

In the chapter that follows, the reader will bare witness to the characterization of the deplorable nature of the house of Judah that was said to exist in many of King David's own sons. Incredibly, this assessment did not come from a political exile or future enemy of Solomon, rather; on the contrary, King David himself spoke this testimony in the very last words leading up to his death. In the following historical account, still other aspects of the Lord's divine judgment will be revealed including the resurrection of condemnation and many other subtle aspects of Christ's ministry and teaching. This scriptural account will ascribe to the Lord's power over the grave as well his rendering of a fiery judgment at the end of the current earth age.

Artemis of Ephesus modeled after the goddess Ashtoreth
Goats ascending in rows of two form the hair.(Fig 1.a)

Breasts as a cluster of grapes (Fig 1.b)

VI
The Sons of Belial

Belial is another term for Satan that is prevalently found in the Old and New Testament. Its innately shameful connotations, while translated frequently as a proper name, still retains its adjectival meaning as defined by words such as worthlessness or hopeless ruin.(1) The oldest form of the word Beliar is possibly from a phrase signifying "Lord of the forest," while in the New Testament the word is used to denote a system of impure worship especially connected with the cult of Aphrodite.(2) As a proper name the word seems to imply an unnatural other- worldly quality, which poses a strong link to the name Satan.

The notion that individuals were actually referred to by the name Belial, supports the principle belief that these individuals could be born to a particularly shameful life and would eventually die without ever having tasted repentance.

One of the most graphic examples of the belief that such individuals existed is supplied in the book of Jude in the New Testament.

Jude 1 vs. 12

These are spots in your feasts of charity, when they feast with you, feeding themselves without fear: clouds they are without water, carried about of winds; trees whose fruit withered, without fruit, twice dead, plucked up by the roots;

13 Raging waves of the sea, foaming out their own shame; wandering stars, to whom is reserved the blackness of darkness forever.

The term "Sons of Belial" seems to take on a shameful more obscure connotation, since any honorable person would probably avoid having any association with it's meaning. Usages are frequently attributed to dissidents involved in the rabble of political discord, (1 Sam 10 vs. 27) or to individuals who turn aside to idolatry. (Deut 13 vs. 13) In most cases references are short and disdainful. The book of Judges describes how the moral decay in Gibeah, largely attributed to idolatrous practices, gave rise to an incident of extreme sexual abuse on the part of certain sons of Belial. (Judges 19 vs. 22)

It is in this surprising context in which King David shares an intimate revelation regarding the future of his house in his famous last words when in an unprecedented move David clearly refers to his very own sons as sons of Belial who are set to experience the fire of God's judgment. The spiritual dark ages that Israel eventually falls into as a result of Solomon's folly is clearly represented in this prophetic utterance.

II Samuel 23 vs. 1

NOW these be the last words of David, David the son of Jesse said, and the man who was raised up on high, the anointed of the God of Jacob, and the sweet psalmist of Israel, said,

2 The Spirit of the Lord spake by me, and his word was in my tongue.

3 The God of Israel said, the Rock of Israel spake to me, He that ruleth over men must be just, ruling in the fear of God.

4 And he shall be as the light of the morning, when the sun riseth, even as a morning without clouds: as the tender grass springing out of the earth by clear shining after the rain.

5 Although my house be not so with God; yet he hath made with me an everlasting covenant, ordered in all things, and sure: for this is all my salvation and all my desire, although he make it not to grow.

6 But the sons of Belial shall be all of them as thorns thrust away, because they cannot be taken with hands:

7 But the man that shall touch them must be fenced with iron and the staff of a spear; and they shall be utterly burned with fire in the same place.

In his last words David clearly conveys the demise of his royal house by describing his descendants as sons of Belial that will be utterly burned with fire. The very nature of this revelation, whereby the Rock of Israel clearly spoke to David concerning his house, proves that the nature of the anti-Christ was well established among David's direct descendants. The images presented thus far, seem to support the claim that Solomon may clearly be implicated among these sons of wickedness. The mentioning of God's everlasting covenant is consistent with the notion that Solomon would temporarily exploit the Lord's irrevocable word. The fact that these sons of Belial "cannot be taken with hands" is a direct reference to God's supernatural anointing, and how this form of rebellion merits a more eternal form of judgment.

The Question of Lineage

Since the descendants of David implicated in this scripture are the result a dynasty that named Solomon as it's immediate successor, the question of Solomon's claim as the legitimate forerunner of this dynasty may henceforth be raised. Although Solomon is never directly described as illegitimate, the fact that his birth was the result of marital infidelity is clearly stated in the genealogical records of the New Testament. (Matthew 1 vs. 6) Traces of Solomon's historic fall into perdition may have been foreshadowed by Solomon's ancestry and the subsequent events leading up to his birth. In the same way, the house of David's eventual decline could have been influenced by Solomon's infidelity under the guise of the Lord's supernatural law, which stipulates that the iniquities of the fathers would be visited unto the third and fourth generations. (Exodus 20 vs. 5) Upon closer examination one will find that Solomon's ancestry uncovers a shameful secret. Only Judas Iscariot rivals this shocking betrayal, as another well-known incarnation of the son of perdition. (John 17 vs. 12) In fact, the images conjured by the events in question are surely echoed by Judas Iscariot's violent death and suicide by hanging.

Ahithophel, Solomon's great grandfather on the side of his mother Bathsheba, was also considered a wise man, known best for the counsel he gave David's eldest son, Absolom. Although King David had considered Ahithophel to be a trusted advisor, Ahithophel was poised to unleash a very morbid form of treachery against David his king. (II Sam 16 vs. 23) When Absolom came to covet his father's throne and schemed to overcome him, Ahithophel advised Absolom that he should go in to his father concubines in order to establish himself a mortal enemy and adversary to his father David.

(II Sam 16 vs. 21) With an army of ten thousand men Ahithophel then planned to attack David in order to ambush and kill him. (II Sam 17 vs1) Ahithophel's disgrace was made complete when his wisdom, (likened unto the oracle of God itself) was blatantly disregarded by Absolom. Ahithophel promptly put his house in order, and hanged himself on a tree when he saw that his advice was not followed. (II Sam 17 vs. 23)

The suggestion that Absolom should go in to David's concubines could well have been taken from Ahithophel's knowledge of another oracle that was spoken as a result of David's sin. David plotted to take Bathsheba, the wife of Uriah the Hitite, as his own. By sending Uriah to the front lines to fight in the battles fiercest point, David effectively has Uriah put to death. After David takes Bathsheba as his own wife the Lord sends Nathan the prophet to reveal the eternal consequence of David's sinful actions.

II Samuel 12 vs. 7

And Nathan said unto David, Thou art the man. Thus saith the Lord God of Israel, I anointed thee king over Israel, and I delivered thee out of the hand of Saul;

8 And I gave thee thy master's house, and thy master's wives into thy bosom, and gave thee the house of Israel and of Judah; and if that had been too little, I would moreover have given unto thee such and such things.

9 Wherefore hast thou despised the commandment of the Lord to do evil in his sight? Thou hast killed Uriah the Hittite with the sword, and hast taken his wife, and hast slain him with the sword of the children of Ammon.

10 Now therefore the sword shall never depart from thine house, because thou hast despised me and hast taken the wife of Uriah the Hittite to be thy wife.

11 Thus saith the Lord, Behold, I will raise up evil against thee out of thine own house, and I will take thy wives before thine eyes, and give them unto thy neighbor, and he shall lie with thy wives in the sight of this sun.

12 For thou didst it secretly: but I will do this thing before all Israel, and before the sun.

When one searches the scriptures it becomes evident that this prophecy, which could only be fulfilled from one who would originate from David's own house, was probably best represented by Solomon's actions in taking Abishag the Shunammite to wife. As was previously mentioned the civil unrest that eventually emerged from within the nation of Israel was a direct result of Solomon's rampant polygamy. A 'sword' of division soon overtook the nation of Israel as Solomon slipped further and further into idolatrous practices. Solomon's seven hundred wives and princesses and three hundred concubines (1 Ki. 11 vs. 3) would easily qualify Solomon for the fulfillment of this prophecy.

Legacy of Perdition

As the spiritual conditioning of the nation of Israel continued to decline, the Lord took measures in order to keep the momentum of Solomon's divine promise at bay. The succession of political enmity arrayed against Judah eventually took on a supernatural quality that lingered mysteriously in its opposition to the hierarchy of Solomon's satanic order. In this harrowing account the Lord stirs up a supernatural adversary against Solomon and the kings of Judah in fulfillment of prophecy of the sword that would not depart from Israel. Israel is eventually split into the dichotomy of two opposing remnants that prevailed over one another at different points in history.

In terms of God's prophetic anointing, subtleties exist in scripture that imply that the Lord was faithful in his judgment towards Solomon. According to scripture the Lord is careful to exact judgment by supernatural means that would otherwise go unnoticed, if the Lord's ability to transcend the limits of death were not known. It is within this capability that the true reckoning of God's standing as "Lord over the spirits of all flesh" is amply realized. (Num. 27 vs. 16)

The other worldly quality of the sons of Belial, stems from a wave of satanic influence and fractioning of powers spread as a result of Solomon's abuse of God's anointing. Despite the outright rebellion committed against God, scripture clearly suggests that the Lord's judgment was easily entreated against Solomon. Prophetic scriptures regarding the demise of this satanic figure are clearly fulfilled by the subtle events directly following Solomon's reign.

1 Kings 11 vs. 14

And the Lord stirred up an adversary unto Solomon, Hadad the Edomite: he was of the king's seed in Edom.

15 For it came to pass, when David was in Edom, and Joab the captain of the host was gone up to bury the slain, after he had smitten every male in Edom:

16 (For six months did Joab remain there with all Israel, until he had cut off every male in Edom:)

17 That Hadad fled, he and certain Edomites of his father's servants with him, to go into Egypt: Hadad being yet a little child.

21 And when Hadad heard in Egypt that David slept with his fathers, and that Joab the captain of the host was dead, Hadad said to Pharaoh, Let me depart, that I may go to mine own country.

23 And God stirred him up another adversary, Rezon the son of Eliadah, which fled from his lord Hadadezer king of Zobah:

24 And he gathered men unto him, and became captain over a hand, when David slew them of Zobah; and they went to Damascus, and dwelt therein, and reigned in Damascus.

25 And he was an adversary to Israel all the days of Solomon, beside the mischief that Hadad did: and he abhorred Israel, and reigned in Damascus.

Hadad and Rezon were more than just hired mercenaries for the Lord. The Bible suggests that they were raised up as adversaries against Solomon. At first glace, scripture does not yield many clues as to the supernatural nature of these adversaries, however, a consistent line of succession seems to follow these individuals in their rivalry against Solomon and his descendants. In fact in this line of succession of supernatural adversaries, reasonable suspicion is raised when one traces this opposition to its root, which would imply that Bible references are often connected to a single individual. Even in the scripture quoted above the fact that Hadad the king of Edom could have gained such privilege with Pharaoh and Rezon could suddenly find himself reigning over Damascus, which is a city in Syria, suggests that these individuals had supernatural favor with both God and men. Furthermore, the fact that this seamless transition was made gives rise to the suspicion that God purposely raised up an opponent that would be kept alive supernaturally until this role as adversary could be completed.

Over the span of nearly two hundred years to which Syria was involved in this conflict against Israel, a common origin and name may be traced to this opposition. Ben-hadad (which means son of Hadad in the original Hebrew) is a name that is synonymous with the Syrian opposition exerted against Solomon's regime. Curiously, historians meet with obvious confusion surrounding the personalities represented by this name as to the time and actual duration of their reign since, over the span of four generations; this office is kept by a succession of individuals that keep the same name. Although this coordinated attack against the nation of Israel reveals a common spirit of opposition against Solomon, Syria meets with limited success against Israel due to the consistent cowardice of it's leadership. Ben-hadad's hesitancy in asserting this opposition becomes an issue for the Lord when on five separate occasions this pathetic figure flees the battlefield and on at least two occasions a treatise is temporarily struck with Israel against God's will.

1 Kings 20 vs. 17
And the young men of the princes of the provinces went out first; and Ben-hadad sent out, and they told him saying, there are men come out of Samaria.
18 And he said, Whether they be come out for peace, take them alive; or whether they be come out for war take them alive.
19 So these young men of the princes of the provinces came out of the city, and the army which followed them.
20 And they slew every one his man: and the Syrian's fled; and Israel pursued them: and Ben-hadad the king of Syria escaped on a horse with the horsemen.

The source of fear that captivated Solomon's opponent shows a strange irony since God's anointing would have undoubtedly given them a full measure of God's protection. The possibility that this adversary incurred abuses against God's anointing that were similar to that of Solomon seems entirely likely. Although God never violates his ordinance of free will, there are times in history suggested by Holy Scripture where God's inexhaustible resources are utilized in a unique way. With the dawning of the Christian movement, a growing anticipation of God's righteous judgment had reached its climax. Many of Christ's followers embraced the notion that ancient prophecy could find its fulfillment in a way not conventionally accepted by the mainstream religious movement of the day. Consistent with Christian thought, the token proof of perdition was identified by the drawing back of one's resources in performing God's will, which in turn encouraged the Lord to achieve his purposes by other means.

Philippians 1 vs. 27
Only let your conversation be as it becometh the gospel of Christ: that whether I come and see you, or else be absent, I may hear of your affairs,

that ye stand fast in one spirit, with one mind striving together for the faith of the gospel;

28 And in nothing terrified by your adversaries: which is to them an evident token of perdition, but to you of salvation, and that of God.

29 For unto you it is given in the behalf of Christ, not only to believe on him, but also to suffer for his sake;

30 Having the same conflict which ye saw in me, and now hear to be in me.

With the failure of more conventional methods and as a result of Syria's continued military defeat, the Lord is finally forced to exact judgment out of his own resources in a way that was in keeping with prophetic scripture. Specific prophecy exists that warns of an eternal judgment for all those who are left to serve in the enemy's tabernacle. (Job 20 vs. 26) For Satan himself a specific fate is implied in scripture that shows God's punishment is a direct and tangible reality. The unconventional demonstration of God's power in this formal judgment will be more effectively explored towards the end of this chapter.

The Seeds of Judgment

The supernatural power base of Solomon's regime, since it was established by divine order, challenged the early church to proclaim its message of reform in a way that was subtle. Jesus frequently spoke in parables when imparting the mysteries of the kingdom of God. Salvation, for all intents and purposes, becomes a way of spiritually purging oneself of this tainted world system in order to see the spiritual reality of God's true government.

On the opposite front, true religious authority remained in the hands of the Sadducees descended from Zadok and Solomon's regime which disclaimed the notion of a coming resurrection.(3) The temple itself was overcome by a more capitalist mentality and became a popular center for commerce and trade. (Mt. 21 vs. 13) Economic and political powers, which posed a significant challenge to the spread of Christ's saving gospel, were clearly identified by Jesus as the true force of anti-Christ in the world.

John the Baptist, Christ's forerunner emerges out of the plains of the desert to proclaim the coming Christ. John sternly warns the religious authorities of the day to brace for this reform by preaching the coming of the Messiah who will have full spiritual authority in accomplishing this radical change.

Matthew 3 vs. 7

But when he saw many of the Pharisees and Sadducees come to his baptism, he said unto them, O generation of vipers, who hath warned you to flee from the wrath to come?
8 Bring forth therefore fruits meet for repentance:
9 And think not to say within yourselves, We have Abraham to our father: for I say unto you, that God is able of these stones to raise up children unto Abraham.
10 And now also the axe is laid unto the root of the trees: therefore every tree which bringeth not forth good fruit is hewn down, and cast into the fire.
11 I indeed baptize you with water unto repentance: but he that cometh after me is mightier than I, whose shoes I am not worthy to bear: he shall baptize you with the Holy Ghost, and with fire:
12 Whose fan is in his hand, and he will throughly purge his floor, and gather his wheat into the garner; but he will burn up the chaff with unquenchable fire.

The threshing floor illustrated in this passage is reminiscent of the threshing floor of Aurnan the Jebusite which was purchased for the sight of the building of the Temple. (1 Chr. 21 vs. 23-26) John the Baptist is therefore serving notice to the Pharisees and Sadducees of how God's righteous judgment would soon fall. The religious strongholds of the enemy were soon to be shaken at their lowest foundation as a result of Jesus ministry. Through his own admission, Jesus explains how by speaking in parables those that are blinded by this worldly system of government may be lured away into the divine light of God's kingdom. (Matt 13 vs. 15) For those that remain the consequence of God's eternal judgment is also served by this preaching method.

In the following parable, which bares a striking similarity to David's last words, Jesus explains this methodology whereby the Lord's righteous seed will prevail in the Day of Judgment.

Matthew 13 vs. 24
Another parable put he forth unto them, saying, The kingdom of heaven is likened unto a man which sowed good seed in his field:
25 But while men slept, his enemy came and sowed tares among the wheat, and went his way.
26 But when the blade was sprung up, and brought forth fruit, then appeared the tarres also.

27 So the servants of the householder came and said unto him, Sir, didst not thou sow good seed in thy field? from whence then hath it tares?
28 He said unto them, An enemy hath done this. The servants said unto him, Wilt thou then that we go and gather them up?
29 But he said, Nay; lest while ye gather up the tares, ye root up also the wheat with them.
30 Let both grow together until the harvest: and in the time of harvest I will say to the reapers, Gather ye together first the tares, and bind them in bundles to burn them: but gather the wheat into my barn.

Scripture clearly differentiates between those seeds that were sown in good faith and those seeds, which were sown by the enemy who are reserved for the fires of judgment. A similar look at David's last words illuminates the possibility that Jesus Christ is qualified in the fulfillment of this prophecy as sewing the seeds of God's righteous judgment against Solomon and his descendants.

II Samuel 23 vs. 2

The Spirit of the Lord spake by me, and his word was in my tongue.
3 The God of Israel said, the Rock of Israel spake to me, He that ruleth over men must be just, ruling in the fear of God.
4 And he shall be as the light of the morning, when the sun riseth, even as a morning without clouds: as the tender grass springing out of the earth by clear shining after the rain.
5 Although my house be not so with God; yet he hath made with me an everlasting covenant, ordered in all things, and sure: for this is all my salvation and all my desire, although he make it not to grow.
6 But the sons of Belial shall be all of them as thorns thrust away, because they cannot be taken with hands:
7 But the man that shall touch them must be fenced with iron and the staff of a spear; and they shall be utterly burned with fire in the same place.

Although several of Solomon's abuses of God's anointing have already been investigated in this treatise for their diverse outcomes, many other abject articles of prophetic scripture exist which describe the particularly violent end that this wicked man from God would soon be subjected to. The ancient prophets and all those who were effectively flowing in God's anointing quickly identify the nature of God's power and ability to fulfill this prophecy in a more unconventional way. Towards the end of the successive opposition asserted against Solomon and his descendants the scripture chronicling this period in history invites further speculation into the specific nature of God's judgment towards Solomon.

A Prophecy Fulfilled

Theologians have often speculated about the events surrounding eternal judgment of Satan and his angels as they are cast into the eternal lake of fire. Many prophecies exist which indicate Satan's demise. When one looks closer however, these prophecies seem to be fulfilled at least on an interim bases, in the events directly following King Solomon's reign. The revelation of the anti-Christ's secret identity being revealed is a consistent theme among these prophecies. (Isa.14 vs. 16) The following examples in scripture reveal a list of specific criteria stipulated for the fulfillment of the demise of this anti-Christ figure.

In the following prophecy the specifics of this formal judgment are outlined predicting a violent end for this individual, by stating how the bow of steal shall strike him through. (This prophetic word is consistent with the prophetic utterance spoken against the serpent in the Garden of Eden whereby the serpent's head shall be bruised by Eve's offspring. (Gen 3 vs. 15)) This prophecy goes on to suggest how heaven shall reveal his iniquity; and the earth shall rise up against him. Finally, in a statement that is repeated in various points in scripture through out the Bible, scripture mentions how judgment will be poured out on all those who choose to remain in his tabernacle.

Job 20 vs. 22

In the fullness of his sufficiency he shall be in straits; every hand of the wicked shall come upon him.

23 When he is about to fill his belly, God shall cast the fury of his wrath upon him, and shall rain it upon him, while he is eating.

24 He shall flee from the iron weapon, and the bow of steel shall strike him through.

25 It is drawn, and cometh out of the body; yea, the glittering sword cometh out of his gall: terrors are about him.

26 All darkness shall be hid in his secret places: a fire not blown shall consume him; it shall go ill with him that is left in his tabernacle.

27 Then heaven shall reveal his iniquity; and the earth shall rise up against him.

28 The increase of his house shall depart, and his goods shall flow away in the day of his wrath.

29 This is the portion of a wicked man from God and the heritage appointed unto him by God.

Elsewhere in scripture it is suggested that men will marvel when they consider the true identity of this satanic figure. This individual's effort to exalt himself above God's throne, as was brought out in the second chapter of this treatise, was a major offence that was committed by Solomon against God. This scripture goes on to describe the antithesis of the resurrection of condemnation. This event is centered on God's irrevocable word, which stipulates that this anti-Christ figure, although left to live in relative safety for his remaining life, would eventually awaken to eternal condemnation.

Isaiah 14 vs. 12

How art thou fallen from heaven, O Lucifer, son of the morning! how art thou cut down to the ground, which didst weaken the nations!

13 For thou hast said in thine heart, I will ascend into heaven, I will exalt my throne above the stars of God: I will sit also upon the mount of the congregation, in the sides of the north:

14 I will ascend above the heights of the clouds; I will be like the most High.

15 Yet thou shalt be brought down to hell, to the sides of the pit.

16 They that see thee shall narrowly look upon thee, and consider thee, saying, Is this the man that made the earth to tremble, that did shake kingdoms;

17 That made the world as a wilderness, and destroyed the cities thereof; that opened not the house of her prisoners?

18 All the kings of the nations, even all of them, lie in glory, everyone in his own house.

19 But thou art cast out of thy grave like an abominable branch, and as the raiment of those that are slain, thrust through with a sword, that go down to the stones of the pit; as a carcase trodden under feet.

Scripture further promises that this individual will die the death of the uncircumcised as those who are slain in the midst of the seas. If Solomon were truly the individual that this scripture was pertaining to, questions arise as to how these scriptures were fulfilled. In the following excerpt from Ezekiel this scripture bares an eerie consistency with those shared previously. Collectively these scriptures seem to point to yet another mystery discovered in scripture.

Ezekial 28 vs. 8

They shall bring thee down to the pit, and thou shalt die the deaths of them that are slain in the midst of the seas.

9 Wilt thou yet say before him that slayeth thee, I am God? but thou shalt be a man, and no God, in the hands of him that slayeth thee.

10 Thou shalt die the deaths of the uncircumcised by the hand of strangers: for have spoken it, saith the Lord.

In order to touch on the answer to these mysteries one must look to the successive opposition that was initially instated against the house of Judah. Despite the fact that this opposition remains as a significant force against Israel, this role as an adversary is interrupted when Israel inadvertently chose to enter into a peace treatise with Syria and Judah simultaneously. Scholars of history explain how the fratricidal wars between Israel and Judah resulted in a treatise when Ahab arranged a marriage between the princess Athaliah and Joram, the crown prince of Judah. This triangulated peace was in clear violation of the lord's intentions in keeping the dispersion of Solomon's satanic forces at bay.(4)

The token proof of perdition is clearly exemplified when Ben-hadad grovels before Ahab the king of Israel in sack-cloth and ashes. The strange repercussions that follow seem to explain the Lord's handling of this unsanctioned treatise.

I Kings 20 vs. 32

So they girded sackcloth on their loins, and put ropes on their heads, and came to the king of Israel, and said, Thy servant Ben-hadad saith, I pray thee, let me live. And he said, Is he yet alive? he is my brother.

33 Now the men did diligently observe whether anything would come from him, and did hastily catch it: and they said, Thy brother Ben-hadad. Then he said, Go ye, bring him. Then Ben-hadad came forth to him; and he caused him to come up into the chariot.

34 And Ben-hadad said unto him, The cities, which my father took from thy father, I will restore; and thou shalt make streets for thee in Damascus, as my father made in Samaria. Then said Ahab, I will send thee away with this covenant. So he made a covenant with him, and sent him away.

The fulfillment of these ancient prophecies is overshadowed by the principle nature of God's power. With the barrier of death finally crossed, by the power of Christ's son- ship and anointing, the Lord ultimately has his way with 'the spirits of all flesh'. By the specific nature of this power, God shows how he is able to reinstate any individual into bodily form in order to fulfill divine prophecy and have his perfect will obeyed. The signature of this ability is denoted in the subtle reference to 'the sons of the prophets'. The meaning of the term 'sons' in this subtle reference to 'the sons of the prophets' is to those things that are drawn out of a prophetic understanding, implying the presence of those things that only God's prophetic office can attain to. Thus when 'the sons of the prophets' are referred to one must be prepared for scripture to be revealed under the guise of this unique power. The concept of this ability will be thoroughly dealt with in the next chapter of this treatise.

The application of this power is subjugated to God's holy prophets where by the transition of God's anointed purposes is passed on from generation to generation as the Lord sees fit. Philosophically speaking, the essence of these purposes is a very pure form of man's created nature. This power of God seems to suggest that these individuals have the ability to be incarnated with these particular purposes for the time and season of God's choosing.

Directly following the peace treatise that was struck between Israel and Syria in the chain of events that follow it becomes evident that God is exerting his power as 'Lord over the spirits of all flesh' so that scripture can be adequately fulfilled. It is within the personality of the 'prophet' mentioned in this scripture that Solomon's hidden character swiftly meets with the Lord's judgment. Ahab, the reigning king of Israel, because of the treaty he made with Syria, is also destined to bear the brunt of this curse. The 'utter destruction' that Ben hadad was appointed to is symbolic of his opposition to the wave of satanic influence that was unleashed upon the world as result of Solomon's abuses.

I KINGS 20 vs. 35

And a certain man of the sons of the prophets said unto his neighbor in the word of the Lord, Smite me, I pray thee. And the man refused to smite him.

36 Then said he unto him, Because thou hast not obeyed the voice of the Lord, behold, as soon as thou art departed from me, a lion shall slay thee. And as soon as he was departed from him, a lion found him and slew him.

37 Then he found another man and said, Smite me, I pray thee. And the man smote him, so that in smiting he wounded him.

38 So the prophet departed, and waited for the king by the way, and disguised himself with ashes upon his face.

39 And as the king passed by he cried unto the king: and he said, Thy servant went out into the midst of the battle; and behold, a man turned aside, and brought a man unto me, and said, Keep this man;

if by any means he be missing, then shall thy life be for his life, or else thou shalt pay a tallent of silver.

These initial passages of scripture bear an other-worldly quality suggestive of God's divine interventions in these unfolding events. The Lord's ability to raise up a prophet who would eventually take the brunt of God's formal judgment becomes a surprising example of the many attributes of God's power. Although on the surface this prophetic figure seems to be unbeknownst to the exact intention of God's purpose, God's word is obeyed without question when the prophet encourages a man to strike him. As the nature of these occurrences is brought to a climax the Lord's displeasure is voiced and the curse of this adversarial role is suddenly shifted to include Israel and it's king.

I Kings 20 vs. 41

And he hasted, and took the ashes away from his face; and the king of Israel discerned him that he was of the prophets.

42 And he said unto him, Thus saith the Lord, Because thou hast let go out of thy hand a man whom I appointed to utter destruction, therefore thy life shall go for his life, and thy people for his people.

43 And the king of Israel went to his house heavy and displeased, and came to Samaria.

God has the power to do as he will regarding the spirits of all flesh The notion that an individual like Solomon can suffer death and then be brought back for his untimely judgment does not contradict any of the spiritual principles accustomed to in the Judeo-Christian tradition. In the book of Revelations scripture speaks of "the beast whose deadly wound was healed" (Rev 13 vs. 3) to whom the world wondered after. Scripture that follows later mentions how "those who dwell on the earth would wonder who's names were not written in the book of life from the foundations of the world, when they behold the beast that was, and is not and yet is." (Rev 17 vs. 8) Although the belief in this form of reincarnation is not presently identified by the Christian church as a whole, the belief and practice of this reality was clearly accepted by the early church as will soon be discovered.

In what is regarded as probably the oldest book of the Bible, God's prophetic word provides a very exact account of this event to underscore the divine nature of God's judgment. Scripture's description of how the wicked man believing not that he will return out of darkness where he is waited for of the sword could well refer to the process of returning Solomon in order for the Lord's divine judgment to be fulfilled.

Job 15 vs. 17
I will shew thee, hear me; and that which I have seen I will declare.
18 Which wise men have told from their fathers, and have not hid it:
19 Unto whom alone the earth was given, and no stranger passed among them.
20 The wicked man travaileth with pain all his days, and the number of years is hidden to the oppressor.
21 A dreadful sound is in his ears: in prosperity the destroyer shall come upon him.
22 He beleiveth not that he shall return out of the darkness, and he is waited for of the sword.
23 He wandereth abroad for bread, saying, Where is it? he knoweth that the day of darkness is ready at hand
24 Trouble and anguish shall make him afraid; they shall prevail against him, as a king ready for battle.
25 For he stretcheth out his hand against God, and strengtheneth himself against the Almighty.

Another common adage that commonly resurfaces in prophetic scripture also prevalent in the book of Ecclesiastes is Solomon's long discourses on vanity. (Eccl 1 vs. 2) "Vanity of vanities, all is vanity," says Solomon, yet this scripture discourages the reader from trusting in vanity, for vanity shall be his recompense. Finally, consistent with the divine prophecy from a variety of sources, this particular scripture reminds us of how fire shall consume the tabernacles of bribery.

Job 15 vs. 29
He shall not be rich, neither shall his substance continue, neither shall he prolong the perfection thereof upon the earth.
30 He shall not depart out of darkness; the flame shall dry up his branches, and by the breath of his mouth shall he go away.
31 Let not him that is deceived trust in vanity; for vanity shall be his recompense.
32 It shall be accomplished before his time, and his branch shall not be green.
33 He shall shake off his unripe grape as the vine, and shall cast off his flower as the olive.

34 For the congregation of hypocrites shall be desolate, and fire shall consume the tabernacles of bribery.
35 They conceive mischief and bring forth vanity, and their belly prepareth deceit.

In the next chapter, the revelation of the sons of the prophets will be fully examined, along with the key individuals to whom it pertains. In the early Christian church the growing expectancy that the timing of the fulfillment of God's prophecy was drawing near, met with this more unconventional reality of God's power on more than one occasion. The possibility that many key personalities from the Bible were included in this subtle process will be thoroughly explored. God's promised inheritance as it pertains to the Gentile race will be further substantiated as a result of this unique power.

VII
Sons of The Prophets

In the previous chapter a new aspect of God's power was investigated whereby the Lord's ability to return any human soul to bodily form was realized. God's dominion over the spirits of all flesh is reaffirmed in this ability. A further investigation into the ancient culture and belief of God's chosen people renders a more detailed account of this particular revelation; an understanding aptly referred to as the revelation of the sons of the prophets. This terminology denotes the existence of certain key personalities incarnated with a divine purpose, which may only be identified as a result of this prophetic understanding. As expected, these things, as they pertain to the oracles of prophecy, would remain supernaturally sealed if not for the spiritual insight revealed through the death and resurrection of Jesus Christ, God's only son.

John the Baptist, who readily identified Jesus as being the son of God (Matt. 3 vs. 17) ascribed to this unique power. As John was overseeing the baptism of the multitudes, knowing the people's thoughts, he warned them "and do not think to say to yourselves 'we have Abraham as our father,'" John continues by making a public declaration of God's ability to "take any one of these stones and turn it into a son of Abraham." (Matt. 3 vs. 9) (John the Baptist is clearly engaged in this particular belief in a variety of ways as will soon be explored.) From the standpoint of John the Baptist's ministry from the banks of the Jordan River, upon commenting on the sons of Abraham, John's attention could well have been fixed on those stones that were gathered as a memorial to Joshua's triumphal passage into the Holy Land when the waters of the Jordan parted before the Ark of the Covenant. John's stones, the same stones that were gathered as a memorial of this triumphal entry when the waters of the Jordan parted, were also placed as a witness to God's supernatural power. (Joshua 4 vs. 6) The symbolic virtue of these stones is largely consistent with 'the rock of revelation' previously mentioned. Clearly, the revealing nature of these mysteries inspires a deeper understanding of one's unique identity in Christ. This symbolism is reiterated in the book of Revelations.

Rev 2 vs. 17

He that hath an ear, let him hear what the Spirit saith unto the churches; To him that overcometh will I give to eat of the hidden manna, and will give him a white stone, and in the stone a new name written, which no man knoweth saving he that receiveth it.

In this context it one discovers how God's purposes are entreated with an existence that transcends the reality of birth and death. In this realm an individual's personable existence is open to a new level of discovery that would otherwise go uninvestigated. The theory that God has many anointed purpose at his disposal validates the potential for uniqueness in every human being. Likewise the possibility that every individual has a unique historical tie to God's eternal purposes remains unrenowned to most human beings since these purposes bear an ancient existence that remains foreign to one's immediate reality.

The Anointing of Elijah

John the Baptist remains one of the more enigmatic characters of the gospels. His beliefs have been linked to that of the Essenes* since the community of Qumran was not far from where John the Baptist would have preached.(1) The source of mystery surrounding this personality is encountered early on in the gospels when a procession of Levite priests are sent to investigate John the Baptist's true identity. The Levite priests, by their speculation, are lead to believe that John could be the prophet Elijah back from the dead, a prospect that John flatly denies. (John 1 vs. 21) Mary"s visit to Elizabeth, the mother of John reinforces John"s otherworldly character, when the gospels state "the babe in her womb lept for joy" and Elizabeth was filled with the Holy Spirit. (Luke 1 vs. 41,44) John's ministry of water baptism is consistent with the gospel's portrayal of John's primary role of preparing the people for the coming Christ. Still, the notion of John's connection to the prophet Elijah persisted based entirely on the prophecy of Malachi (Mal. 4 vs. 5), which states that the prophet Elijah would return before "the great and terrible day of the Lord." Jesus' disciples inquire further on this point to which Jesus clearly explains that Elijah has already come, suggesting that Jesus was speaking of John the Baptist. (Matt. 17 vs. 12,13)

In the final analysis, it is clear that the belief that God has the power to return any individual to bodily form in order to fulfill scripture is clearly considered within the realm of possibility among Christ's disciples. Jesus himself posed the question, "who do men say that I am?" Jesus' disciples answered "some say that thou art John the Baptist: some, Elijah; and others, Jeremiah, or one of the prophets." (Matt. 16 vs. 13, 14) These answers reflect the belief of the times whereby God's capability in this realm of birth and death is clearly implied.

To settle the question of John the Baptist's true identity, the fact remains that he was who he was. Given the truths previously expounded it is also reasonable to suggest that John came in the power and anointing of Elijah so that this essential ministry could be carried out. Distinct parallels have been drawn, which not only link John the Baptist with the anointing of Elijah, but with the even more ancient prophet, Moses.(2) This substantiates John's ministry of Baptism in a new way since Moses means, "drawn out of the water."(3) Baptism, as a unique spiritual preparation recon's one self to a unique individual calling consistent with the nation of priests and prophets that God had foreordained. (Ex. 19 vs. 6) John's ministry, existing largely on the outskirts of Jerusalem is reminiscent of Moses' exile which occurred as a consequence of his striking the rock when the Lord specifically instructed him to speak to the rock. (Num 20 vs.11, 12)

The Lord's Covenant With Abraham

During the course of this chapter a number of unique identities will be explored in scripture which seem to validate Jesus Christ's special calling as a light of revelation to the Gentiles. The universal appeal served by the Christian church will be substantiated by a very ancient spiritual calling which shows itself superior to any calling after the flesh, either by race or nationality. This calling further asserts Jesus of Nazareth's birthright and ministry as the only Son of God by the prophetic fulfillment of this Holy Scripture. God's supernatural seal is modeled after an earlier type and shadow of the Lord's sanctification. According to the covenant God made with Abraham, every male child was to be circumcised on the eighth day of his life as the sign of the seal in flesh (Rom 4 vs. 11) imparted to Abraham and his descendants. Since it remains true that God's immutable intention to raise up Abraham's offspring as a kingdom of priests, this seal in the flesh becomes an enduring symbol of God's supernatural anointing. The number eight carries with it a symbolically prophetic connotation as a result of this connection.

Historically, the rite of circumcision becomes the source of some debate in the early Church. (Acts 15 vs. 1) In the process of fulfilling ethical and legal requirements of Levitical law, the question of precedence between these two types of sanctification arose. For all intents and purposes, the seal of God, which is wrought by the spirit of Christ, is seen as the more essential circumcision of the heart described in the New Testament. (Phil 3 vs. 3) Likewise, the Old Testament draws this parallel, whereby the people of God are asked to circumcise the flesh of their hearts on more than one occasion. (Jer. 9 vs. 26) (Ez. 44 vs. 9) Aspects of this ancient belief may be traced back to when this ordinance was originally instated in God's covenant with Abraham. The subtle instruction delivered to Abraham surrounding this practice clearly proves how the mind of God transcends the more natural, linear based understanding which mankind is accustomed to.

The Lord's historic interaction with Abraham and Sarai, Abraham's wife, is a clear example of the intimacy which exists between God and his worshippers and the subtlety and detail in God's word that may be examined as a result of this relationship. At one point Sarai, whose name was changed to Sarah, laughs to herself when she considers God's promise to give her a son since she is beyond the years of child bearing. The Lord reading her thoughts promptly asks, "wherefore did Sarah laugh? ... Is anything to hard for the Lord?" (Gen 18 vs. 11,13) A similar intimacy may be examined in the events leading up to the instatement of God's covenant with Abraham.

Genesis 15 vs. 3

And Abram said, Behold, to me thou hast given no seed: and, lo, one born in my house is mine heir.

4 And, behold, the word of the Lord came unto him, saying, This shall not be thine heir: but he that shall come forth out of thine own bowels shall be thine heir.

5 And he brought him forth abroad, and said, Look now toward heaven, and tell the stars, if thou be able to number them: and he said unto him, So shall thy seed be.

6 And he believed in the Lord; and he counted it to him for righteousness.

7 And he said unto him, I am the Lord that brought thee out of Ur of the Chaldees, to give thee this land to inherit it.

8 And he said, Lord God, whereby shall I know that I shall inherit it?

The scripture clearly explains how Abraham believed in the Lord and how the Lord counted it to him for righteousness, but the perfect nature of this simple faith is short-lived. A subtle nuance exists that is expounded based on the sacrifice that God requires at Abraham's hand, which would suggest that Abraham sinned presumptuously. Not satisfied with merely believing, Abraham boldly asks, "whereby shall I know that I will inherit it," implying that Abraham was requesting to know on the basis of fact. In due course it was likely that God was preparing to make his covenant with Abraham, but what Abraham was asking was unprecedented for a covenant relationship. God's covenants are traditionally based on faith alone. (Gen 8 vs21)

The likelihood that Abraham, as a prophet of God (Gen 20 vs7) had some inclination into what he was requesting remains possible, since foreknowledge of the glory of Christ is stipulated in all prophecy. (1 Pet 1 vs. 10,11) The revelation to follow, which proves itself beyond the constraints of time is a further example of the supernatural properties spanning God's living word.

Abraham's Sacrifice

When Abraham makes this unprecedented request, the Lord promptly orders that Abraham offer up a sacrifice according to his specific instruction. The items of this sacrifice include one young heifer; the sacrifice customarily used in association with defilement after touching a dead body, (Num 19 vs. 1-10) one young he goat, traditionally offered if one sins through ignorance, (Lev 5 vs15) one she goat, the offering given if one sins by ignorantly swearing with a vow of self will, (Lev 5 vs. 6) (also used if a person touches something dead) and a turtle dove and a young pigeon, half the sacrifice used ceremonially in the rite of circumcision.(Lev 12 vs. 8) According to God's instruction the animals of the sacrifice were cut in two, where as the birds were to remain whole. The sacrifice Abraham offers seems consistent with the notion that Abraham sinned presumptuously in vowing that he should know if he would receive this inheritance.

The self same day God's covenant to circumcise every male child on the eighth day of his life, as a lasting ordinance passed down from generation to generation is furbished. (Gen 15 vs. 18) Even if sin did exist as a result of Abraham's request, the Lord remains curiously silent. Millenniums would pass with nothing more than scarce references to this occurrence to be found in Holy Scripture.

Eventually, a few references emerge in the context of those things that were to be sealed up that lead to a startling revelation to the rites of sanctification mentioned previously. Prophetic scripture insists that the Lord of hosts himself be sanctified. With this scripture in question, the notion of Christ coming in the flesh must be entertained since the Lord of hosts needs no sanctification, the Lord must be speaking of the circumcision, the lesser type and shadow* of sanctification, which would be a significant platform to proclaim the Lord's arrival in the flesh. The scripture further orders that this testimony should be sealed up among the Lord's disciples where the Lord's children are set for signs and wonders in Israel.

Isaiah 8 vs. 13
Sanctify the Lord of hosts himself; and let him be your fear, and let him be your dread.
14 And he shall be for a stone of stumbling and for a rock of offence to both the houses of Israel, for a gin and for a snare to the inhabitants of Jerusalem.
15 And many among them shall stumble, and fall, and be broken, and be snared, and be taken.
16 Bind up the testimony, seal the law among my disciples.
17 And I will wait upon the Lord, that hideth his face from the house of Jacob, and I will look for him.
18 Behold, I and the children whom the Lord hath given me are for signs and for wonders in Israel from the Lord of hosts, which dwell in mount Zion.

This scripture speaks of the preparation of the gospel ready to be brought before all people and the sanctification that is centered on the mind of Christ through the revelation of the Holy Spirit. The key components of this ministry, as explored previously, were clearly represented in Christ's teachings as well as the subsequent ministry of Christ's disciples. Collectively, the legacy of scripture that would follow bears witness to the account of Christ's sanctification and was indeed sealed up among Christ's early followers.

Abraham's Promise Fulfilled

The question of Abraham's secret heart- vow when he requested that he be able to know for a surety that he would receive the inheritance promised by God, takes on a new emphasis where these two types of sanctification intersect. Incredibly, scripture seems to dictate that Abraham was present, in one form or another, to witness Christ's arrival in the flesh. Two separate Gospel references along with Old Testament prophecy seems to pinpoint the exact nature of the disciples sealed testimony. In fact, not long after this testimony is mentioned in prophetic scripture, in subsequent chapters scripture goes on to describe the monumental revelation that would follow for all of the nations of the world. (Is. 9 vs. 2) It is from this revealing platform that Christ's ministry is first heralded to the Gentile nations.

According to Jesus' testimony Abraham did rejoice to see his day and Jesus further asserts how he, meaning Abraham, saw it and was glad. Historically Bible scholars have speculated regarding Christ's intended meaning of these passages. In light of the revelation of the sons of the prophets the potential for scripture to be fulfilled according to this theme is entirely possible. Similar to that of John the Baptist, Jesus enters into a long discourse, warning his critics that their genealogical ties to Abraham will not save them. (John 8 vs39)

John 8 vs. 54
Jesus answered, If I honour myself, my honour is nothing: it is my Father that honoureth me; of whom ye say, that he is your God:
55 Yet ye have not known him; but I know him: and if I should say, I know him not, I shall be a liar like unto you: but I know him and keep his saying.
56 Your father Abraham rejoiced to see my day: and he saw it and was glad.

Jesus' critics go on to reason among themselves thinking how Jesus, being a young man, could not possibly have seen Abraham. (John 8 vs. 57) This response is typical of the linear based understanding to which mankind is accustomed. Still, the question of how Abraham was able to see Jesus would seem to challenge every natural avenue of one's intelligence. The idea that Jesus was speaking figuratively or even spiritually in this case seems unlikely, since such an answer would not be in keeping with the tone of this passage.

When one considers God's goodness and pleasure in fulfilling his word in a way that is most fulfilling, it would seem infinitely appropriate if Abraham would have been able to see Jesus in the flesh in one form or another. Abraham's covenant, which was consecrated by the seal in flesh as a symbol of the Lord's sanctification, bears a heart-felt connection to the true sanctification that is given by faith through Jesus Christ alone. In the Lord's eternal nature an almost seamless transition exists between those things of an ancient origin, and the things, which pertain to the current age. In the following passage the notion that Abraham would be present during Jesus' rite of sanctification, which is his circumcision, is subtly implied in this prophetic scripture.

Isaiah 29 vs. 22
Therefore thus saith the Lord, who redeemed Abraham, concerning the house of Jacob, Jacob shall not now be ashamed, neither shall his face now wax pale.
23 But when he seeth his children, the work of mine hands, in the midst of him, they shall sanctify my name, and sanctify the Holy One of Jacob, and shall fear the God of Israel.
24 They also that erred in spirit shall shall come to understanding, and they that murmured shall learn doctrine.

The tone of this scripture is consistent with the Lord's dealings with Abraham and Sarah as documented in the book of Genesis. The suggestion that "they that murmured shall learn doctrine" could well imply that the Lord is prepared to meet Abraham's request whereby he desired to know that he would receive his trusted inheritance. Again, in this passage, the two types of sanctification intersect, whereby the Holy one of Jacob should be sanctified. This passage is clearly referring to Jesus Christ's circumcision in the flesh and how Abraham himself would come to witness these proceedings. The sacrifice Abraham offered as a result of God's instruction is in keeping with the fulfillment of this promise with the sacrifice of the turtledove and the young pigeon, half the ceremonial requirement for circumcision. Since Jesus was conceived by the power of the Holy Spirit, the sin offering portion as a token of original sin may have been omitted. (Lev. 12 vs. 8)

In order to discover how it would be possible for Abraham to witness Jesus' circumcision, one must turn to scripture to examine the Gospel's record of these events. The fulfillment of this promise is yet another example of God's power and the unusual impact it had on those who would stand as witnesses. By the reaction of a certain key individual involved in seeing this coming of age for the baby Jesus, a sure notion of God's handiwork is implied.

God Has Heard

According to the Gospel record an individual who came by the spirit into the temple would bare witness to the rite of circumcision performed for Jesus. As instructed, the old man would be blessed to see the Lord's Christ before he died, as this promise was revealed to him from the Holy Spirit. The old man promptly takes Jesus up in his arms and begins quoting, for the fulfillment of scripture, the prophetic utterances of old pertaining to Christ's coming in the flesh.

Luke 2 vs. 21
And when eight days were accomplished for the circumcising of the child, his name was called Jesus, which was so named of the angel before he was conceived in the womb.
25 And, behold, there was a man in Jerusalem, whose name was Simeon; and the same man was just and devout, waiting for the consolation of Israel: and the Holy Ghost was upon him.
26 And it was revealed unto him by the Holy Ghost, that he should not see death, before he had seen the Lord's Christ.
27 And he came by the Spirit into the temple: and when the parents brought in the child Jesus, to do for him after the custom of the law,
28 Then took he him up in his arms, and blessed God, and said,
29 Lord, now lettest thou thy servant depart in peace, according to thy word:
30 For mine eyes have seen thy salvation,
31 Which thou hast prepared before the face of all people;
32 A light to lighten the Gentiles, and the glory of thy people Israel.

Simeon, who's name in the Hebrew means "God has heard" (4) seems to be incarnated with the spirit and anointing of Abraham, causing him to see and know for a certainty of the inheritance that would be brought before all people as a result of Christ's death and resurrection. Not only are the staggering implications of this ancient but time-honored request fulfilled by these occurrences, but the true calling of the Gentiles is authenticated in this claim and the tangible existence of a new glorified nature that transcends time seems to be fully supported. The variety of sources compiled in this inheritance and the remarkable consistency of the subject matter of Old and New Testament scripture alike, miraculously converges.

New Testament Application

When ascribing to Abraham, shortly after the day of Pentecost, Peter makes mention of the fulfillment of Abraham's covenant, testifying to the Jewish people that they were the most- likely recipients of God's promised salvation as the designated sons of the prophets. (Acts 3 vs. 25) Peter further explains how this process of sanctification had garnered God's promise to similarly bless all the kindred of the earth through Abraham's descendants. (Gen. 12 vs. 3) This claim suggests that a further investigation into the principle application of the sons of the prophets ought to be extended to include other Bible figures from the Old and New Testament.

The life and anointing of the Apostle Paul bear's a remarkable similarity to the Old Testament prophet Jonah. Both were known for their calling as popular evangelists. This designation, although extremely rare in Jonah's day, is nonetheless applicable to his life and ministry as examined in the book bearing his name. Paul, likewise emerged to be one of the great evangelists and preachers of his time. (Acts) Despite their unwavering success in these ministries, both showed reluctance in answering God's calling. Paul himself was originally reputed as a persecutor of the early Christians (Acts 8 vs. 1) whereas Jonah at first denied his prophetic calling altogether. (Jo. 1 vs. 3) Jonah was known have made his getaway to Tarshish, a well-known seaport and belonging to a popular trade route; (Jo. 1 vs. 3) Paul himself hailed from the city of Tarsus; also a seaport, similar in name and purpose by all accounts. (Acts 9 vs. 11)

Their seafaring journeys are equally compelling when examined in scripture. Both accounts in scripture entail a terrible storm during their ocean voyages. Jonah was essentially blamed for this turn of events so he was thrown overboard when the captain of the ship cast lots in order to inquire of the Lord as to the cause of their misfortune. (Jo. 1 vs. 15) In a similar but opposite way, Paul, who was accredited with keeping his fellow passengers safe, (Acts 27 vs.

22) prayed for his captors as they jumped overboard. (Acts 27 vs. 43) In God's persuasion to encourage these men to answer their calling, Paul is blinded and remains on a fast for three days, (Acts 9 vs. 9) whereas Jonah is swallowed up and stays in the belly of a whale for three days. (Jo. 1 vs. 17) In what has been acknowledged as the foremost sign of the resurrection, Jesus once told the scribes and Pharisees, which could well have included Paul the soon to be Apostle, that "no sign would be given them except the sign of the prophet Jonah". (Matt 16 vs. 4)

The Valley of the Shadow of Death

When Jesus indicated how Abraham rejoiced to see his day and that he saw it and was glad the word day takes on a unique depth of application. Day, which in the original Hebrew is frequently used to denote the dawning or beginning of a time, (5) represents the starting point of Jesus' life and ministry. The rite of circumcision or seal in the flesh is followed by the ceremonial offering for purification of two turtledoves and two young pigeons for every male child that openeth the womb. (Lev. 12) At the dawning of this earthly existence, as this life is set in motion within the confines of humanity's linear reality, one's sense of self is first developed. Similarly, scripture tells of how the people that walked in darkness in the valley of the shadow of death have seen a great light. (Is. 9 vs. 2)

Subject to this ancient supernatural anointing and calling are many God driven purposes set about in order to reveal an aspect of his divine wisdom. For those who are called to these preordained purposes, Christ's preeminent nature* is eventually revealed with the understanding that this calling was predestinated in God before the world began. Nevertheless, when an individual first enters their corporeal existence in the flesh, that individual is essentially lost to the awareness of their former estate, hence the analogy of the valley of the shadow of deat' is appropriated.

For one Bible figure, the unique revelation and ability to look into this former estate seemed to exist. The cosmological force and precursor to mankind's earthly existence in the flesh, discussed at great length in various points in scripture, is identified by this individual as the true blame for setting his fleshly existence in motion.

Job's Annointing

The book of Job and its revelation is based on Job's tremendous suffering as a result of the satanic attack allowed in Job's testing. Job's tremendous sorrow at the loss of his family, his deteriorating health and the loss of his goods, (Job 1,2) hails in comparison to grief of knowing the cataclysmic cosmological events that shaped the destiny of mankind long before the world began. Unlike the more natural occurrence and false assurance of self given to mankind at birth, Job's awareness of this former age had remained untainted. (Job 8 vs. 8) Observed as more of a curse than a blessing, yet channeled by the very depths of Job's sorrow, Job's knowledge of the cataclysmic events akin to this former estate are subtly implied throughout the book of Job. Similarly, the book of Revelations chronicles the clash between the forces of good and evil as a war of epic proportion ensued in heaven and Satan and his angels were cast out. (Rev 12 vs. 9) Humanity's pilgrimage through the valley of the shadow of death and how one's existence indirectly stems from these events was well known to Job.

In the tradition of the ancient Hebrews the primordial waters of the world's existence contains a serpent creature of colossal proportions, which eventually emerges as a cosmological force representing the workings of chaos and disorder.(6) In the process of this war (above) scripture suggests that this creature, known as Leviathan in the ancient world, was awakened out of its primordial state only to unleash this reckless force upon a third of the stars of heaven. (Job 3 vs. 8, Rev 12 vs. 4)

Leviathan, which maintains an ancient symbolic tie with the Babylonian civilization,(7) is representative of mankind's unrestrained ability to accomplish anything their imagination conceives. (Gen 11 vs. 6) The existence of this force of chaos raises suspicion that some type of cosmic force was unleashed, powerful enough to cast a third of the stars of heaven to earth (Rev 12 vs. 4) that could well have triggered the events that set humanities natural existence in motion. The stars, mentioned above, a likely representation of the descendants of Abraham's inheritance who were promised to be as innumerable as the stars of heaven are also symbolic of the times and seasons of divine purposes that navigate the lives of men. Mysteriously, Job is given the unique ability to see past the barrier imposed by this fleshly existence, but this uncanny ability only seemed to arouse more sorrow as a result of the knowledge of these cataclysmic events.

In the following passage Job unwittingly curses his day as he quietly reflects on this unwelcome ability unstained by the shadow of death.

Job 3 vs. 1

AFTER this opened Job his mouth, and cursed his day.

2 And Job spake, and said,

3 Let the day perish wherein I was born, and the night in which, There is a man child conceived.

4 Let the day be darkness; let not God regard it from above, neither let the light shine upon it.

5 Let darkness, and the shadow of death stain it; let a cloud dwell upon it; let the blackness of the day terrify it.

6 As for that night, let darkness seize upon it; let it not be joined unto the days of the year, let it not come into the number of the months.

7 Lo, let the night be solitary, let no joyful voice come therein.

8 Let them curse the day, who are ready to raise Leviathan.

9 Let the stars of the twilight thereof be dark; let it look for light, but have none neither let it see the dawning of the day:

10 Because it shut not up the doors of my mother's womb, nor hid sorrows from mine eyes.

In the progression of Job's faithful struggle a choice sublimely emerges. Despite his wife's encouragement to curse God and die (Job 2 vs. 9), Job is faced with deciding between the death and chaos inflicted as a result of his testing, or submitting to the power and authority of God. The image of Leviathan reemerges as a symbol of chaos; the ill-favored alternative to Job's plight. (Job 41 vs. 4) The clear analogy may be drawn between the slow disintegration of the natural order that leads to death and chaos, and God's eternal covenant, which is enacted by faith alone. In the same sense, scripture suggests that all of humanity is faced with a similar choice in choosing for themselves as to the true source of their existence.

Consequently, mankind encounters two schools of ideology throughout their lifetime, one that would discount human existence suggesting that it is vain and meaningless, (Ecc. 1 vs. 2) and the other ascribing to the proclamation of the kingdom of God and the profound notion of justice and equity from which it stems. (Matt 6 vs. 19) Humanity enters their fleshly existence in submission to one power or another. Thus, Jesus flatly charges his critics, since they found themselves unable to listen to his speech, as being of their father, the Devil (John 8 vs. 43, 44) who "was a murderer from the beginning, and abode not in the truth." (John 8 vs. 44)

In the following passage of scripture the Lord, God of all creation, remonstrates with Job to make the right choice and to remain faithful to his calling.

Job 41 vs. 1

CANST thou draw out leviathan with an hook? or his tongue with a cord which thou lettest down?

2 Canst thou put an hook into his nose? Or bore his jaw through with a thorn?

3 Will he make many supplications unto thee? Will he speak soft words unto thee?

4 Will he make a covenant with thee? Wilt thou take him for a servant forever?

5 Wilt thou play with him as with a bird? Or wilt thou bind him for thy maidens?

6 Shall the companions make a banquet of him? Shall they part him among the merchants?

7 Canst thou fill his skin with barbed irons? Or his head with fish spears?

8 Lay thine hand upon him, remember the battle, do no more.

9 Behold the hope of him is in vain: shall not one be cast down even at the sight of him?

10 None is so fierce that dare stir him up: who then is able to stand before me?

34 He beholdeth all high things: he is king over all the children of pride.

This earthly existence and one's journey through the valley of the shadow of death is based entirely on this decision whereby one's affiliation to one of these sources is ultimately decided. The creation of the world and humanity, created and configured to reinforce this freedom of choice, does not preclude the effort of Satan and his forces to appeal to mankind's more selfish tendencies. The covert secular personality of the son of perdition whose character is carefully detailed in previous chapters of this treatise, continually seeks to negate this choice.

The King of Terrors

Within the depths of experience of the human psyche, there is none more primitive than those that emerge at night while one sleeps. The spiritual tone of this experience is clearly indoctrinated in scripture. Old Testament scriptures speak of waves of desolations that haunt men's dreams, which bears a unique connection with the otherworldly existence that pervades the origins of humanity. (Job 30 14-17) These experiences as in any culture or society went on to shape the essential structure and belief of God's people in a variety of ways.

Jesus himself taught how every kingdom divided against itself will be brought to desolation. (Matt 12 vs. 25) Defilement, the act of becoming ceremonial unclean, is based on the consequence of being cut off from God, due in part to ill effects of sin on any given individual. Cut off from the true light of God's presence, an individual is left to the demise of spiritual emptiness as a result of this desolation. This phenomenon and the reputation that precedes it are based on the common occurrence of the sensation of being spiritually attacked in the process of one's sleep. Such an occurrence is well documented in the book of Job, when as a result of his testing, God momentarily turns his back on Job and these terrifying episodes ensue.

Job 30 vs. 14

They came upon me as a wide breaking in of waters: in the desolation they rolled themselves upon me.

15 Terrors are turned upon me: they pursue my soul as the wind: and my welfare passeth away as a cloud.

16 And now my soul is poured out upon me: the days of affliction have taken hold upon me.

17 My bones are pierced in me in the night season: and my sinews take no rest.

18 By the great force of my disease is my garment changed: it bindeth me about as the collar of my coat.

19 He hath cast me into the mire, and I am become like dust and ashes.

Contrary to the more traditional belief, Jesus himself teaches that the true nature of defilement* occurs when evil thoughts, attitudes, and imaginations are allowed to come from within from the very depths of the heart of mankind. (Matt 15 vs. 18) According to this principle the experience of defilement is the spiritual equivalent of being cast into outer darkness where "there shall be weeping and gnashing of teeth." As apposed to Job's experience (above) these terrifying episodes are usually short-lived. Traditionally, Levitical practice and the laws in keeping with ceremonial uncleanness and defilement is constant with a physical explanation of this phenomenon bearing in on explanations that range from eating a bad lunch before sleeping to any oppressive burden as the result of the conflict of sin.

As was explained previously, most individuals seldom relate to spiritual attainment upon entering this physical existence, nor do they have the guarantee of the Lord's salvation. It could be, as in Job's case, that individuals remain susceptible to this phenomenon upon entering into any spiritual experience without the promise of the Lord's sanctification. As Jesus clearly states in his teachings whom the son sets free is free indeed (John 8 vs. 36) which could also be taken for the revelation of Christ's son-ship and resurrection.

For the anti-Christ, the opposite is true, having thwarted his existence against God; this individual is doomed eternally to the fate of this terrorizing.

Job 18 vs. 5

Yea, the light shall be dark in his tabernacle, and his candle shall be put, and the spark of his fire shall not shine.

6 The light shall be dark in his tabernacle, and his candle shall be put out with him

7 The steps of his strength shall be straightened, and his own counsel shall cast him down.

11 Terrors shall make him afraid on every side, and shall drive him to his feet.

12 His strength shall be hunger bitten, and destruction shall be ready at his side.

13 It shall devour the strength of his skin: even the firstborn of death shall devour his strength.

14 His confidence shall be rooted out of his tabernacle, and it shall bring him before the king of terrors,

15 It shall dwell in his tabernacle, because it is none of his; brimstone shall be scattered upon his habitation.

Clearly, the bulk of this defilement* evidently coincides with the efforts in evicting this antichrist personality out into the outer darkness previously described. The religious connotation implied in mentioning the tabernacle that is none his, maintains the possibility that this form of judgment may be laid up for a specific identity. The notion that this individual is to be brought before the king of terrors implies that a specific judgment has been carefully tailored for this individual. Lastly, remaining consistent with the fiery judgment consistently examined throughout the Bible regarding Satan's demise, scripture declares that brimstone will be scattered upon his habitation.

The Resurrection of Condemnation

The type of anointing decided exclusively by each individual soul is reflected in the type of resurrection one receives. (John 5 vs. 28-29) Detailed within the annals of creation, scripture suggests that the existence of each category of nature created by God, had it's appointed time or day, a connotation that was possibly used to denote each individual type of sanctification for God's created purposes. (Gen.1) Jesus' claim to being Lord of the Sabbath (Mar.2 vs. 28) may well be symbolically rooted in the Lord's sanctification of the seventh day recorded in Genesis. (Gen 2 vs. 3) Likewise, the Apostle Paul categorizes the many types of flesh of a variety of animals, as well as the glory of celestial and terrestrial bodies to which mankind shares a common bond under God's creative authority. (1 Cor. 15 vs. 37-42) As was explored in the initial chapter of this treatise, all of God's purposes were formed in Christ as the substance of all things created. (Col 1 vs. 16) Inherent to these purposes is the form of the sanctification chosen and subsequent resurrection to follow, as was predetermined in Christ before the world began. From the standpoint of humanity, a reckoning exists in determining the type of resurrection that will be attained. For those who are faithful, these individuals are promised to attain to the resurrection of the righteous, corruption will put on incorruption in a miraculous transformation. (1 Cor. 15 vs. 53) For those who entertained the belief and following of the anti-Christ, another type of resurrection is profiled otherwise known as the resurrection of condemnation. (John 5 vs. 29) Without hesitation, scripture seems to identify the existence of a historical figure that best typifies the process of this shameful reanimation. In keeping with the precepts consistently applied in previous chapters of this treatise, God gives his servants the ability to discern the true character and content behind this spiritual force. The existence of this individual reaffirms the reality of an antichrist figure, poised to walk the earth in order to deceive its inhabitants. Scripture explains how such an individual will be shamed with the detriment of this resurrection of condemnation to emerge as distinguished and separated from that of the resurrection of the righteous.

Isaiah 14 vs. 12
How art thou fallen from heaven, O Lucifer, son of the morning! how art thou cut down to the ground, which didst weaken the nations!
13 For thou hast said in thine heart, I will ascend into heaven, I will exalt my throne above the stars of God: I will sit also upon the mount of the congregation, in the sides of the north:
14 I will ascend above the heights of the clouds; I will be like the most High.
15 Yet thou shalt be brought down to hell, to the sides of the pit.
16 They that see thee shall narrowly look upon thee, and consider thee, saying, Is this the man that made the earth to tremble, that did shake kingdoms;
19 But thou art cast out of thy grave like an abominable branch, and as the raiment of those that are slain, thrust through with a sword, that go down to the stones of the pit; as a carcass trodden under feet.

This mystery is reiterated and foretold by Jesus in his famed parable of the wedding feast. Evidently, the notion that this individual will be brought to an open shame is an unmistakably recurring theme in scripture. In this particular parable, the anti-Christ is identified as the guest who came in, not wearing a wedding garment, whom the king notices and promptly expels. Contrary to the popular belief, this portrayal strengthens the argument of Satan's apparent mortality, casting this individual as somewhat more benign than what was previously thought. Satan's mortal existence was clearly implied in the Gospel of John, when Jesus is witnessed as calling Satan a murder from the beginning. Later on in John's epistle this notion is further emphasized when John explains how "he who hateth his brother is a murderer; and ye know that no murderer hath eternal life abiding in him." (1 John 3 vs. 15) The unsettling eventuality for those who settle for the resurrection of condemnation is the shame of being cast out into outer darkness where there will be weeping and gnashing of teeth.

Matthew 22 vs. 1
AND Jesus answered and spake unto them again by parables and said,
2 The kingdom of heaven is like unto a certain king, which made a marriage for his son.
3 And sent forth his servants to call them that were bidden to the wedding: and they would not come.
9 Go therefore into the highways, and as many as ye shall find, bid to marriage.

10 So those servants went out into the highways, and gathered together all as many as they found, both bad and good: and the wedding was furnished with guests.
11 And when the king came in to see the guests, he saw there a man which had not on a wedding garment:
12 And he saith unto him, Friend, how camest thou in hither not having a wedding garment? And he was speechless.
13 Then said the king to the servants, Bind him hand and foot, and take him away, and cast him into outer darkness; there shall be weeping and gnashing of teeth.

To the extent that one's earthly father bears a resemblance to his offspring, the notion that humanity will emulate the true source of one's existence is clearly supported in scripture. The anti-Christ, an obvious example of this precept, has been clearly identified in his connection with the serpent creature in the garden of Eden. Jesus, when addressing the Pharisees for their estranged doctrine identifies them as a generation of vipers. (Matt 12 vs. 34) In previous chapters, Jesus, describing the workings of Satan, explains how a kingdom divided against itself is brought to desolation. (Matt 12 vs. 25) What Jesus is subtly implying is that the kingdom of Satan himself is full of dissention and is destined to erode into total and utter ruin.

In the next chapter subtleties in the transfer of political and religious powers will be examined at various points in scripture in order to shed light on some of the more pivotal moments in history which better illuminate the extent of the satanic influence Solomon inflicted upon the world. Revelation, regarding the key of the house of David, will be expounded along with a look into the scriptures fulfilled as a result of this revelation. Finally a hint regarding Israel's future glory as well as a glimpse into the mercies of God and his unfailing intentions, despite Satan's futile opposition, will be thoroughly examined.

VIII
The Key of The House of David

As was examined in previous chapters, as a result of Solomon's manipulation the nation of Israel was split into two opposing forces. When either of these two opposing remnants gained power, the balance of Israel's religious and political control often shifted predominantly in favor of either group. Through out the more pivotal moments in history, as the dominating cultural and religious values belonging to one of these two rivals were made manifest in Holy scripture, trace evidence of this rift becomes increasingly apparent. The inner workings and political overtones of this split may be seen at various points during Solomon's dynastic succession and through the turmoil of exile and returning from exile, surrounding Israel's Babylonian captivity.

During the upheaval of this civil unrest and even through the military threat of neighboring countries, the religious artifacts and emblems of each successive regime were torn down and systematically dismantled in an attempt to regain political and religious domination. God's awesome power in defeating the military foes that violated his will is clearly documented in Holy Scripture whereby opposing kingdoms were laid waste, and entire regions were brought to desolation. (2 Ki. 19 vs. 35) The Bible warns of the presence of cruel haunts (Ps. 74 vs. 20), and the nymph-like creatures of the night that inhabited these desert wastelands. (Is. 13 vs. 21) In the case of such examples in scripture the terrible consequence of the Lord's displeasure is clearly weighed out.

At the true heart of this disappointment are the weight of grief surrounding Israel's own defiance towards God, and the false security that arose on account of Solomon's exploitation of God's many privileges. For the majority of God's people this betrayal would remain a mystery, kept hidden for the appointed time, when the revelation of the word of God would effectively draw out God's true followers from the fate that was sealed against mankind. (2 Thes 2 vs. 7) In order to authenticate the claim of this unthinkable fate, certain individuals were given a heightened sense of awareness and a successive knowledge of this mystery.

The procession of this knowledge, passed down from generation to generation, is known as the revelation of the key of the House of David. The remnant of God's faithful and true servants, best represented by this office, included Eliakim the son of Hilkiah who lived during the reign of Hezekiah, (Is. 22 vs. 20-22) Asaph the Levite priest and chief song leader from the time of the Temple's original construction (Psalm 73), and Ezra, the scribe and levitical priest who took part in Temple reconstruction during the second Temple period. (Ezra 9 vs. 8) The succession of God's faithful calling is based on eyewitness accounts and the insight into the mystery of lawlessness perpetuated by Solomon and his followers down through the ages. A sympathetic appreciation was clearly extended to those individuals willing to shoulder the burden of understanding against these heinous crimes.

Eliakim, Son of Hilkiah

After the succession of a number of Kings who did wickedly in the sight of the Lord, there finally came the reprieve of a righteous king who obeyed God and began the task of rebuilding Israel. (II Ki. 18 vs. 3) Hezekiah, who secured his reign around 728-686 B.C. began the restoration of the original Temple and brought about immediate religious reforms.(1) Historically, Hezekiah was well known for excavating a tunnel through 1,748 feet (533 meters) through Jerusalem's ancient bedrock in order to provide a constant source of water within the fortified city walls of Jerusalem.(2) It was during this period of reconstruction that the discovery of an unlikely archeological find would shake the foundations of the Temple's religious authority to it's very core.

As Hezekiah made it his resolve to do what was right according to God's law, the tide of Israel's political fortune began to turn. In the midst of this changing political and religious climate, a young scribe, Eliakim, son of Hilkiah emerged to the rank of steward over the royal household. As a result of the repercussions stemming from centuries of moral and heretical abuses against God, Eliakim's divine appointment to this sacred office did not come without a full measure of revelation against Solomon's civil and religious disobedience. A hint of political intrigue may be seen to exist even as the balance of political and religious authority tipped in Eliakim's favor. Eliakim was sent to witness Assyria's military strong-arming against Israel as its ambassadors gathered by the conduit of the old pool. Here the Assyrian leaders reasoned among themselves how that by Hezekiah's dismantling of Israel's many idolatrous high places, the God of Israel would not defend his people against Assyrian attack. To the contrary, with the help of mentors like Isaiah the prophet, Eliakim emerged with a full revelation of the moral victory wrought by Hezekiah's religious reforms.

1 Kings 18 vs. 17

And the king of Assyria sent Tartan and Rabsaris and Rabshakeh from Laschish to king Hezekiah with a great host against Jerusalem. And they went up and came to Jerusalem. And when they were come up, they came and stood by the conduit of the upper pool, which is in the highway of the fuller's field.

18 And when they had called to the king, there came out to them Eliakim, the son of Hilkiah, which was over the household, and Shebna the scribe, and Joah the son of Asaph the recorder.

21 Now behold, thou trustest upon the staff of this bruised reed, even upon Egypt, on which if a man lean, it will go into his hand and pierce it: so is Pharaoh king of Egypt unto all that trust on him.

22 But if ye say unto me, We trust in the Lord our God: is not that he, whose high places and whose alters Hezekiah hath taken away, and hath said to Judah and Jerusalem, Ye shall worship before this altar in Jerusalem?

Eliakim himself was likely a witness into the idolatrous practices found etched on the ancient stone relics recovered by Hezekiah's many rebuilding projects. Through Eliakim's obvious affiliation with the prophet Isaiah and upon examining the chapter in the book of Isaiah that identifies the reasoning behind this divine appointment, the burden of knowing the extent of

Solomon's deception is clearly implied. This passage of scripture carries an ominous tone of discovery following the surmountable archeological evidence gathered over the generations of Solomon's satanic abuses. In the midst of this discovery, the Lord states his concern regarding the presence of a sepulcher found hewn out of the bedrock of Israel's most holy site.

Isaiah 22 vs. 9

Ye have seen also the breaches of the city of David, that they are many: and ye gathered together the waters of the lower pool.

11 Ye made also a ditch between the two walls for the water of the old pool: but ye have not looked unto the maker thereof, neither had respect unto him that fashioned it long ago.

12 And in that day did the Lord God of hosts call to weeping, and to mourning, and to baldness and to girding with sackcloth:

13 And behold joy and gladness slaying oxen, and killing sheep, eating flesh, and drinking wine: let us eat and drink: for tomorrow we shall die.

15 Thus saith the Lord God of hosts, Go, get thee unto this treasurer, even unto Shebna, which is over the house and say,

16 What hast thou here? and whom hast thou here, that thou hast hewed thee out a sepulcher here, as he that heweth him out a sepulcher on high, and that graveth an habitation for himself in a rock?

17 Behold, the Lord will carry thee away with a mighty captivity, and will surely cover thee.

The discovery of a sepulcher known to exist at Jerusalem's Temple mount, the antecedent to Eliakim's divine appointment, was representative of the mounting evidence gathered against Solomon and his descendants. The notion that an individual would knowingly prepare a place of burial in God's most holy site underscores the brazen disregard shown by those who would have had access to God's Holy Temple. Along with this abomination, a host of other archeological finds also sets the mood. Later references to this sepulcher suggested that this consecrated ground was at some point defiled by the presence of human remains. (Ez 43 vs. 9) Although Shebna, the former treasurer of the house of David was clearly held accountable for allowing the existence of this ancient burial chamber, the simple fact that a body is at some point known to have occupied this space effectively clears Shebna of any suspicion of title to ownership over this burial site.

Ezekiel 43 vs. 8

In their setting of their thresholds by my thresholds, and their post by my posts, and the wall between me and them, they have even defiled my holy name by their abominations that they have committed: wherefore I have consumed them in mine anger.

9 Now let them put away their whoredom, and the carcasses of their kings far from me, and I will dwell in the midst of them forever.

The known existence of an ancient cave that is believed to predate the Dome of the rock.(3) may be clearly seen from infrared imaging of the Temple's ancient foundation. Some archaeologists believe that this cave may even have been used as an ancient burial site.(3) (Lev.26 vs. 30) The existence of a burial site at the confirmed location of God's Holy Temple represents a blatant violation of religious law suggesting that the Temple itself had been defiled *precisely as scripture had foretold.

The consequence based on the discovery of this ancient burial chamber was that Shebna the scribe was eventually relieved of his duties as treasurer, to whom Eliakim was duly appointed. Despite the wealth and honor associated with the office of treasurer that would normally apply, the existing description of this official undertaking is incurred as more of a burden to bear. In the opening verses of Isaiah's account of these happenings, a passage of scripture aptly entitled "the burden of the valley of vision," the reference to the key of the house of David is subtly used to imply the treasury of a supernatural God-given revelation. Although this revelation is made clear to Eliakim, scripture suggests that the burden of the knowledge surrounding the existence of this ancient oppression would not be cut off till the arrival of the Lord's coming Christ.

Isaiah 22 vs. 20

And it shall come to pass in that day, that I will call my servant Eliakim the son of Hilkiah,

21 And I will clothe him with thy robe, and strengthen him with thy girdle, and I will commit thy government into his hands: and he shall be a father to the inhabitants of Jerusalem, and to the house of Judah.

22 And the key of the house of David will I lay upon his shoulders: so he shall open, and none shall shut; and he shall shut, and none shall open.

23 And I will fasten him as a nail in a sure place; and he shall be for a glorious throne to his father's house.

24 And they shall hang upon him all the glory of his father's house, the offspring and the issue, all vessels of cups even to all the vessels of flagons.

25 In that day, saith the Lord of hosts, shall the nail that is fastened in the

sure place be removed, and be cut down, and fall: and the burden that was upon it shall be cut off; for the Lord hath spoken it.

The key of David laid upon his shoulders suggests the succession of a sacred trust that was to be handed down from one generation to the next to be carried among the remnant of those who were deemed faithful and true to God's high calling. The power and authority to open while none shall shut and to shut while none shall open, is God's certified promise that the light of this truth would not be put out. This promise also contains the advancement of a divine trust regarding the truth of this revelation and the promise that the personal expression of this license would not be violated.

Ezra the High Priest

At the turn of the fourth century B.C. (458 B.C.) at the beginning of the postexilic era upon Israel's return out of Babylonian captivity, a similar eyewitness account is captured in time, as if by chance, that would suggest that something indeed existed within the ancient ruins of the original Temple. Although the details surrounding this sighting are never directly explained, the tumultuous outcry that was sparked as the result of examining these ruins and the strangely divided reaction to this sighting in and around the Temple grounds suggests that the rift of these two ancient subcultures indeed existed. The lack of any formal explanation to this occurrence could imply that the wounds of this division were still fresh, and that the cause of this mixed reaction was rooted in some ancient taboo that defied expression. If, on the other hand, this sighting was clearly based on the evidence of some satanic influence present on the Temple grounds, the ancient wisdom associated with the significance of such a finding may not have appealed to all of the eyewitnesses present.

The following is scripture's historical record of this eyewitness account and the untoward public response that would follow.

Ezra 3 vs. 10

And when the builders laid the foundation of the temple of the Lord, they set the priests in their apparel with trumpets, and the Levites the sons of Asaph with cymbals, to praise the Lord, after the ordinance of David, king of Israel.

12 But many of the priests and Levites and chiefs of the fathers, who were ancient men, that had seen the first house, when the foundation

of this house was laid before their eyes, wept with a loud voice; and many shouted aloud for joy:

13 So that the people could not discern the noise of the shout of joy from the noise of the weeping of the people: for the people shouted with a loud shout, and the noise was heard afar off.

The fact that this audience included ancient men who had seen the first Temple, lends support to the notion that some source of controversy was precipitated in the shadow of this historic moment in time. Ezra, the undisputed author of this book of the Bible, clearly had his reasons for including this account among the annals of Bible history. From the standpoint of historic loyalties, a consignment of individuals known as the Nethinims, (Ez 2 vs. 58) (1 Ki 9 vs. 20-21) the bearers of burdens, hewers of wood and stone masons of the Temple reconstruction (Ez 8 vs. 20) trace their genealogies to a group of hired workers who were all but handpicked by Solomon. The irony behind this loyalty is that the people who were originally consigned as stone masons for the building of the original Temple were not Jews at all, but rather strangers in the land of Israel. (2 Chr. 2 vs. 18) (1 Ki 9 vs. 20-21)

Ezra already stated as included among those who had aspired to shoulder the burden of succession regarding the key to the house of David, (Ez. 9 vs. 28) clearly had insight into the fragile peace as it was fostered by a very small remnant of God's faithful followers. (Ez. 9 vs. 8) In later references to the key to the house of David this remnant is clearly distinguished from those would-be servants who are not Jews at all, a distinction that is perhaps better made by the attitude of indifference that might have been held by any hired worker at the Lord's disposal.

The nail or peg, a significant ensign used to indicate one's God given authority over the house of David, is positively identified in the following scripture. Consistent with the analogy of those more willing workers and servants, Ezra truly celebrates the opportunity for renewal in line with the succession to the key of the house of David eternally beholden to the promise of God's mercy.

Ezra 9 vs. 8

And now for a little space grace hath been shewed from the Lord our God, to leave us a remnant to escape, and to give us a nail in his holy place, that our God may lighten our eyes, and give us a little reviving in our bondage.

9 For we were bondman; yet our God hath not forsaken us in our bondage, but hath extended mercy unto us in the sight of the kings of

> Persia, to give us a reviving, to set up the house of our God, and to repair the desolations thereof, and to give us a wall in Judah and in Jerusalem.

Ezra's steadfast hope in God's eternal promise is traceable to another more ancient eye witness account representative of the burden of truth surrounding Solomon's satanic opposition. The final example of this heart-felt burden already examined in the third chapter of this treatise, is that of Asaph, the Levite priest and gate keeper in God's Holy Temple. (1 Chr. 26 vs1) The heavy-hearted devotion described in Asaph's psalms which epitomizes the burden of grief familiar to this special office is next in line to be examined.

Asaph the Temple Gatekeeper

Although the key of the House of David is never specifically mentioned in Asaph's psalms, the burden of discovery regarding Solomon's deception does weigh heavily upon his shoulders. Asaph, an unlikely hero according to current historical standards, emerges as a champion of the causes of truth and justice in what could very well be considered Israel's darkest period in History. Although no formal protest is ever launched against Solomon on Asaph's behalf, Asaph's dilemma, already examined in this treatise, is written about in the Psalms of Asaph. "If I say I will speak thus," as Asaph carefully explains, "I should offend against the generation of thy children." (Ps 73 vs. 15) The psalms attributed to Asaph's authorship beginning at psalm 50 followed by a significant break. Asaphs' psalms resume after what is quoted as being David's final psalm (Ps 72 vs. 20) a psalm closely associated with Solomon's inauguration. This places the bulk of Asaph's body of inspired work towards the beginning of Solomon's reign.

Courageously, Asaph never does hold his silence. Even though Solomon exercises his resolve by having his own brother put to death (1 Ki. 2 vs25) Asaph continues his protest through the gift of song as the Lord's psalmist. In psalms 50, the earliest known psalm attributed to Asaph, Asaph's historic protest against Solomon's ordered execution of his brother Adonijah is subtlety voiced. Although the 50th psalm is slightly out of sync historically where it is included among the psalms of David, it is considerable that Asaph's 50th psalm, along with his remaining psalms, 73-83, are placed most appropriately towards the beginning of King Solomon's reign. This supports the theory that this particular psalm, as far as its authorship goes, could be attributed to Asaph's remaining psalms 73-83 consistent with the strong tone of judgment against wickedness in high places.

Psalm 50 vs. 16

But unto the wicked God saith, Why hast thou to do to declare my statutes, or that thou shouldest take my covenant in thy mouth?

17 Seeing thou hatest instruction, and castest my words behind thee.

18 When thou sawest a thief consentedst with him, and hast been partaker with adulterers.

19 Thou givest thy mouth to evil, and thy tongue frameth deceit.

20 Thou sittest and speakest against thy brother; thou slanderest thine own mother's son.

21 These things hast thou done, and I kept silence; thou thoughtest that I was altogether such a one as thyself: but I will reprove thee, and set them in order before thine eyes.

For Asaph, his protests and pleading before God may be seen in the psalms ascribed to his additional authorship of Psalms 73 -83. For the avid reader, these psalms take on a sharp tone of criticism against the political and religious leadership having been overrun by Solomon's wayward regime. Nowhere is such a sharp historic contrast regarding Solomon's true character ever implied as in the case of Asaph's psalms. It seems that Asaph was one individual who history may yet identify as being truly outspoken for his time. Musical and lyrical talent was held in high regard as the token proof of a deeper prophetic endowment, which was clearly employed by Asaph in this form of worship. (4)

The following psalm is no less intense than Asaph's opening remarks, yet is far from any figurative interpretation that could possibly be entertained. These portions of scripture, strangely overlooked for their historical implications, seem suggestive of Solomon's maniacal tendencies gone awry. At this point in history Israel did not succumb to any foreign invasion, nor was it given to any obvious civil or religious unrest. The obvious explanation to be entertained is that Solomon was currently exercising his absolute power over religious and political values in a way that met with Asaph's expressed protest.

Psalm 74 vs. 1

O God, why hast thou cast us off forever? Why doth thine anger smoke against the sheep of thy pasture?

2 Remember thy congregation which thou hast purchased of old; the rod of thine inheritance, which thou hast redeemed; this mount Zion, wherein thou hast dwelt.

3 Lift up thy feet unto the perpetual desolations; even all that the enemy hath done wickedly in the sanctuary.
4 Thine enemies roar in the midst of thy congregations; they set up their ensigns for signs.
5 A man was famous according as he had lifted up axes upon thick trees.
6 But now they break down the carved work thereof at once with axes and hammers.
7 They have cast fire into thy sanctuary, they have defiled by casting down the dwelling place of thy name to the ground.
8 They said in their hearts, Let us destroy them together: they have burned up all the synagogues of God in the land.
9 We see not our signs: there is no more any prophet: neither is there among us any that knoweth how long.

Despite Asaph's dramatic wake-up call, his historic plea fails to make an impression and the signs of the times go unheeded. The images of synagogues being deliberately set ablaze at a time that historians normally describe as a time of peace gives rise to the theory that a campaign of religious censorship was being inwardly waged against the nation of Israel. Comparable to other periods of political and religious oppression, this censorship could well have been established to preserve some new self-serving ideology. Even as the ensigns of Solomon's regime were being set up the subtle influence of a new and elaborate political and religious agenda was secretly being employed.

For one final example from a group of psalms that what would otherwise considered required reading in revealing Solomon's true character, (Ps 50,73-83) Asaph's final effort at counseling Solomon falls on deaf ears. The tone of this psalm is clearly consolatory, suggesting that it was aimed at reproving someone in authority, namely Solomon. The righteous judgment of one in authority is the recurring theme. The references to the horn identified in this psalm is typically the Bible symbolism used to identifies a king, or ruler (Zech 1 vs. 18-21) (Rev 17) where Asaph clearly cautions; lift not up your horn on high.

Psalm 75 vs. 3

The earth and the inhabitants thereof are dissolved: I bear up the pillars of it Selah.

4 I said unto the fools, Deal not foolishly: and to the wicked, lift up not the horn:

5 Lift not up your horn on high: speak not with a stiff neck.
6 For promotion cometh neither from the east, nor from the west, nor from the south.
7 But God is the judge: he putteth down one and setteth up another.

In a statement that further describes the cumbersome burden that Asaph continued to bear as a result of Solomon's disobedience, Asaph describes how even the inhabitants of the earth dissolve, to which Asaph courageously adds, "I bare up the pillars of it." At this point the initial shock and dismay of Solomon's willful intentions seems to have subsided as Asaph asserts God's righteous and immutable authority as judge over the whole earth.

A Pillar In the Temple of My God

Despite the prolonged period of oppression for the inhabitants of Israel as a result of Solomon's scheming, it becomes apparent that those individuals who follow after God's supernatural calling are systematically drawn out of this existing oppression, and into the light of God's true kingdom. Those who attain to the weight of shouldering this burden of truth, effectively align themselves with the prophets and sages of old to whom this ancient calling was a burden. In the Lord's address to the seven churches, the truth of the key of the house of David, God's high calling, reemerges, as once again scriptures tendency to transcend the limits of time is clearly heard.

Revelations 3 vs. 7
And to the angel of the church in Philadelphia write; These things saith he that is holy, he that is true, He that hath the key of David, he that openeth, and no man shutteth; and shutteth, and no man openeth;
8 I know thy works; behold, I have set before thee an open door, and no man can shut it; for thou hast a little strength, and hast kept my word, and hast not denied my name.
9 Behold, I will make them of the synagogue of Satan, which say they are Jews, and are not but do lie; behold, I will make them to come and worship before thy feet, and to know that I have love thee.
10 Because thou hast kept the word of my patience, I also will keep thee from the hour of temptation, which shall come upon the earth.
11 Behold, I come quickly: hold that fast which thou hast, that no man take thy crown.

12 Him that overcometh will I make a pillar in the temple of my God, and he shall go no more out: and I will write upon him the name of my God, and the name of the city of my God, which is new Jerusalem, which cometh down out of heaven from my God: and I will write upon him my new name.
13 He that hath an ear, let him hear what the Spirit saith unto the churches.

In sharp contrast to the original burden posed by the revelation of the key of the house of David, the Lord concomitantly showers blessings upon those who vow to make the truth an enduring priority. The procession of truth that follows this revelation, aside from it's candid appeal to God's supernatural seal and the accepted proof of God's choosing, God's ability to identify his servants by this high calling is validated. This ability is denoted when the new name of God and the new name of God's city is written on the forehead of the bearer. This revelation is concurrent with the notion that true evil does indeed exist, and is uncovered by the individual's earnest desire to bear with the scruples of the weak. (Eph. 4 vs. 2) God empathetically recognizes this weakness, and promises that the same Satanic forces that at one time opposed this effort will at last be kept at bay.

In a classic depiction of this existing authority, the prophet Zechariah receives an open vision of Joshua of the High Priest standing before the angel of the Lord, and Satan standing present to resist him. As it happens the Lord eventually corrects Joshua, assuring that his way will not be blocked forever, but that those who keep the Lord's charge will also judge the Lord's house. In this case the spirit of the seven churches is clearly represented by the seven eyes engraved in stone and the righteous branch is the Lord's Christ who brings salvation to the world. In this incredible statement God promises how the iniquity of the world's ancient imbalances will finally be settled.

Zechariah 3 vs. 1

AND he showed me Joshua the high priest standing before the angel of the Lord, and Satan standing at his right hand to resist him.
6 And the angel of the Lord protested unto Joshua, saying,
7 Thus saith the Lord of hosts; If thou wilt walk in my ways, and if thou wilt keep my charge, then thou shalt also keep my charge, then thou shalt also keep my courts, and walk among these that stand by.
8 Hear now, O Joshua the high priest, thou, and thy fellows that sit before thee: for they are men wondered at: for, behold, I will bring forth my servant the branch.

9 For behold the stone that I have laid before Joshua; upon one stone shall be seven eyes: behold, I will engrave the graving thereof, saith the Lord of hosts, and I will remove the iniquity of the land in one day.

Satan's mortality and, more importantly, his existence as a human being is implied in these passages whereby the Lord says, "thy fellows that sit before thee are men wondered at." This suggests that though God's people may be temporarily opposed, they have as much right, and an equal anointing and access as Satan, regarding the privileges that are secretly kept by God. The apparent truth of how the abuses of Satan originated, as the result of man's infidelities and unfaithfulness to God is undeniable when all scripture based evidence is examined. God's word duly notes how the world will wonder after "those who's names were not written in the Lamb's book of life" (Rev 17 vs. 8) and how Lucifer, after the fall, will be wondered at when men ask, "is this the man that made the earth to tremble?" (Is 14 vs. 16) The book of Ezekiel states how Satan will be put to ashes and brought before kings. (Ez. 28 vs. 17,18)

The Promise of Understanding

In the discovery of any revelation of scripture, it is important to realize that anything that the Lord chooses to reveal is ordered in his original plan of salvation. Regarding the hour of temptation that shall come upon the whole earth, it is clearly promised in scripture how those who hold close to the revelation of the key of the house of David will be saved from the hour of trouble that will come upon the earth. (Rev 3 vs. 10) This recurrent theme, magnanimously supported in scripture, reveals a subtle urgency to God's plan.

Ezekiel the prophet reiterates this sense of urgency stating how if Noah, Daniel and Job were faced with this calamity they would still only be able to save themselves. This particular prophecy describes how an ancient remnant shall emerge from out of the annals of history who's works will be made plainly visible, and how by the enlightenment of this understanding, God's faithful followers will be comforted regarding the nature of God's final judgment.

Ezekiel 14 vs. 20

Though Noah, Daniel, and Job, were in it, as I live saith the Lord God, they shall deliver neither son nor daughter; they shall but deliver their own souls by their righteousness.

21 For thus saith the Lord God; How much more when I send my four sore judgments upon Jerusalem, the sword, and the famine, and the noisome beast, and the pestilence, to cut off from it, man and beast?
22 Yet, behold, therein shall be left a remnant that shall be brought forth, both sons and daughters: behold, they shall come forth unto you, and ye shall see their way and their doings: and ye shall be comforted concerning the evil that I have brought upon Jerusalem, even concerning all that I have brought upon it.
23 And they shall comfort you, when ye see their ways and their doings: and ye shall know that I have not done without cause all that I have done in it, saith the Lord God.

The remnant in question, mentioned above, could be best represented by the existence of those who are presently engaged in Solomon's ancient deceit. The known civilized world seems to be fixated on Solomon as a model of worldly success and power. A vast majority of the world's citizens could be engaged in the stronghold of these forces, and remain inconspicuous, making the identification of those belonging to such a group difficult if not impossible. The prospect of the existence of an ancient elite belonging to the structure of this power base has a high probability in light of the burden of evidence presented thus far.

The notion that God's people will enter blindly into the supernatural events surrounding the Lord's appointed time of judgment and emerge unscathed is highly unlikely. In fact, scripture clearly states that only those who endure to the very end will be saved. (Matt 10 vs. 22) Furthermore, those who eventually attain to this salvation will do so on account of the divine light of God's wisdom. (Dan 12 vs. 9) Even the truth behind the cosmological forces that have shaped mankind's destiny from the foundations of the world could realistically emerge as common knowledge among many of the earth's inhabitants. The book of Daniel promises that "those who are wise shall shine like the brightness of the firmament and those who turn many to righteousness like the stars forever and ever." (Dan 12 vs. 3)

In the midst of the current explosion of knowledge and information that has taken the world by storm, the notion that God is somehow making a distinction between those who are called according to his purpose and those who are not seems entirely possible. Historically Noah and his family were well versed in the knowledge of the floodwaters that were set to overtake the land. (Gen 6 vs. 15) Moses was well instructed by the Lord regarding the Lord's

Passover when the Lord clearly distinguished between Israel's firstborn and the firstborn of Egypt. (Ex 11 vs. 7) In the same way scripture clearly implies that this same pattern of disclosure will be followed at the time of the Lord's judgment.

In the following scripture a distinction is clearly made between those who know God and respect his covenant, and those who do wickedly. For those who disregard the Lord's covenant, the Lord promises to corrupt with flattery, whereas those who know their God will carry out great exploits. (Dan 11 vs. 32) In the same way Jesus flatly warns his disciples, "woe unto you, when all men speak well of you! For so did their fathers to the false prophets." (Lu 6 vs. 26) At the same time, the promise of understanding is clearly extended to those who strive after the Lord's wisdom.

DANIEL 12 vs. 8

And I heard but I understood not: then said I, O my Lord, what shall be the end of these things?

9 And he said, Go thy way Daniel: for the words are closed up and sealed till the time of the end.

10 Many shall be purified, and made white, and tried; but the wicked shall do wickedly: and none of the wicked shall understand; but the wise shall understand.

The Bible speaks of a time of great delusion when only those who have developed an inherent love for the truth will be saved. When this process of delusion is unfurled, the voice of reason for God's people will be rooted in this love. For the rest of the inhabitants of the earth, apathy and indifference will clearly rule the day as these individuals remain unmoved by the lie that settles over them. The most profound implications exist in the notion that when this ancient evil is to be revealed then the end of the age is said to be very near. At this point in history scripture states how those who lettest must let until they be taken out of the way," which could well refer to the Lord's promise to save those who have understanding, from the hour of trouble which is poised to be unleashed upon the earth. (Rev 10 vs. 3)

2 Thessalonians 2 vs. 1

Now we beseech you, brethren, by the coming of our Lord Jesus Christ, and by our gathering together unto him,

2 That ye be not soon shaken in mind, or be troubled, neither by spirit, nor by word, nor by letter as from us, as that the day of Christ is at hand.

3 Let no man deceive you by any means: for that day shall not come,

except there come a falling away first, and that man of sin be revealed, the son of perdition:

4 Who opposeth and exalteth himself above all that is called God, or that is worshipped; so that he as God sitteth in the temple of God, shewing himself that he is God.

5 Remember ye not, that, when I was yet with you, I told you these things?

6 And now ye know what withholdeth that he might be revealed in his time.

7 For the mystery of iniquity doth already work: only he who now letteth will let, until he be taken out of the way.

8 And then shall that wicked be revealed, whom the Lord shall consume with the spirit of his mouth, and shall destroy with the brightness of his coming:

9 Even him, whose coming is after the working of Satan with all power and signs and lying wonders,

10 And with all deceivableness of unrighteousness in them that perish: because they received not the love of the truth, that they might be saved.

11 And for this cause God shall send them strong delusion, that they should believe a lie:

12 That they all might be damned who believed not the truth, but had pleasure in unrighteousness

This New Testament scripture is consistent with the promise of understanding mentioned previously, whereby it is stated that the mystery of iniquity already at work will be revealed. The notion that God himself allowed this sense of delusion so that a distinction could be made between his true and faithful followers shows how the methodology behind God's plan goes far beyond human reasoning. While it seems apparent that God's faithful witnesses are being drawn out into the light of this divine truth, the possible existence of a plan of contingency identifiable in ancient scripture merits further investigation. When the historical events surrounding Solomon's manipulations are first implied, incredibly, the foundations of the Lord's true intentions are already set in motion in scripture.

God's Original Plan

Evidence in Holy Scripture would suggest that the Lord was willing and able to turn the earth into a utopia of unparalleled beauty and abundance in

Solomon's time had he chosen to be obedient. (2 Chr. 7 vs. 14) Ironically Solomon's disobedience in keeping with God's original plan, is what facilitates the preservation of these intentions. Scripture speaks of this contingency in describing how the world's oceans were to be healed so that this abundance of life could be brought about for the inhabitants of the earth. (Ez 47 vs. 9) Under careful scrutiny God's word reveals how the good that Solomon rejected in his lifetime is clearly ready to unfold.

In the chapter that follows, God's original plan for mankind will be thoroughly examined, along with what scripture seems to imply, is an alternate location for the construction of a new and glorious Temple that will be built, based on the Lord's specifications. The assurance of God's ability to withstand Satan's deceit is clearly dealt with in these passages of scripture, followed by further geographical and archeological evidence in substantiating these claims. In addition, the existence of an ancient spring of a supernatural quality and origin will be examined for it's miraculous healing properties.

IX
The Temple of God

Despite the defilement* of the former Temple and the moral corruption of both the political and religious authorities of the day, the existence of a divine alternative is at work well before the onslaught of Solomon's civil disobedience is ever deployed. Incredibly, Holy Scripture clearly shows how Solomon's deviant behavior was out-stepped by God's eternal plan from the very beginning. Biblical and geographical evidence supports the existence of a new, yet original location, chosen for the eventual construction of a new Holy Temple, which, as a result of Solomon's waywardness, was more in keeping with God's original plan.

Zion traditionally heralded as the mountain of God's holiness (Psalm 48 vs. 1) abounds as an enduring symbol of Israel's national glory. The historic connotation to this symbolism, although ancient, has not been devalued in Christian theology for its sense of generativity towards the gentile nations. In Holy scripture, Zion is immortalized as an eternal beacon set for the gathering in of all nations and tongues where the revelation of God's eternal word will be enjoyed. (Is. 2 vs. 3) Known also as the throne of God's righteous judgment, where the citizens of the world shall seek God's correction, the righteousness of the saints follows a similar revelation in the declaration of God's promise. (Psalm 50 vs. 2-6) In more modern theological circles this analogy has come to represent Christ himself, a reasonable assumption based on the revelation of Christ's son-ship; the designated key that unlocks this knowledge. The true blessing of Christ, however, is how the miraculous properties of God's living word points to further revelation which includes the blueprint for a new and glorious Temple. At the height of the establishment of this new Temple, the mystery of the Lord's inexhaustible resources is promised to be revealed as the unique geological formations indigenous to this location will give rise to a scientific breakthrough that will astonish and astound the world's scientific community.

The Jebusite City

The historical account of how the original site for Solomon's Temple was chosen leaves some room for speculation. One will recall how David was persuaded or moved by Satan to perform a census of the nation of Israel and how Joab, David's trusted advisor, considered this an abominable request, since it was traditionally understood that God would multiply the nation of Israel to be "as the stars of heaven" (Genesis 15 vs. 4) and "as the dust of the earth." (Genesis 13 vs. 16) As a result of this census God's displeasure is voiced, and the nation of Israel is given a choice of three punishments; famine, plague, or sword. David chooses the Lord's pestilence stating, "Let me fall into the hands of the Lord for his mercy is very great." (1 Chr. 21 vs. 13) After the death of seventy thousand of his men the Lord requested that David build an alter on the threshing floor of Araunah the Jebusite. The Angel of the Lord then appeared on the threshing floor and the Lord finally relented. (1 Chr. 21 vs1 6, 25, 26) David eventually purchased this property for six hundred sheckles of gold, for what would become the future sight of the Temple of God. When one carefully considers the events leading up to the choosing of the site for the Lord's Holy Temple, several points need to be considered. Firstly, nowhere in scripture does God specifically command that a Temple should be built for his name's sake. The construction of this Temple is clearly based on a sense of mutual good will between the Lord and David, his servant. David is inspired to build the Temple as a result of God's mercy in saving Israel from further wrath. What the Lord does stipulate is that David should not build a house unto the name of the Lord because of the blood that was shed as a result of David's many military campaigns. In observance of the laws of defilement, Solomon was specifically chosen for the task of building the Lord's Temple. (1 Chr. 22 vs. 9) The traditional laws of defilement, which played an integral role in establishing the early Temple, would also play a crucial role in the need to eventually relocate the Temple as the result of Solomon's abuses. The laws of defilement* clearly state that once the land has been defiled by blood shed then no atonement can be made for it except by the blood of him who shed it. (Num 35 vs. 33) Sadly, the probability that Solomon's Temple was defiled in this way is very high, considering the early Temple's long history of impropriety.

The site originally identified as "Mount Zion" was traditionally affiliated with the mountain stronghold that protected the Jebusite city; the same city that David's army was alleged to have overthrown. (2 Sam 5 vs. 6-10) Shortly after the throngs of this historic victory, David purchases the threshing floor of Araunah the Jebusite, which the Bible mentions is the original historical landmark for the Lord's Temple. The strangers of the land, the likely descendants of the Jebusite nation who were counted among the nations that Israel failed to drive out, (Jud 1 vs. 21) were probably hired by David as stone masons to engage in the process of beginning this construction. It was David who ultimately chose this site as the alter of burnt offering for Israel. (1 Chr. 22 vs. 1) From the standpoint of Holy Scripture, this Jebusite city, later known as "mount Zion," holds a definite connection with the future glory of the Lord's restored Temple.

In the twentieth year of Babylonian captivity the Lord raises up a prophet whose principle mission is to share his divinely inspired vision of the Temple's future glory with the nation of Israel. At the beginning of the fortieth chapter of the book that bears his name, in visions, the hand of the Lord is said to bring Ezekiel to the land of Israel where he is set upon a very high mountain which was said to be "as the frame of a city on the south." (Ez 40 vs. 2) In what would seem to be a clear indication of the Lord's intentions, Ezekiel is given the sacred blueprint for another glorious Temple to be erected in a previously undisclosed location, save for the physical description which bears a strong resemblance to the Jebusite city formally known as mount Zion. In keeping with the original geographical designation, scripture consistently names this location as the chosen site of the Lord's Temple to be restored. (Isa 2 vs. 3) (Psalm 48 vs. 1)

Ezekiel 40 vs. 1

IN the five and twentieth year of our captivity, in the beginning of the year, in the tenth day of the month, in the fourteenth year after that, the city was smitten, in the selfsame day the hand of the Lord was upon me, and brought me, thither.

2 In the visions of God brought he me into the land of Israel, and set me

upon a very high mountain, by which was as the frame of a city on the south.

3 And he brought me thither, and behold, there was a man whose appearance was like the appearance of brass, with a line of flax in his hand, and a measuring reed; and he stood in the gate.

4 And the man said unto me, Son of man, behold with thine eyes, and hear with thine ears, and set thine heart upon all that I shall show thee; for to the intent that I might show them unto thee art thou brought hither: declare all that thou seest to the house of Israel.

As a result of repeated scripture references, the general appeal of this particular location, along with the presence of key landmarks specific to Ezekiel's vision that have yet to be described, make mount Zion a reasonable site for Temple reconstruction. Political and religious opposition to rebuilding the Temple in its former location could well have contributed to this regions long history of political tensions and instability. It is also noteworthy that through obedience to God's will, Temple reconstruction in this new location might be interpreted as an act of clemency of unprecedented scale on the part of the Jewish authorities, which Holy scripture states will usher in an era of unparalleled peace. (Is 2 vs. 4) Aside from these incidental considerations, the realization that the site of Israel's former Temple was utterly defiled makes this particular site a viable alternative for Temple reconstruction.

The following scripture captures the general tone of impropriety surrounding the former location of the Temple and goes on to suggest that the house of Israel should measure the pattern of Ezekiel's blueprint. The presence of the man with the measuring reed in hand mentioned above in the presence of this historic site, logically suggests that measurements should be taken of this framed city, namely mount Zion, as a token proof of God's definitive choice for this location. The possibility that the perimeter of mount Zion measured at the site of the former wall of the Jebusite city might render a similar measurement, as those outlined in Ezekiel's vision would be a truly miraculous discovery. (Ez 40 vs. 6) Scripture further suggests how the whole limit of this mountain is to be considered most holy. The overall tone of this portion of scripture lends suspicion to possibility that this sacred site could well have been the original site of the threshing floor of Araunah the Jebusite that would have been placed more appropriately behind the fortified walls of the Jebusite city.

Ezekiel 43 vs. 5

So the spirit took me up, and brought me into the inner court; and behold, the glory of the Lord filled the house.

6 And I heard him speaking unto me out of the house; and the man stood by me.

7 And he said unto me, Son of man, the place of my throne, and the place of the soles of my feet, where I will dwell in the midst of the children of Israel for ever, and my holy name, shall the house of Israel no more defile, neither they, nor their kings, by their whoredom, nor by the carcasses of their kings in their high places.

9 Now let them put away their whoredom, and the carcases of their kings, far from me, and I will dwell in the midst of them forever.

10 Thou son of man, show the house to the house of Israel, that they may be ashamed of their iniquities: and let them measure the pattern.

12 This is the law of the house; Upon the top of the mountain the whole limit thereof round about shall be most holy. Behold, this is the law of the house.

Another issue that needs to be taken into account in considering the plausibility of relocating the Lord's Temple is those scriptures pertaining to the Temple's future glory, and the mentioning of key landmarks found in and about the proposed site. Unlike the European landscape, the ancient landmarks of any prehistoric significance are scarce. With the foundations of many generations being rebuilt in this ancient location the accumulation of rubble has made Jerusalem's underlying bedrock very porous. The ancient clues pointing to the existence of these landmarks written about in Holy Scripture are said to be below Jerusalem in its ancient bedrock.

An Ancient Landmark

Early on in history, the local inhabitants frequently ascribed mystical and supernatural qualities to the ancient waterways of Mesopotamia. In a region known for it's vast deserts and a hot, often inhospitable climate, these ancient waterways and their ability to transform the landscape into a thriving agricultural center, gained a mythological reputation for their ability to sustain life. From the standpoint of the Judeo-Christian tradition and the eternal nature of God's word, at least one of these ancient waterways and its miraculous properties has endured in Jewish and Christian belief systems all the way to the present day.

Of the four heads of the waterways identified in the book of Genesis recognized for keeping the Garden of Eden well irrigated, the Euphrates River is the only waterway that is presently identified with any certainty. From a linguistic standpoint, there is very little difference in the Babylonian tongue between river and irrigation ditch, which leads some scholars to believe that the Gihon was in fact a major irrigation ditch that can no longer be located.(1) Even more peculiar to this particular waterway is the survival of the name Gihon as an ancient spring of water that was evidently held as very sacred by the inhabitants of Jerusalem.(2) Among Jerusalem's exiting waterways both Old Testament and New Testament scripture contain eyewitness accounts that substantiate the existence of naturally occurring springs in and around Jerusalem.

One historical account has Solomon drinking from the spring of Gihon on the day of his coronation.(3) (1 Ki 1 vs. 38) If this ancient spring did in fact have some miraculous quality to it, it would have been Solomon's prerogative to keep this waterway under his control. Shortly after being invigorated by the source of this miraculous spring, the Lord speaks to Solomon, first reminding him of his sacred duty as king, then by way of a conditional promise the Lord reveals his desire to heal the land for the very first time in scripture. Thus the supernatural promise extended to Solomon is implied to have been far greater if Solomon would have stayed true to the Lord's conditions of kingly rule.

The following scripture is an account of this initial promise, at the point in which the Lord's divine intentions are first revealed.

2 Chronicles 7 vs.12

And the Lord appeared to Solomon by night, and said unto him, I have heard thy prayer, and have chosen this place to myself for an house of sacrifice.

13 If I shut up heaven that there be no rain, or if I command the locusts to devour the land, or if I send pestilence among my people;

14 If my people which are called by my name, shall humble themselves, and pray, and seek my face, and turn from their wicked ways; then will I hear from heaven, and will forgive their sin, and will heal their land.

19 But if ye turn away, and forsake my statutes and my commandments, which I have set before you, and shall go and serve other Gods and worship them;

20 Then will I pluck them up by the roots out of my land which I have given them, and this house, which I have sanctified for my name, will

I cast out of my sight, and will make it a proverb and a byword among the nations.

Historically it is known that Solomon failed to heed the words of this prophecy, but rather, chose to disobey God in what would appear to be outright rebellion. The existence of a fountain sealed mentioned in Solomon's "Song of songs" (Cant 4 vs. 12) adds to the possibility that Solomon was going about his own selfish objective in creating a personal utopia for himself and his many wives. Though the opulence and wealth of Solomon's personal status can be scarcely imagined, the possibility that Solomon was hording this resource as his own, lends a very morbid twist to Solomon's personal existence. A growing dependency on this resource cut off from the lives of Israel's ordinary citizens further reinforces the existence of a Satanic elite whose membership was extended to the privileged few. The pathetic tone of such an existence seems to mimic all the gothic details of Bramstoker's mythic account of the nosfuratu.

Elsewhere in scripture the sense of insult the Lord must have felt at this refusal is clearly expressed. The waters of shiloah, which means small stream in the ancient Hebrew tongue,(4) is the reference used when the Lord's disapproval is officially announced. The possibility remains that as the result of selfishness and greed the miracle that the Lord intended is sadly opposed. As with many other examples of the Lord's responses, the expression of this frustration does not follow man's linear view, rather the response is made in the Lord's chosen time.

The following is an account of the Lord's displeasure being voiced in the prophetic utterances spoken through the prophet Isaiah.

Isaiah 8 vs. 6

For as much as this people refuseth the waters of Shiloah that go softly, and rejoice in Rezin and Remaliah's son;

7 Now therefore, behold, the Lord bringeth up upon them the waters of the river, strong and many, even the king of Assyria, and all his glory: and he shall come up over all his channels, and go over his banks:

8 And he shall pass through Judah; he shall overflow and go over, he shall reach even to the neck: and the stretching out of his wings shall fill the breadth of thy land O Immanuel.

The fact that Israel rejoiced in Rezin and Remaliah's son is a reference to the successive opposition chronicled in the sixth chapter of this treatise when an unauthorized peace is struck between Israel and Syria. The analogy of floodwaters of a different sort is then implied, as the Assyrian army is consequently arrayed against Israel.

The Spring of Gihon

According to Holy Scripture, Zion's future glory promises to be unrivalled for it's international appeal in reaching out to the very basic and fundamental spiritual needs of the world's inhabitants. Scripture describes an ingathering set to occur on a global scale and accompanied by a newfound zeal whereby the Lord's faithful servants will be supernaturally compelled to respond to this calling. In the context of this major influx, due in part to the divine trust to which this new Temple will be established, Holy scripture invites the Lord's faithful servants to expect the miraculous, as the benefit of the Lord's resources are supernaturally tapped.

The geographical location of the spring of Gihon identified in part for it's supernatural reputation, coincides with the new location of the Lord's holy Temple to be reconstructed at the top of mount Zion, the site that was once the Jebusite city. This connection is clearly established in the dramatic climax of Ezekiel's wondrous vision. In one of the final chapters of the book of Ezekiel the proximal location of the Lord's new Temple with the presence of this ancient spring, culminates in grand detail as the miraculous potential of God's resources is choreographed.

Ezekiel 47 vs. 1

AFTERWARD he brought me again unto the door of the house, and behold, waters issued out from under the threshold of the house eastward: for the forefront of the house eastward: for the forefront of the house stood toward the east, and the waters came down from under from the right side of the house, at the south side of the alter.

2 Then brought he me out of the way of the gate northward, and led me about the way without unto the utter gate by the way that looketh eastward; and, behold, there ran out waters on the right side.

5 Afterward he measured a thousand; and it was a river that I could not pass over; for the waters were risen, waters to swim in, a river that could not be passed over.

7 Now when I had returned, behold, at the bank of the river were very many trees on the one side and on the other.

The exquisite detail of Ezekiel's vision is consistent with God's plan to regenerate the earth by means of his own unseen resources. The geographical location of the spring of Gihon as well as other ancient waterways including Hezekiah's tunnel and the Siloam pool in and about the ancient foundations of mount Zion the original site of the Jebusite city, lends credence to the suggestion that Ezekiel's vision pertains to Zion's future glory; a new and glorious Temple. The map provided, an accurate depiction of Old Testament Jerusalem, clearly places the Gihon spring near the eastern side of mount Zion with Hezekiah's tunnel flowing to the southern Siloam and lower pools.(5) (Fig. b1)

Images of lush vegetation embanked beside the river, the first indication of this water's miraculous healing properties, is consistent with many other inspired prophecies and visions dispersed throughout God's inspired word. As Ezekiel's vision reaches it's ultimate climax, this water's supernatural transforming ability is emphatically implied as the leaves of the trees yield their life-giving medicine. Scriptures many references to the healing virtue of these resources could be seen as stemming back to the Lord's initial promise to Israel to heal the land. (2 Chr 7 vs. 12) The cause and effect relationship presented on behalf of this ancient spring, along with the implied political nuances, places humanities freedom of choice as a major cosmological force with the capability of inviting the Lord's supernatural remedy for the ills of mankind.

Ezekiel 47 vs. 10
And it shall come to pass, that the fishes shall stand upon it from Engedi even unto Eneglaim; they shall be a place to spread forth nets; their fish shall be according to their kinds, as the fish of the great sea, exceeding many.
11 But the miry places thereof and the marishes thereof shall not be healed; they shall be given to salt.
12 And by the river upon the bank thereof, on this side and on that side, shall grow all trees for meat, whose leaf shall not fade, neither shall the fruit thereof be consumed: it shall bring forth new fruit according to his months, because their waters they issued out of the sanctuary: and the fruit thereof shall be for meat, and the leaf thereof for medicine.

Through the many aspects of Ezekiel's incredible vision, the Lord demonstrates his ability to transform, both by the supernatural resources at his disposal, as well as by way of spiritual salvation in the ministration of a new Holy Temple. Concurrent with Ezekiel's vision are the inspired words of many other Old Testament prophets proving that the creation of this garden utopia was not exclusive to Ezekiel's particular vision, but rather a universal theme among God's intended purposes. In the book of Joel the spiritual and geographical survey situating the new Temple in this location, and the presence of this ancient spring set to bring forth rivers of living water becomes the token proof that the Lord has chosen this location for his dwelling place.

Joel 3 vs. 16
The Lord also shall roar out of Zion, and utter his voice from Jerusalem; and the heavens and the earth shall shake; but the Lord will be the hope of his people, and the strength of the children of Israel.
17 So shall ye know that I am the Lord your God dwelling in Zion, my Holy mountain: then shall Jerusalem be holy, and there shall no strangers pass through her any more.
18 And it shall come to pass in that day, that the mountains shall drop down with new wine, and the hills shall flow with milk, and all the rivers of Judah shall flow with waters, and a fountain shall come forth of the house of the Lord and shall water the valley of Shittim.

For many theologians the fine balance between the spiritual and figurative implications of these passages interfaces with the more tangible physical realities of these prophetic utterances. The mystical connotation to these visions gives the sense that some analogy or ancient allegory may be derived from these scriptures, yet both Old Testament and New Testament scripture seems to consistently prove that certain fountains and pools in and around Jerusalem did in fact contain supernatural healing properties. Likewise, the interest in the Lord's ability to turn the desert landscape into a garden paradise is a commonly recurring theme in scripture. The following passage, far from any figurative interpretation, is suggestive of the Lord's tender care in looking after the poor of the land by way of the Lord's supernatural provision.

Isaiah 41 vs. 17
When the poor and the needy seek water, and there is none, and the tongue faileth for thirst, I the Lord will hear them, I the Lord will not forsake them.
18 I will open rivers in high places, and fountains in the midst of the valleys: I will make the wilderness a pool of water, and the dry land springs of water.
19 I will plant in the wilderness the cedar, the shitah tree, and the myrtle, and the oil tree; I will set in the desert the fir tree, and the pine, and the box tree together:

20 That they may see, and know, and consider, and understand together, that the hand of the Lord hath done this, and the Holy one of Israel hath created it.

The Old Testament account of the Lord's official plan for temple reconstruction, coupled with visual and prophetic accounts of a sacred stream to be flowing out of this new Temple, raises the question of how these recurring themes present themselves in New Testament theology. A closer examination of scripture shows how the balance of figurative and literal interpretations of New and Old Testament scripture as well as the various eyewitness accounts, clearly supports the existence of this miraculous spring water in and about Jerusalem.

New Testament Accounts

The Gospel of John, central to all of the themes previously explored in this treatise, continues to play a central role in supporting the prophetic utterances mentioned above. Although the substance of the Old Testament scriptures presented thus far are far from being resolved, according to the eyewitness accounts documented in this gospel, a window of possibility is clearly left open. On at least one occasion scripture proves beyond a shadow of a doubt, that the spring waters in question were believed to contain miraculous healing properties. (John 5) Similar possibilities seem to reverberate in the images belonging to John's incredible vision from the book of Revelations, (Rev 22) which fully supports the occurrences outlined in Ezekiel's miraculous vision.

In John's account of some of Jesus' earliest preaching, Jesus confides that he knows of the whereabouts of the living water that for the drinking shall be as "a well of water springing up into everlasting life." (John 4 vs. 10) With the revelation of Jesus Christ as the official capstone to this revelation, this figurative analogy remains conducive to the line of reasoning presented in this treatise thus far. The figurative accounts of Christ's rivers of living water are equally compelling for their spiritual implications. Although these descriptions are clearly indicative of the Holy Spirit and anointing of Christ, such a figurative reference is also in keeping with the notion that God's supernatural resources do in fact exist.

The next chapter of John's gospel describes the existence of an ancient pool called Bethesda that was surrounded by the presence of a picturesque colonnade having five porches. The location suggested by historians places the existence of this ancient pool near the Sheep gate at the entrance to the former Temple.(6) According to scripture's description of the characteristics unique to this holy site, the claim that ancient spring waters of a miraculous nature existed here is obviously implied.

John 5 vs. 1

AFTER this there was a feast of the Jews; and Jesus went up to Jerusalem.

2 Now there is at Jerusalem by the sheep market a pool, which is called in the Hebrew tongue Bethesda, having five porches.

3 In these lay a great multitude of impotent folk, of blind, halt, withered, waiting for the moving of the water.

4 For an angel went down at a certain season into the pool, and troubled the water; whosoever then first after the troubling of the water stepped in was made whole of whatsoever disease he had.

Another miraculous occurrence that suggests a possible connection between Jerusalem's natural spring water and Christ's supernatural healing power is entailed in the healing of the blind man. Jesus explains to his disciples how this man was not blind as result of any sin, but rather to the intended purpose that the works of God should be made manifest in him. After taking the initial steps in order to heal this man who was said to be blind from birth, Jesus sends him to wash in the pool of Siloam located at the southern tip of what is formally known as mount Zion, otherwise identified as the former site of the Jebusite city. Even as Jesus is careful to acknowledge that it was purposed for the blind man to be healed "so that the works of God could be made manifest in him," it seems evident that John's gospel mentions this particular miracle to draw some attention to this Holy site. One would argue that by the accounts given from the other gospels, Jesus clearly had the spiritual authority to heal this man in the manner of his own choosing. Howbeit, as Jesus clearly states, " I must work the works of him that sent me." This statement in itself implies that the instruction Jesus gave came about according to the will of his heavenly Father, and that some divine purpose was served by drawing attention to this location.

The following is provided as a full account of this miracle according to the gospel of John.

John 9 vs. 1

AND as Jesus passed by, he saw a man, which was blind from his birth.

2 And his disciples asked him, saying, Master, who did sin, this man, or his parents, that he was born blind?

3 Jesus answered, neither hath this man sinned, nor his parents: but that the works of God should be made manifest in him.
4 I must work the works of him that sent me, while it is day; the night cometh, when no man can work.
5 As long as I am in the world, I am the light of the world.
6 When he had thus spoken, he spat on the ground, and made clay of the spittle, and he anointed the eyes of the blind man with the clay.
7 And said unto him, Go wash in the pool of Siloam, (which is by interpretation, Sent) He went his way therefore, and washed, and came seeing.

The remarkable detail in which Old Testament scripture is fulfilled in the New Testament leaves little doubt that Christ's mission and teachings were rooted in this traditional belief. Even to the very intimate details passed along by the ancient prophets, Christ's teachings and doctrines seem to remain true. In Jesus' lengthy address concerning the time of the end, no favorable report is given surrounding the plight of Solomon's Temple and it's current location. With his disciples marveling over the brilliant architecture and the grand scheme of the former Temple, Jesus is careful to point out how "there shall not be left here one stone upon another that will not be thrown down." Likewise, the apocalyptic climate surrounding the establishment of the new Temple seems to be a dominant characteristic surrounding similar portions of scripture.

Apocalyptic Considerations

God's awesome power and majesty is known primarily by his creative powers in forming the universe in all its intricacy and mystery. The foundational doctrinal footing of this treatise is rooted in the principles of Christ's salvation and sanctification, may also be seen in the principle nature of all of creation. The net properties and aspects of creation, each committed to their appointed time are given over to the same transforming power exhibited in Christ's resurrection. The possibility that a similar rebirth will take place for our earthly existence is, therefore, more than likely. The Apocalyptic overtones prevalent in scripture represent a certain coming of age for the earth and it's inhabitants when a miraculous change is set to recreate the earth according to this new glorified nature. In and about this time the ravages of war are said to take place as all nations are gathered against

Jerusalem in what is said to be final Armageddon. (Zec 14 vs. 1) Christ's return is then eminent, as he is expected to touch down on the Mount of Olives with the return of the saints. The mount olives itself will be split in two at the shear power and majesty of Christ's return. (Zech 14 vs. 4) The moon and the sun are consistently said to be darkened. (Joel 2 vs. 10) (Matt 24 vs. 29) In the midst of this calamity a transformation is set to occur that seems to outdo every earthly consideration known to man with the formation of a new heavens and a new earth. (Is 65 vs17)

Despite this awesome display of the Lord's creative power, the subject of the former offenses surrounding the glory of the former Temple are still remembered. As part of this apocalyptic climate the Lord promises to choose their delusions and to bring their fears upon them. This statement is concurrent with the aspects of God's judgment already mentioned in this treatise whereby the Lord promises to send them strong delusion that they should believe a lie for all those who had pleasure in unrighteousness. (2 Thes 2 vs. 11,12) In the final chapter of the prophet Isaiah, a chapter that deals primarily with Zion's future hope, the pride associated with the Temple's original construction is finally put in its proper perspective.

Isaiah 66 vs. 1

THUS saith the Lord, The heaven is my throne, and the earth is my footstool: where is the house that ye build unto me? And where is the place of my rest?

2 For all those things hath mine hands made, and all those things have been saith the Lord: but to this man will I look, even to him that is poor and of a contrite spirit, and trembleth at my word.

3 He that killeth an ox is as if he slew a man; he that sacrificeth a lamb, as if he cut off a dog's neck; he that offereth an oblation, as if he offered swine's blood; he that burneth incense, as if he blessed an idol. Yea, they have chosen their own ways, and their soul delighteth in their abominations.

4 I also will choose their delusions, and will bring their fears upon them; because when I called, none did answer; when I spake they did not hear; but they did evil before mine eyes, and chose that in which I delighted not.

The true Throne of Lord's majesty is described in elaborate detail in the final chapter of the final book of the Holy Bible. As with many principle images from the book of Revelations the very ancient of ways remarkably converges with the Lord's holy power for future regeneration. This final appeal as a result of John's revealing vision, while supporting the existence of a train of theology spanning the succession of many generations, also encourages the possibility that John himself was blessed with some inclination to its revolutionary understanding.

In the context of this convergence a similar image emerges; that of the Lord's throne high and lifted up, and a crystal sea flowing out like a river with its supernatural transforming power regenerated in the presence of the great tree of life. Despite the many levels of figurative and literal interpretations speculated in theological thought passed down through the ages, the consistency to Ezekiel vision regarding the images featured here are undeniable. While the leaves for the healing of the nations seems to answer the Lord's former promise to heal the land reiterated at various points in scripture, the existence of the tree of life on the banks of this crystal stream reveals how the eternal nature of God's word eventually comes full circle. With the great tree of life identified on the banks of this river, the potential for eternal life that was previously offered in the Garden of Eden will clearly be reestablished.

Revelation 22 vs. 1

AND he showed me a pure river of water of life, clear as crystal, proceeding out of the throne of God and the lamb.

2 In the midst of the street of it, and on either side of the river, was there the tree of life, which bare twelve manner of fruits, and yielded her fruit every month; and the leaves of the tree were for the healing of the nations.

3 And there shall be no more curse; but the throne of God and of the Lamb shall be in it; and his servants shall serve him;

4 And they shall see his face; and his name shall be in their foreheads.

5 And there shall be no night there; and they need no candle, neither light of the sun; for the Lord giveth them light; and they shall reign forever and ever.

As the final chapter of the final book of the Bible draws to a close, one cannot help but wonder how the relentless struggle between good and evil will play out on the final stage of world history. John's exile to the island of Patmos, just one example of the intense persecution faced by the early church and a symbol of the church's undying fidelity, is also rooted in a historical tradition that stays true to the various degrees of this epic struggle. In the same way that the satanic forces infiltrated the ancient Jewish belief system, the early Christian church is eventually faced with similar challenges. John's inspired address to the seven churches in the book of Revelation, further proof of this engagement, is a valid glimpse into the fundamental nature of this struggle.

Moral Considerations

Of the many aspects of Bible theology, its moral considerations, although rarely praised by the secular world, could well pose the highest degree of understanding and reasoning our intellectual capacity has to select from. Representative of the bulk of the Lord's covenants, which are enacted by a faith relationship alone, this moral aspect forms a temporal boundary for those who are unable to accept its graces. In the final analysis of those things that pertain to the establishment of the Lord's Temple the existence of such a boundary will henceforth be explored.

The clear spiritual connotation that exists is that, to the shame of those individuals who refuse to comply with the moral and legal requirements of God's law, no admittance will be granted. The nature of this absolution points to one final harrowing look into the outer darkness where there will be weeping and gnashing of teeth. The inner sanctum of the Lord's sanctuary will then be supernaturally sealed against anything profane or unholy.

In the book of Revelations closing statements, a sense of finality ensues, when at the approach Lord's final judgment, the remnant of the Lord's chosen people will take their place inside the sanctified walls of God's holy city, while the souls that deny his graces will be driven out into outer darkness.

Revelations 22 vs. 10

And he saith unto me, Seal not the sayings of the prophecy of this book: for the time is at hand.

11 He that is unjust, let him be unjust still: and he which is filthy, let him be filthy still: and he that is righteous, let him be righteous still: and he that is holy, let him be holy still.

14 Blessed are they that do his commandments, that they may have right to the tree of life, and may enter through the gates into the city.

15 For without are dogs, and sorceres, and whoremongers, and murderes, and idolater, and whosoever loveth and maketh a lie.

The innate purpose of Christ's saving sacrifice is to make the realm of God's holiness accessible to God's people. Without the grace of this atoning sacrifice humanities petty distractions, misunderstandings, mistrust, and self-centeredness would make this access impossible. The freedom based on this covenant relationship and its ability to root out the vanity of mankind's self-will is the same spiritual authority that will effectively gather God's chosen people from all nations and tongues to the domain of God's holy mountain.

This subtle claim is reiterated in popular Psalm of king David attributed to the joyous expectation of the final approach up the steeps of mount Zion.

Psalm 24

THE earth is the Lord's, and the fullness thereof; the world, and they that dwell therein.

2 For he hath founded it upon the seas, and established it upon the floods.

3 Who shall ascend into the hill of the Lord? Or who shall stand in his holy place?

4 He that hath clean hands, and a pure heart; who hath not lifted up his soul unto vanity, nor sworn deceitfully.

5 He shall receive the blessing from the Lord, and righteousness from the God of his salvation.

6 This is the generation of them that seek him, that seek thy face, O Jacob. Selah

7 Lift up your heads, O ye gates; and be ye lift up, ye everlasting doors; and the King of glory shall come in.

8 Who is this King of glory? The Lord strong and mighty, the Lord mighty in battle.

9 Lift up your heads, O ye gates; even lift them up, ye everlasting doors; and the King of glory shall come in.

10 Who is this King of glory? The Lord of hosts, he is the King of glory, Selah.

Though moral excellence is obtainable, only Christ and the saving power of his graces serve any real hope for admittance into this holy realm. The true covenant of the Lord's counsel is that which was paid in the blood sacrifice of God's own son. The saving atonement of this sacrifice, however, does not stop at the Lord's death and crucifixion, rather it continues on into the miracle of his resurrection. As Jesus clearly states at the beginning of John's gospel "destroy this Temple and in three days I will raise it up." (John 2 vs. 19) In saying this Jesus was speaking of the Temple of his body, and the miracle of his resurrection.

In the chapter that follows the ravages of the epic struggle between the forces of good and evil will be examined as the elements of the satanic forces described in this treatise are reexamined for their place in world history. Remnants of this satanic elite will be identified for their more covert operations as well as for the resurgence of the more obvious indiscretions perpetrated in the name of modern religion. The many cross-cultural considerations familiar to this satanic movement will also be thoroughly explored along with the historic influence impacted on mankind.

X
History of the Satanic Movement

Despite the inner workings of several millenniums of evolution, the principles outlined in this treatise suggest a relatively simple beginning for the original dispersion of Solomon's satanic movement. Although the covert operations of this occult activity was doomed to stand in the shadow of God's true favor, evidence suggests that many times in history, beginning with Solomon's reign at about 1000 B.C., it gathered to itself a sizable following. Not only can the original form of satanic worship be identified in major centers of the civilized world from the beginning of Christian era, but the existence of a cross-cultural appeal is also presented here in convincing detail.

Originally operating from within the guise of the Jewish faith, during this volatile period in history, the eventual challenge posed to the benefactors of this Satanic influence was to tap into the Christian movement as close to its source as possible, then to reestablish its covert base of operations. Although other cultural motifs served a similar attraction and purpose, establishing this order from within the Christian church itself would be this movement's crowning achievement. From out of these traditions some occult movements of legitimate origin survived into our modern era, whereas still others stemmed from a known resurgence of occult activity based on individual efforts to malign the Holy name of God.

Diana of Ephesus

The original onslaught of Solomon's satanic propaganda had clearly reached the major centers of the known civilized world well before Christianity at around 600 B.C.(1) For Judaism it came in the form of the covert activities investigated previously in this treatise. For ancient Rome this preservation can be seen in the popularity of the goddess Diana who was the Roman counterpart of Artemis of Ephesus. The Temple of Artemis of Ephesus, once hailed as one of the seven wonders of the ancient world, (2) contained an image of Artemis carved out of an ancient meteorite that fell from the heavens. In the vein of interpretation already described, Ashtoreth, the goddess who served as the copy to which this colossal structure was erected, (3) is likely the whore of Babylon who is depicted as sitting on many waters. (Rev 17 vs. 8) Likewise, in the book of Revelations a star called "wormwood" described as falling from the heavens (Rev 8 vs. 10,11) is a symbolic representation of this statue of Artemis at Ephesus that was carved out of a meteor.

Scripture goes on to describe how the star is said to have fell upon the fountains of waters causing a third part of the waters to become as wormwood and how many men died of the waters because they were made bitter. (Rev 8 vs. 11) Later in the book of Revelations the angel in John's vision clearly explains that "the waters where the whore sitteth" are to be understood as peoples, and multitudes and nations and tongues. (Rev 17 vs. 15) This interpretation as depicted in the book of Revelations leaves the massive undertaking of the erecting of this idol as highly suspect for originating from Solomon's initial satanic movement.

Aside from this interpretation, when compared to the images seen depicted in The Song of Solomon investigated in the fifth chapter of this treatise remarkably similar images are presented. If the idols at Ephesus were derived out of a more ancient form as experts suppose, then The Song of Solomon seems to be one possible source for this blueprint. The flock of goats that is spoken of is clearly represented in the statue of Artimes that was recovered from Ephesus. In the photograph depicting this image, goats can clearly be seen carved into the hair as ascending in rows of two on either side of the head. (Cant 6 vs. 6) (See fig. 1a) (4) The "two breasts that are like two young roes that are twins," describes the fact that this image actually has many breasts with an initial layer of six seen depicted on the image from Ephesus.

(Cant 7 vs. 3) (Fig 1.a) 5 The distinct reality of this image is reinforced when the idols breasts are likened to "a cluster of grapes," thus the breasts that are being described are not one, but many. A more detailed examination of The Song of Solomon is provided in the fifth chapter of this treatise.

From a Biblical standpoint, evidence suggests that the statue of Artemis existed and was documented early on during the Apostle Paul's evangelistic ministry. According to Holy Scripture a rivalry of more of a curious nature did breakout between the inhabitants of Ephesus against the Apostle Paul and those engaged in assisting in his evangelical mission. For the inhabitants of Asia minor it seems unusual for individuals engaged in the worship of the ever popular goddess Diana to feel as threatened as they were in the presence of Paul's preaching. In this passage of scripture the obvious anxiety displayed on behalf of a certain man named Demetrius, a silversmith who made shrines for Diana, is identified as one individual among many who posed an obvious effort to frustrate Paul. The town's clerk then came to Paul's defense with an exhortation, which includes the description of the image of the goddess Diana as it was said to have fallen down from the heavens.

Acts 19 vs. 24

For a certain man named Demetrius, a silversmith, who made silver shrines for Diana brought no small gain unto the craftsmen;

25 Whom he called together with the workmen of like occupation, and said, Sirs, ye know that by this craft we have our wealth.

26 Moreover ye see and hear, that not alone at Ephesus, but almost throughout all Asia, that Paul hath persuaded and turned away much people saying that they be no gods, which are made with hands:

30 And when Paul would have entered in unto the people, the disciples suffered him not.

31 And certain of the chief of Asia, which were his friends, sent unto him, desiring him that he would not adventure himself into the theater.

32 Some therefore cried one thing, and some another; for the assembly was confused; and the more part knew not wherefore they were come together.

35 And when the town clerk had appeased the people, he said, Ye men of Ephesus, what man is there that knoweth not how that the city of the Ephesians is a worshiper of the great goddess Diana, and of the image which fell down from Jupiter?

As Solomon's satanic influence unfurled, a concerted effort was devoted to evangelize the known civilized world in order to head off and curtail the expected ministry of the coming Christ. The spread of this cultic ministry was at its zenith in Asia minor at around the time of 600 B.C., 200 years after Solomon began his reign.(6) In Rome, the exact features of Artemis of Ephesus were copied down to the smallest detail where another massive sanctuary was provided on the Aventine.(7) With Rome as the conquering force of the civilized world, it would seem as though this Satanic ministry would safely accomplish it's objective, yet the true spiritual battle for all of Christendom had yet to be waged.

Developments at Asia Minor

As the Christian faith began to evangelize it was also faced with the sharpest opposition Rome could deliver. Christians were systematically murdered and tortured and were often used for sport in the ancient Roman arenas. For this reason Christianity was left to develop in secrecy hidden away from the tortures that awaited them should the Roman authorities discover them. In the midst of this persecution the Christian movement was faced with the challenge of enduring and maintaining sound doctrine. In a spirituality that was already beholden to many mysteries, the secretive nature of this developing faith gave rise to the expectancy of hidden knowledge or gnosis that would further establish the church's spiritual authority and serve to unify the diversity of it's members.

As Holy Scripture will support, this early period consequently gave rise to a startling number of heresies based on this initial development. Despite beliefs and religious practices that were often grossly exaggerated, the church remained tolerant, but not without correction. Without the guiding hand of the Holy Spirit these developing beliefs would be subject to a melting pot effect where the desired religious influence of it's growing membership would endeavor to be included. Conveniently, the best example of this melting pot effect in the face of complex diversity may be seen in the developing faith of the many churches of Asia Minor, the selfsame churches to which John the Apostle would address his untimely vision in the book of Revelations.

The foothold of the Jewish Dispersion is also evident in Asia Minor as early as 546 B.C. due in part to the military exploits of Cyrus of Persia.(8) The Apostle John went about his ministry in this area exposed to the richness of this diversity in which many Jewish and Old Testament teachings were faithfully preserved. The Hellenized Hebrew monotheism, rich in allegory and symbolism, made a venerable foundation for John's holy vision. This environment, on the other hand, did nothing to avert the growing Gnostic movement that was determined to refuel the advancement of satanic insurgence. The existence of one of these early heretical movements is documented in the book of Revelations, namely the Nicolaitanes is cited as one example of the occasion for heresy. (Rev 2 vs. 15)

It was in this particular environment that selected books from the Old Testament, still of intrinsic value to the Christian Church, were presented by petition to be included as part of what would one day become the Christian Bible Canon. With the foothold of Satanic idol worship prevalent in this region, including Artemis of Ephesus and the Cybeline cults in Phrygia, the fact that The Song of Solomon was among those books petitioned to be included comes as no surprise. Worship of the idol Cybele, which was at it's peak at around 800 B.C.,(9) bears a number of remarkable similarities to it's counterpart Artemis of Ephesus, which was at it's zenith 200 years later. Among modern scholars it is understood that goddesses like Cybele, Ashtoreth, and Artemis bared a strong affiliation with one another. One similarity in particular that is worth noting between the cults of Cybele and Artemis is how both bear a strange connection to a meteorite rock. Where Artemis was entirely carved out of this rock, the known existence of another meteorite, possibly the same one, was said to be a sacred icon to the great Phrygian mother Goddess.(10) This qualifies Moses' prophetic utterance regarding the rock that is not like our rock (Deut 32) and the subsequent anti-Christ quality credited with Satan's return to the garden of Eden. The existence of such similarities further substantiates the claim that an ancient network responsible for propagating these beliefs was established. Unlike the Christian faith, the cult status of these idols was advanced by diplomacy from the upper echelons of government, and imposed upon the general populace by its leaders.

Out of this long tradition of fertility worship found in Phrygia, a strain of feminism became apparent in the early church at this location. Coupled with the migration of acquired beliefs from that of the Mithras, the sun worship of central Rome, a concealed effort, conscious or unconscious, was made for the preservation of certain beliefs. Strangely, just before religious freedom was officially declared in Rome, the ritual worship of the Mithras began being practiced in underground temples known as caves where inductees were poised to go through seven grades of initiation. According to sources the religious practices of the cult of Cybele were similar in most respects.(11) On occasion high-ranking church official proved to be sympathetic to many aspects of these beliefs.

Melito, a known ascetic in Phrygia who fit the profile of one of these sympathizers, was also known to have made a pilgrimage to Palestine where he compiled a list of Old Testament books comparable to a similar list that was sanctioned by the Jewish Rabbis at Jamnia.(12) One such Rabbi named Akiba spoke in Jamnia in favor of the inclusion of The Song of Solomon.(13) Given Melito's many affiliations, his sympathy towards this particular cult raises many questions regarding the permeability of the early Church in this region. A fragment from Melito's second century writings shows distinct parallels being drawn in the context of pagan myth familiar to that of Mithraism.

As when a copper globe full of fire within, flashing much light, is washed in cold water with a great noise, but the fire within is not quenched but again flashes fierily; so the sun, burning like lightening, is washed wholly but not extinguished....washed in a mystic baptism, he rejoices exceedingly....He rises as a new sun to men; driving out the darkness of night, he begets the light of day. On this course also the motion of the stars and the moon, is washed in the ocean, why not Christ too in the waters of the Jordan? King of kings and governor of creation, the sun of the east who also appeared to the dead in hell and to mortals in the world, shone forth from heaven as the only sun.(14)

Out of the many centers evangelized by the Christian Church, the provinces of Asia Minor became very influential. After nearly 300 years of persecution, the Roman emperor Constantine, the first emperor to declare himself a Christian, initiated many of the sweeping changes to the Roman Empire. Constantine, despite his obvious influence over the Christian church, was not baptized.(15) Nevertheless; Constantine begins an immediate effort to transfer the Roman capital to Constantinople. Not far away, in 325 A.D. Constantine presided over the council of Nicaea where the Nicene Creed was first formulated.(16) In a statement that was equally sympathetic to that of Mellito's, Constantine declares Sundays to be a holiday known as the venerable day of the sun.(17)

These new developments effectively established Asia Minor as the future European gateway to the Byzantine Empire. Regardless of these drastic changes, the unmistakably Johnine influence in this region as those churches that were under his original apostolic jurisdiction remained prevalent and was held in high regard. Despite the fall of Rome to the Goths in 410 A.D.,(18) the

Roman city of Constantinople remained a safe haven for the Christian church till it fell to the Turks in 1453.(19) As the Christian faith spread to the west, traces of this ancient subculture survived in the Christian military monastic orders of the crusades where numerous efforts to regain the Holy land were effectively launched.

Succession Into the Modern Age

The same complex spirituality was apparent in the early middle ages among those engaged in the military campaigns to regain the Holy Land. Members of the order of St. John, largely responsible for the care of the sick in Jerusalem after it's liberation from the Saracens,(20) probably served in order to stay true to it's ancient Palestinian ties and came away with a unique spiritual retrospective upon returning to this region. Despite the fact that over six hundred years had passed, the rudiments of an ancient spirituality still existed in the Johnine tradition.

The order, officially ratified by Pope Honrius I in 1128, developed as the result of the continued Saracen threat against Jerusalem. In the region known for its ancient roots in the tradition of the Holy Temple, with a membership now restricted to those obtaining the rank of knight, (21) the Knights of the Templar emerged. Remaining true to the religious vows to which they were accustomed, and from possibility of clinging to the spoils of war, the order bank- rolled massive amounts of corporate wealth.(22)

Those who inherited this wealth could have developed an attitude of control that was similar to that of Solomon when the construction of the original Temple was first underway. In light of what was considered the righteous crusades, the fact that this benevolent cause unwittingly emerged, as a cash-cow is more than likely. The burgeoning spirituality of the Templars, maintaining a plausible connection to it's ancient roots in the Johnine tradition, was often accused of heresy, idolatry and homosexuality, till in 1308 Edward the second succumbed to pressure to confiscate much of the revenue that was amassed.(23) Whether or not a thread of Solomon's original Satanic order survived and was elated by their return to the site of Solomon's Temple cannot be stated with any certainty, but the recurring themes that emerge in the succession of this tradition seems to invite further speculation.

Development of the Freemasons

At first glance the secrecy and cloak-in-dagger rhetoric of the Freemasons seems to be an unlikely threat, spiritually or otherwise, yet the underlying principles of Christ and his salvation are easily offset by a tolerance to the conflicting values that are too often imposed on it's members. In reality, the corporate self-serving image of success is in extreme conflict with all Christ centered teachings. The likelihood that the fundamental mysteries guarded by the Freemasons originated entirely out of the tradition outlined in this treatise remains high, yet one can not help but wonder if the strangle hold of this image of success plays a inherent role in turning individuals away from God.

Even the name Masons, an obvious reference to the construction of Solomon's Temple, seems to bear a timeless connection with the satanic principles thus far described. The covert rituals and secrecy lend a perfect rendering with Solomon's former exploits, and seems to have a far-reaching impact on today's society. The following portions of this chapter will continue to trace the origins of this modern day cult to many of it's significant branches that do little to hide their Satanic influence.

Although the origin of a fraternal order known as the Rosicrucian's is unlikely to stem directly from any formal link to the Knights of the Templar, the appeal of it's former mystic would have extended to many of the individuals privy to it's existence. With the Knights of the Templar formally suspended in 1312 on behalf of Pope Clement V24, a new movement inspired by the practice of alchemy was about to emerge.(25) Christian Rosicrucian was a legendary character who lived between 1378 and 1484 and was thought to have visited the holy land and was said to have made discoveries in the science of alchemy while visiting Damascus and other Christian sites in the near east.(26) Long after this movement had died out, the published report that Christian Rosicrucian's remains had been found without decay, provoked a phenomenal comeback, ascribing to it's popularity throughout Europe, but mainly in England where its principle practice took hold well into the 1600s.(27)

Thus the ancient antiquity of the early church survived covertly into our modern era. By the end of the 19th century, the brotherhood known as Societa Rosicruciana in Anglia (SRIA) was officially born. Although modern Masonry can be dated no earlier than 1781 according to known surviving texts, evidence suggests that at least some of the principles can be found at work in England under a Sir Thomas Dunckerly towards the end of the eighteenth century.(28) Familiar to the tradition outlined thus far in this chapter, Freemasonry is known to be rooted in a long history of allegories and symbols. In the words of the old English constitution, "Freemasonry is a system of morality, veiled in allegory, and illustrated by symbol."(29) Even the symbols of ancient alchemy are likely preserved in this tradition. The militaristic style of the Knights of the Templar may also be seen in the tendency for this organization to ascend in ranks of up to 33 honorary degrees.

By the 1900's when religious tolerance to the world of the occult was slowly being introduced, the cloak and dagger ritual of the Freemasons would have provided many followers safe haven till the issue of religious freedom could be resolved. This explains the many branches of occult practice that stemmed from the Freemasons later on in the 20th century. One consistency among these branches and the most obvious fundamental connection this organization has with the occult is that many of its teachings stem back to Solomon and his early Temple.

Masonic Preoccupation With Lucifer

The most recent development in Freemasonry is that the high level defection of certain high-ranking Freemasons has resulted in further evidence of these organizations satanic tendencies. Drawn out speculation on the part of the media in term's of this organization's fascination with Lucifer has been examined by the public, implying a true connection with the occult. Unrenowned to this general fascination, the satanic attraction to this dogma, is that no matter who we are as human beings, and no matter how far we have come in Christ, there is still the potential for any one person to fall into perdition and die without repentance. Lucifer, as will be further explored in the eleventh chapter of this treatise, is a clear symbol of this potential.

This Luciferian doctrine could well represent an estranged; last ditch effort to entice its followers to gaze into the precipice of occult practice in order to inspire one final plunge into sin. Fortunately and contrary to the lies of the enemy, no such plunge exists as long as repentance is an option. On the other hand, this doctrine could also be rooted in the original possibility that Solomon himself had the potential to ascend to the title of morning star before this possibility was ultimately denied.

Like any movement, the Freemasons had its radicals. In this context such a member might be deemed out of order in their zeal to discredit God's saints, thereby receiving a proverbial slap on the wrist from Mason authorities. Occasional indiscretions regarding references to Lucifer, despite the tendency to leak to the press, have not prevented it's graduates from obtaining the highest degree in Freemasonry.(30) It could be that through years of patronage to King Solomon these individuals are eager to confer a special title in Solomon's honor. Whatever the case, these indiscretions are examined here in brief, as further proof of an anti-Christian sentiment.

One statement made in by high level Masons is quoted as such..."Lucifer is a name of God, Satan doesn't really exist and besides even if he did he is really just doing God's work."(31)

Whether this statement was made out of ignorance, or was purposed to deceive, is indeed another question. Although philosophically these statements hold some weight, what is certain is that the term Satan represents the place of God's anger, and what angers God the most is wasted human potential. Scripture clearly states that "Satan is a liar and the father of it." (Jo 8 vs. 44) Some would argue that the Freemason's enigmatic approach is a cover in order to preserve the truth for higher level masons. The following excerpt from the Masonic author Carl Claudy implies such a theory.

"Cut through the outer shell and find a meaning; cut through that meaning and find another; under it, if you dig deep enough, you may find a third or a fourth—who shall say how many teachings?" (32)

Aside from the endless labyrinth of rhetoric that could be explored, emblems like the Seal of Solomon with it's six points and the double headed eagle, shed further light on this luciferian tradition on the part of the Freemasons. The two headed eagle, it is suggested, is not an eagle at all, but rather, represents the phoenix who is said to wrap itself up in a fiery grave and from it be reborn. In the context of witchcraft, William Schnoebelen states "Most occultists believe that the Phoenix is a symbol of Lucifer who was cast down into flames and who...will one day rise triumphant."(33) The seal of Solomon is a known ensign familiar in the world of sorcery and witchcraft. 34 As one final example of this disquieting link to Lucifer, chosen from a long list of excerpts concerning this allegiance, the following is a letter written by the sovereign Grand commander Albert Pike, (33) degree.

"We shall unleash the Nihilists and Atheists, and we shall provoke a formidable social cataclysm which in all it's horror will show clearly to the nations the effects of absolute atheism, origin of savagery and of the most bloody turmoil. Then everywhere, the citizens, obliged to defend themselves against the world minority of revolutionaries, will exterminate those destroyers of civilization, and the multitude, disillusioned with Christianity, whose deistic spirits will be from that moment without compass, anxious for an ideal, but without knowing where to render it's adoration, will receive the pure doctrine of Lucifer, brought finally out in the public view, a manifestation which will result from the general reactionary movement which will follow the destruction of Christianity and atheism, both conquered and exterminated at the same time." (35)

This excerpt, while showing the true colors of Mason loyalties, is nothing compared to those organizations that emerged from the ranks of the Freemasons to take their place on the platform of religious freedom. Among those branches accredited as off-shoots of the Freemasons; The Hell Fires clubs formed by Francis Dashwood in 1751, The Wicca religion created by Gerald Gardner in the 1940's, and the hard-core Satanism of the Hermetic Order of the Golden Dawn to which the notorious Aleister Crowley was a member. The many similarities between these cults makes it difficult to set them apart, although each did have it's own distinct emphasis into varying degrees in the realm of Satanism.

The Hellfire Clubs

The Hellfire Clubs bear the phenomenal account of Sir Francis Dashwood, a member of English upper class who in his early years lived a life of privilege in an adventuresome style. As an earlier member of the Freemasons, Dashwood went his way independently to form his own club called the Friars of St. Francis of Wycombe, to which members dressed as monks and friars strictly on a pretentious basis. Dashwood gradually gained a reputation for his trendy underground sexual romps among England's upper class.(36)

Although this particular club is often discounted as having no legitimate ties to traditional Satanism, it's obvious tendencies towards sexual promiscuity kept it true to its roots. The long history of sexual orgies realized in pagan times, dates back to Solomon himself and his many wives. Creation of the Hellfire Clubs on the part of Francis Dashwood is often excused as merely an opportunity to engage in sexual orgies. On the other hand, the sexual element of Satanism must not be downplayed since the tendency to practice this satanic art is a principle form of worship towards the ancient goddesses of fertility. A satirical cartoon of Sir Francis Dashwood worshipping the goddess Venus is depicted which adds to the consistency with this theory.37

Among those aspects that helped the Hellfire Clubs maintain an image that was somewhat benign, was it's reputation as a gentleman's club that held an appeal for eligible bachelors given over to gambling and eating and drinking in excess. From the standpoint of modern culture, for the local upper-class to embrace these secretive escapades resembles the modern-day playboy stereotyping but still retains it's dark and sinister association with Satan. As is often the case, by the time Dashwood reached the age of sixty, as the chief organizer, his orgies eventually held little appeal and his Hellfire Club was forced to close.

The Wicca Religion

Gerald Gardner was introduced to Rosicrucian's in the early 20th century then went on to form the main branch of the Wicca religion in the 1940s.(38) Similar to its Freemason counterpart, Wiccans formally deny that Satan has any part in their religion. Ironically, it seems possible that this claim is substantiated in part, due to the fact that Wiccans firmly reject the concept of Satan.(39) This rejection actually plays a diabolical role in Wicca teachings, to which Satan is obviously inherent, at least on an incidental basis.

The main reason the concept of Satan is clearly rejected by Wicca is because it is a purely Christian term meaning "one who stands in the way." For the Wicca there are probably no limits or restrictions imposed that cannot be solved by the proper ritual. Instead, Wicca lays claim to the fact that it originated with the ancient wisdom of nature that predates the concept of Satan. Since religious freedom was declared the Wicca religion clearly exercises its right to be separated from anything Christian. As for its ancient heritage, a barrage of natural principles, rituals, and beliefs from the more practical aspects of ancient culture probably do exist, and have evidently been incorporated into this resurgence of witchcraft. Since the nature of witchcraft was always to work outside of the Christian faith, most of these assertions do hold some truth in their claim to excluding anything satanic. At the same time, the ability to control, influence and deal out retribution to it's enemies, aside from posing a challenge for public relations, is clearly an ability that is not in dispute.

Another unique development in the practice of the Wicca religion is the fact that the personality of Solomon and the unique folklore surrounding his earthly existence seems to have developed quite independently in Wicca teachings. It seems that Solomon's reputation, as a celebrated Wiccan is one aspect of the Judeo-Christian tradition that this religion has not failed to capitalize on. The Wicca belief system readily accepts the principle existence of gods and goddesses in the realm of nature, including many of the ancient gods and goddesses that were recognized by Solomon himself. Other aspects common to Solomon and the Wicca belief system alike are a profound understanding of nature, magic, clairvoyance and the psychic arts, and the existence of benevolent and malevolent spirits, as they exist in nature.

In the world of modern witchcraft, the personality of Solomon is arguably much more central in it's traditional belief than in the Judeo-Christian tradition. This is due in part to the fact that for those engaged in the black arts there is little ambivalence as to where Solomon's true loyalty was placed. In the Judeo-Christian tradition, on the other hand, the well-intended beliefs garnered as a token of Solomon's kingly authority are suddenly cut short, leaving the subject of his true loyalties in question. In the tradition of cultic folklore the image of Solomon as a powerful sorcerer is emphasized, where as his turning from God on account of his many wives is seriously downplayed. In fact the circle of allegiance that these alliances formed is hailed as a virtue of tolerance, to which Solomon emerges as the ideal model of modern Wicca belief.(40)

The following is an excerpt from a current occult encyclopedia that typifies this drastic shift in emphasis subject to its affiliations with the satanic arts.

Solomon had about 700 wives and 300 concubines. Many of the exotic women were in fact living treatise. He sustained alliances by taking wives from the family of every ruler willing to sign a treaty. He even kept mighty Egypt out of Israel by marrying an Egyptian princess, daughter of a pharaoh.

By loving so many foreign women and allowing them to continue their own forms of worship, corrupting the Holy city with their exotic rituals and gods, Solomon not only tolerated this paganism but also participated in it himself. Some say that he became a skilled sorcerer. According to one of the many legends about him, Solomon used pagan magic to imprison 72 rebellious evil kings into a brass vessel, throwing it then into a deep lake, where they were supposed to stay until the end of time. In an attempt to find great treasure, the Babylonians rescued the vessel and broke it open, allowing the demons to escape. These devils became known as the 72 spirits of Solomon. (41)

From a Christian standpoint the number 72 is significant since 70 of Christ's disciples who were sent out in ministry were given authority "to tread on serpents and scorpions, and over all the power of the enemy." (Luke 10 vs. 19) In this excerpt from the occult encyclopedia, to the opposite extreme, Solomon finds himself in authority over 72 demons.

The Bible's Teaching on Witchcraft

The foremost, and final authority on the subject of witchcraft is the covenant of God's faithful law. From this standpoint one is reminded by the eternal nature of the world of spirits, that if such a primal spiritual world exists, then to deny the authority of the spirit of Christ, either by action or inaction, is to be set on the path of destruction set aside for Satan and his angels. The excuses of those given over to the abomination of being caught up in their own fanciful experience of this spiritual domain without the benefit of Christ's witness and protection will be of no consolation when the protection of God's grace is lifted. For those individuals who are of Christ and have learned to test the spirits, whether they are of Christ or not, (1 Jo 4 vs. 1) the eternal nature of this world of spirits is equally real but at far less risk to one's immortal soul.

While the realization of one's spiritual self is innate to humanities existence, the most typical form of rebellion against God is to remain in the comforts of one's personal spirituality by refusing to engage in the true witness of Christ. Witchcraft's mistaken claim to personal protection and its inevitable attraction is most often based on the innocence of this selfish existence. With this mentality the basic tenet of the craft is served "...and it harm none, do what thou wilt."(42) Ironically, since the passing of the fraudulent medium's Act of 1951, (43) this foundational principle of Wicca is legally encouraged. This act gave Wiccans the freedom to practice as long as no harm was inflicted against any other individual. The mythical existence of white magic, a magic that is supposedly based on the benefit of all humanity, further lures would be members into this satanic snare.

The inherent evil of this occult spirit is that it does approach the ancient of days as does every spirit. What this counterfeit cannot supply is the lifeline of salvation that Christ himself came to provide. Instead, in the world of secular anonymity individuals who succumb to this form of occult worship eventually become complacent and refuse to seek out fellowship in the true testimonies of Christ. The every man for himself mentality fostered by the occult and seen in the Wicca religion inevitably becomes the witness of self, a false witness by any standard. (Deut 19 vs. 15) By subscribing to occult loyalties, one is in actuality swept away into a most heinous form of rebellion in an unholy communion with this ancient spirit.

The prophet Samuel has this instruction…

1 SAMUEL 22

And Samuel said, Hath the Lord as great delight in burnt offerings and sacrifices, as in obeying the voice of the Lord? Behold, to obey is better than sacrifice, and to hearken than the fat of rams.

23 For rebellion is as the sin of witchcraft, and stubbornness is as iniquity and idolatry. Because thou hast rejected the word of the Lord, he hath also rejected thee (Saul) from being king.

Samuel the prophet was well aware of this potential snare; since any intentional deviation of God's instruction is teetering on occult practice and witchcraft, as King Saul would go on to learn. Hard pressed to hear from God's spirit, Saul eventually communes with the witch of Endor. (1 Sam 28 vs. 8) From the world's standpoint a similar ultimatum is given in association with identifying God's truth in the time and season of its calling in whatever form it comes. Only in entering into a truly intimate relationship with one's heavenly father will the benefit of God's protection from the spiritual assault of the enemy be secured.

From the standpoint of the oracles of prophecy, at the designated time, when God is poised to pour out his divine wisdom, by virtue of the death and resurrection of his son, a growing hunger for even a spark of the Lord's spirit will offset the world's secular society into a feeding frenzy on the basis of this occult spirituality. As this becomes apparent, the only valid connection powerful enough to qualify an individual as a true believer will be the shared testimony of Christ and the revelation of his son-ship and resurrection. All others will attend to this famine hard pressed to hear God's voice, turning to the occult for even a hint of God's presence.

The following scripture describes the season of this spiritual famine as it approaches our modern times. From the principle nature of this prophecy the key elements of Christ's salvation are made evident, which includes the Testimonies that were passed on to Christ's beloved disciples, and the rock of revelation set for the preservation of God's true saints and all of those who show a willingness to abide in this truth.

Isaiah 8 vs. 12

Say ye not, A confederacy, to all them to whom this people shall say, A confederacy: neither fear ye their fear, nor be afraid.

13 Sanctify the Lord of hosts himself; and let him be your fear, and let him be your dread.

14 And he shall be for a sanctuary; but for a stone of stumbling and for a rock of offence to both the houses of Israel, for a gin and for a snare to the inhabitants of Jerusalem.

16 Bind up the testimony, seal the law among my disciples.

18 Behold, I and the children whom the Lord hath given me are for signs and for wonders in Israel from the Lord of hosts, which dwell in mount Zion.

19 And when they shall say unto you, Seek unto them that have familiar spirits, and unto wizards that peep, and that mutter: should not a people seek unto their God? for the living to the dead?

20 To the law and to the testimony: if they speak not according to this word, it is because there is no light in them.

21 And they shall pass through it, hardly bestead and hungry; and it shall come to pass, that when they shall be hungry, they shall fret themselves, and curse their king and their God and look upward.

22 And they shall look unto the earth; and behold trouble and darkness, dimness of anguish; and they shall be driven to darkness.

According to prophecy, the fate against this present form of complacency has already been sealed. The rise of occult practices in the form of the Wicca style religion is in keeping with this ancient prophecy and is based on the false spiritual hope that mankind will somehow emerge as the true master of its own spiritual destiny. This Wicca style of belief best represents the snare of Satan in its infant state and its potential to grow into full-blown rebellion against God. In the context of religious freedom there exists a satanic elite who turns this rebellion into an obvious reality. With little satisfaction, for the sake of identifying the growing resolve of these satanic forces, the remainder of this chapter will endeavor to take one final glimpse into the modern existence of this satanic movement.

The Hermetic Order of the Golden Dawn

The Hermetic Order of the Golden Dawn, which, by title, ascribes to some of the Luciferian imagery presented earlier, was formed largely on the precepts of its Rosicrucian predecessor, the Freemasons. In the face of growing pressure from its more radical members, The Hermetic Order of the Golden Dawn, took the plunge into self-professed Satanism. This organization peaked, as far as its satanic principles are concerned, around the turn of the 20th century, (44) when a young protégé by the name of Aleister Crowley took to its ranks. Born in 1875, Aleister Crowley acquired an early aversion to Christianity possibly from his parent's involvement in the Plymouth Brethren group, which despite its Christian beliefs, cut itself off from mainstream Christianity.(45)

At the age of 25 with his formal membership into The Hermetic Order of the Golden Dawn, Aleister Crowley began his lifelong devotion to the service of Satan. Unlike the secretive approach of the Freemasons, Aleister Crowley publicly acknowledged his Luciferian beliefs. As a clear departure from witch covens to which Crowley may have been exposed earlier in his life, Crowley aligned himself with the Bibles teachings on Satan when he acclaimed himself as "The Great Beast 666, Prophet of a New Aeon."(46) Through his writing and Satanic doctrine Crowley often expressed his outright defiance against God.

The philosophical stance of this Satanic movement was the declaration of absolute freedom, although the context of this freedom is never clearly identified it suggests freedom from law, freedom from morality, even freedom from self as a potential path to enlightenment. In this mentality modern Satanists take the philosophy of their Wicca counter parts a step further into nonexistent form of emancipation from the world and it's many responsibilities.

In 1904, while traveling to Cairo, Egypt, Crowley claimed to have come in contact with a spirit entity known as Aiwass and with the assistance of his wife wrote his most influential work, known as *The Book of the Law*. Through this heretical work the pagan catch phrase, "Do what thou wilt shall be the whole of the law, Love is the law, Love under Will."(47) The title of this work reveals much of the philosophical web that keeps many of the world's population in the clutches of the master deceiver.

The Luciferian deception, although subtle, is fully exposed and deposed from within Holy Scripture, where will worship, and the worship of angels is incurred as an ultimate deception. (Col 2 vs. 18-23) From what must be the cornerstone of Luciferian doctrine, the sense and ability to worship Satan who transforms himself into an angel of light, (2 Cor 11 vs. 14) subtly produces the desired snare of the enemy. From this tradition, the universal theme of self-transformation, and the world's appeal to one's self will is utterly contemned in its claim to personal salvation apart from God. Although the needed commitment to change and repent will always be a steadfast pillar of theology, the fact that religious Christianity has essentially stalled in the area of this necessity has done nothing to equip its converts to withstand the wave of this Satanic influence.

The irony that Crowley's work, *The Book of the Law,* still gives the impression of some legal requirement, does not serve to strengthen it's position. When it comes to the belief in God and knowledge of his power over creation scripture says, "the devils also believe and they tremble." (Jo 2 vs. 19) In effect what this Luceferian doctrine implies is that a person may do or do not as they please. This juvenile philosophy was well known to Solomon, as was clearly outlined in the beginning chapters of this treatise, suggests that one may passively push the bounds of God's law as it suits them. Having knowledge and faith without obedience is the defining principle of all hypocrisy and in the absence action the Lord's salvation will not be an option.

Another aspect of this satanic wave that scripture is careful to point out is the practice of false humility. In its latent form this deception shows itself in a general neglect of self (Col 2 vs. 23) but can manifest itself in a variety of forms, including self loathing, asceticism, and overall deprivation aimed at lending an advantage in one's efforts for a sympathetic appeal. Usually based on some selfish ulterior motive, this ploy for attention masquerades itself as commonplace in order to win converts to its cause. In an active more creative form, this energy is channeled to disguise those feelings that are clearly full of ego and self in order to pass them off as the opposite reality. While this manipulation may be common in human nature in moments of weakness, for those engaged in satanic practice these expressions become a standardized form of heresy that adds a formidable mystic to potential converts.

This form of creativity, if one can call it that, was not unfamiliar to Crowley's field of expertise. The following is an excerpt from a hymn of tribute to Lucifer written by Crowley, whose publication attributes him as a 33rd degree Freemason.

His body a blood-ruby radiant
With noble passion, sun-souled Lucifer
Swept through the dawn colossal, swift aslant
On Eden's imbecile perimeter.
He blessed nonentity with every curse
And spiced with sorrow the dull soul of sense,
Breath life into the sterile universe,
With Love and Knowledge drove out innocence
The Key of Joy is disobedience. (48)

This, just one small sample of the literature Crowley produced, is the typical style and format of his work. Towards the end of his life Aleister Crowley was given over to a heroin addiction, which he maintained till his death at the age of 72.(49) Sadly, Crowley's reputation of scandal and rebellion against God, went on to serve the pop-culture phenomenon that fueled the satanic movement well into the twentieth century. Today, many individuals mistakenly idolize Crowley for the mystic he created, including musicians like Jimmy Page, the creative talent behind Led Zeppelin, who was reported to buy Crowley's mansion estate out of personal interest.

Collectively, the satanic movement is responsible for more human misery than most earthly catastrophes, and has resulted in the rebellion that temporarily stays God's guiding hand from awarding the meek of the earth their inheritance. Among those who have influenced popular culture, Anton Szandor La Vey, self proclaimed high priest of the Satanic movement, and Charles Manson, whose brand of evolving spirituality shows how satanic principles can be adopted without formal influence or training. The organizations brought out in this treatise, a small token of the satanic network known to have infiltrated various cities and our towns, and in some cases even churches, further presses the urgency to embrace the truths of God as they come, without discrimination.

Those Who Stand in the Way

In the context of the traditional meaning of Satan as "one who stands in the way," everyone with the desire to press on to God's high calling must be careful not to stand in the way of the ebb of God's truth, or to stop up the flow of God's spirit over a personal vendetta, or a conflict of religion. Though human nature often spells out it's own agendas, the hand of God is sure to lend a gentle push, as one allows it, in order for his will to be accomplished. At the time of Jesus' ministry, it was Peter who purposed himself against Jesus, to avoid his triumphal entry into Jerusalem. To this opposition Jesus plainly stated, "Get thee behind me Satan: thou art an offense unto me: for thou savorest not the things that be of God, but those that be of men." (Matt 16 vs. 23) In the same way, this chapter says nothing of those evil acts of retribution that were performed in the name of religion out of selfish motives and direction, but not in keeping with God's intended purposes.

In the next chapter of this treatise, the final chapter in the ongoing saga of the satanic turn of events that went on to shape the destiny of mankind, Lucifer, the fallen angel and his expulsion out of heaven, will be further examined. Scripture's final account of the battle in heaven that ensues, and the scripture and doctrine related to the symbolic virtue of Lucifer's final fall from grace will also be investigated, along with the notion of predestination and mysteries of the angelic realm.

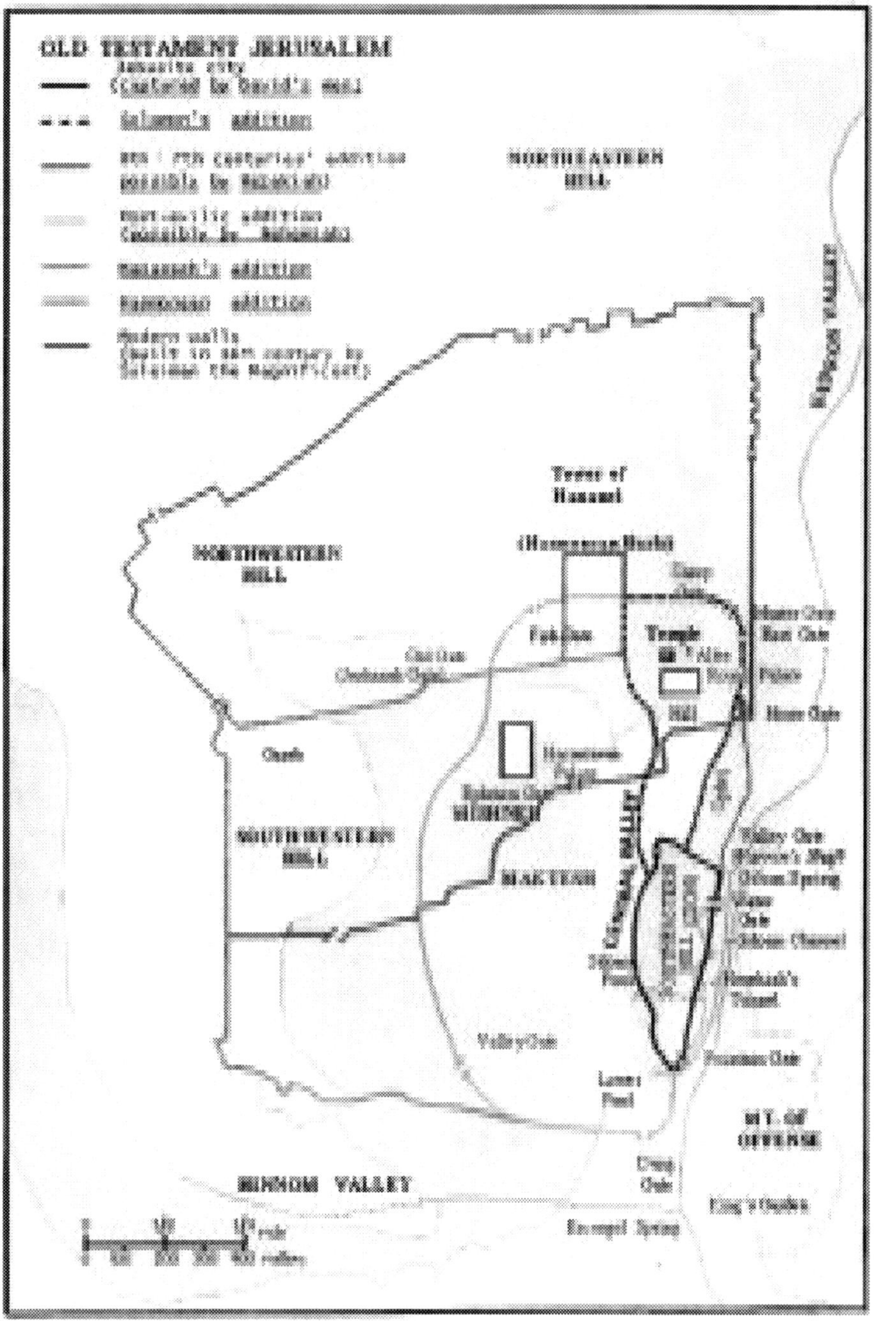
OLD TESTAMENT JERUSALEM
NORTHEASTERN HILL
NORTHWESTERN HILL
SOUTHWESTERN HILL
Tower of Hananel
Temple
Palace
Horse Gate
East Gate
Valley Gate
Lower Pool
MT. OF OFFENSE
Dung Gate
King's Garden
HINNOM VALLEY

Artist's depiction of Baptism in the River Jordan

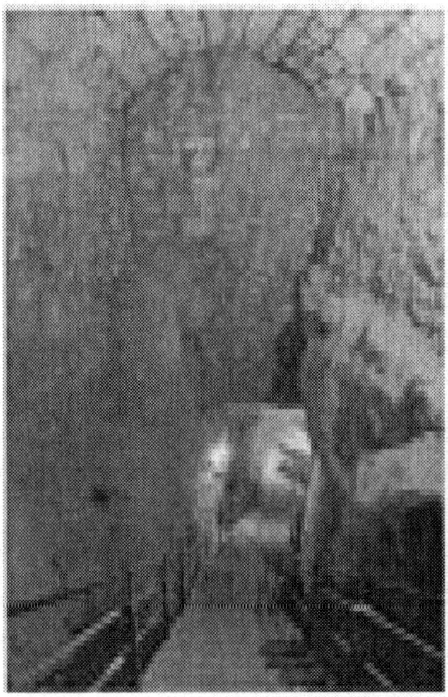

The Spring of Gihon

Hezekiah's Tunnel

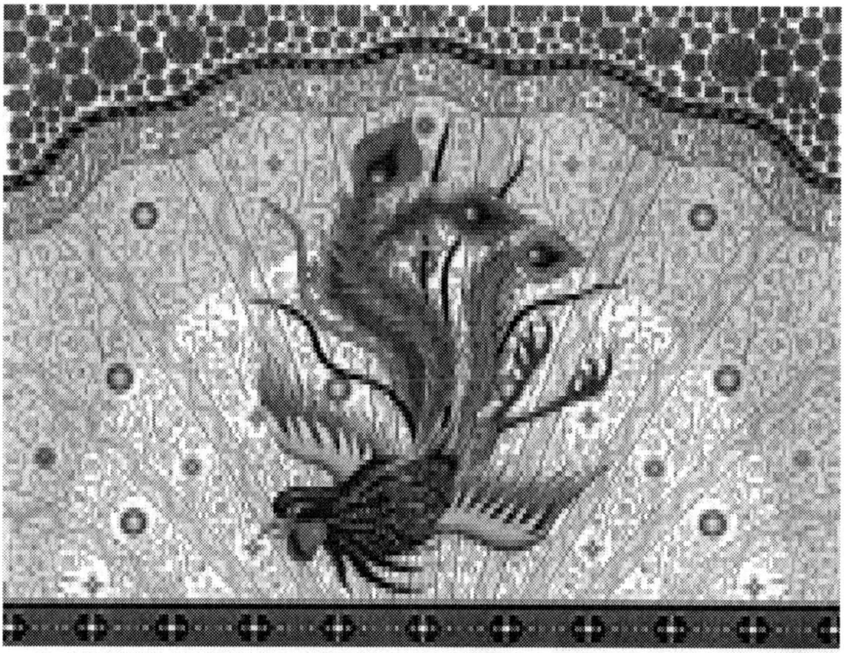

Artist's depiction of the 'phoenix'

Ephesus

Freemason symbol

Seal of Solomon

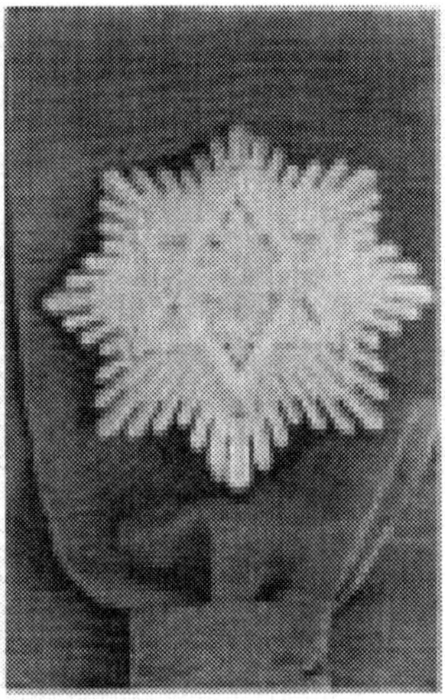

Seal of Solomon

Artemis of Ephesus

Freemason Symbol

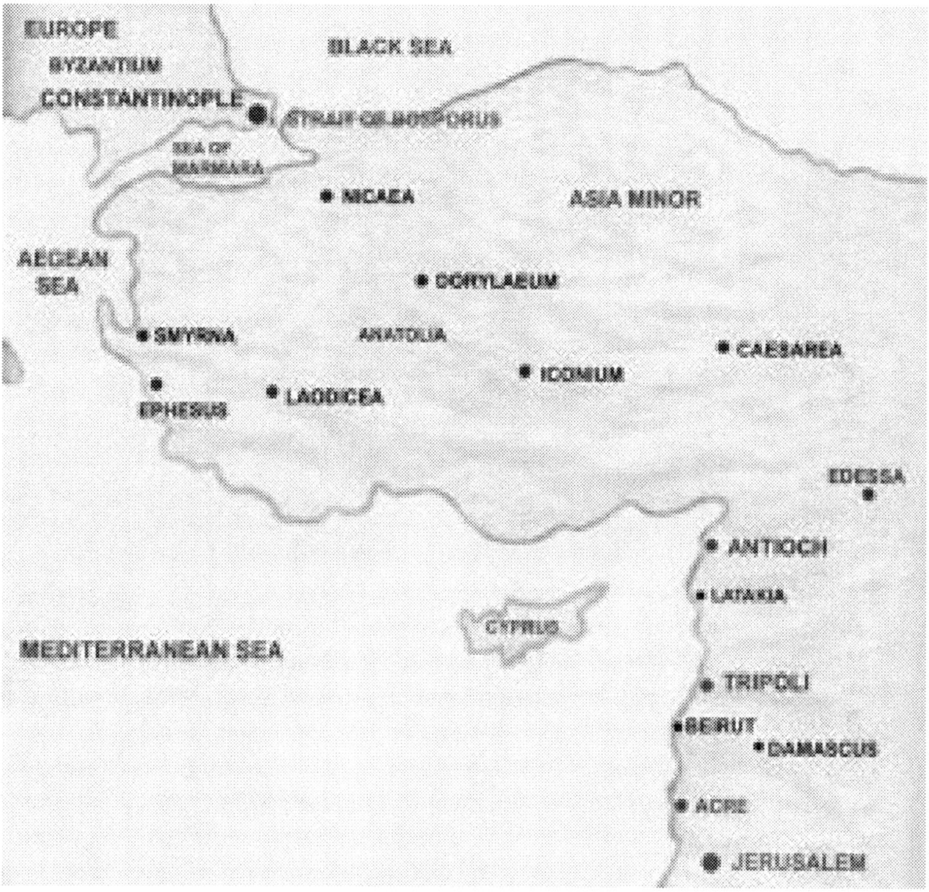

Map of Asia Minor

XI
The Fall of Lucifer

The record of Solomon's mortal existence has long served as a reminder of how wealth and power can corrupt one's moral character. Further to this motif is the inherent challenge of remaining spiritually minded in the realization of God's anointing and privilege. Despite the tremendous honor of coming into a relationship with the known creator of the universe, while the essence of most knowledge has the potential to corrupt an individual, as in Solomon's case, the true value of any God given relationship is primarily to serve in the purpose of salvation.

Aside from the knowledge that Lucifer bares a very real spiritual existence as one of God's sworn enemies, Lucifer remains the foremost symbol of one's potential to fall from God's good graces. In line with this realization, the elementary symbolic representation of Lucifer will be identified in scripture for the moral lesson imparted, along with it's intrinsic property to warn individual's to remain in God's proper service. While the promise of eternal life and God's privilege and anointing* are irrevocable, the choice of eternal condemnation and torture in the lake of fire (which is the second death,) and the choice of eternal bliss in Paradise with one's true heavenly Father is clearly spelled out. Secondarily, the unholy union that Lucifer poses as a spirit of corruption and corrupting hand of Satan will be examined, along with the unique spiritual connection of the preeminent and predestinated natures imparted to every human being in relation to one's angelic counterpart. The spiritual clash between the epic forces of good and evil, the precursor to the spiritual dispersion of Satan and his angels will be identified as the true antecedent to life's moral struggle.

The Morning Star

The symbolic virtue of the stars of heaven as mentioned in Holy Scripture has long been the source of mystery in the realm of divine creation. Held traditionally for signs and for seasons and for days and for years, the navigating principle of these celestial bodies maintained an inseparable bond with the predestined purposes of the lives of ordinary human beings. God's promise to Abraham that he would multiply his seed as the sand on the sea shore, and as the stars of the heavens' bears record of the human element of this symbolic representation. The symbolic representation of the stars of the seven churches of Asia Minor in the book of Revelations clearly maintains a link with the divine as representative of seven angels. In the world of occult practice and belief ancient astrology has placed enormous emphasis on the celestial movement of the stars for their spiritual significance, although such an application is clearly denounced by God as an abominable practice. (Deut 4 vs. 19)

From the dawn of civilization, from the first morning light of the star's first creation, a special significance has gradually taken hold in the designation of the morning star in a variety of cultures. With the popular influence of ancient mariners of Phoenicia and Babylonian astrology, the morning star gradually became a symbol of the peak of modern advancement in the ancient world. Not unlike the cosmological forces of Leviathan, the colossal sea creature that swam in the primordial waters at the beginning of creation, (1) the cosmological features of the morning star became a symbol of mankind's ability to "do anything that the human heart imagines to do." (Gen 11 vs. 6) This unrestrained ability was quickly identified and the symbol of morning star was adopted, partly for Babylonian fascination and influence, (2) at first as a symbol of God's favor and privilege. As the tide of the political climate changed this symbol emerged as a sign of civilization's growing arrogance and pride whose throne endeavored to be exalted above the stars of God. (Is 14 vs. 13)

The original sense of privilege and favor attributed by the designation of morning star has a definite connection with God's anointing and son-ship, and the knowledge of the associated preeminent nature of this calling. Not unlike Jesus Christ and the transformation he received at the time of his resurrection, every human being has the potential to aspire to a similar nature at the time of the resurrection of the righteous. (John 5 vs21) With this possibility clearly understood, the term "morning stars" emerges in connection with the sons of God, whom the Lord suggests existed from the foundation of the world. To the intent of identifying the Lord's privilege, the term Lucifer, which means morning star(3) was the shared designation of the sons of God. The fact that one of these sons exalted his throne above all others is the ongoing topic under investigation in this treatise.

The following scripture entails the shared designation of this privilege as ascribed in the Lord's own words.

Job 38 vs. 4

Where wast thou when I laid the foundations of the earth? Declare, if thou hast understanding.

5 Who hath laid the measures thereof, if thou knowest? or who hath stretched the line upon it?

6 Whereupon are the foundations thereof fastened? Or who laid the corner stone thereof;

7 When the morning stars sang together, and all the sons of God shouted for joy?

The eventuality that one of these sons endeavored to be exalted even above Christ himself is consistent with the spiritual battle that ensues in the heavenly realm, to which Lucifer shows his contention with God's appointed order. From this understanding an unholy alliance is waged against the forces of good in the form of Satan's effort to oppose, the anti-Christ's effort to malign and corrupt God's truth, and Lucifer's spiritual insurgence to appeal to the prideful tendencies of mankind. This unholy trinity, ascribed to one and the same individual, is identified in the different forms of natural and supernatural existence that one attains to before, and after the resurrection. In the form of this unholy union Satan's ability to transform himself into an angel of light is clearly realized. (2 Cor 11 vs. 14)

In Holy Scripture, the fact that Solomon himself subscribes to this belief becomes apparent in a variety of literary forms. In many instances Solomon comes to symbolize the sum of all earthly wisdom, a claim that Solomon does not fail to embellish. Consistent with the designation of morning star in this context Solomon is plain to point out how the Lord possessed him from the beginning of his ways and before his works of old. The sense that Solomon's pride is slowly looming before one's very eyes becomes apparent in a variety of contexts. From Solomon's personal conceits boasting of his personal wealth and his flagrant sexuality in The Song of Solomon, a growing sense of egotism seems to be overtaking Solomon's personal character. The sense of pride coming before a fall seems to be a fitting clich for Solomon, not unlike the flight of Icarus too close to the sun, or the sinking of the Titanic.

The following is one popular example of Solomon's exhortations on the virtues of wisdom, which supports the belief of a preeminent existence* being extended to him as one of God's own sons.

Proverbs 8 vs. 22

The Lord possessed me in the beginning of his way, before his works of old.

23 I was set up from everlasting, from the beginning, or ever the earth was.

24 When there were no depths, I was brought forth; when there were no fountains abounding with water.

25 Before the mountains were settled, before the hills was I brought forth:

26 While as yet he had not made the earth, nor the fields, nor the highest part of the dust of the world.

27 When he prepared the heavens, I was there: when he set a compass upon the face of the depths:

28 When he established the clouds above: when he strengthened the fountains of the deep:

29 When he gave to the sea his decree, that the waters should not pass his commandment: when he appointed the foundations of the earth:

30 Then I was by him, as one brought up with him; and I was daily his delight, rejoicing always before him;

Though the potential for Solomon's personal delusion remains real, the truth that sound theological conclusions are being drawn on Solomon's behalf is also apparent. This reality could well be the source from which the identity of Lucifer and his untimely fall from grace had been birthed, a notion that high level Freemasons seem to embrace, rather with the hope against hope that Lucifer will somehow reemerge as victorious in his struggle against God. From more of an original standpoint, the fact remains that enormous privilege was indeed within Solomon's grasp, and if it were not for his freedom of choice to squander this potential, his existence of one of the Lord's morning stars would have been secure.

New Testament References

The existence of a new glorious nature, sown in death and raised gloriously in the resurrection, is mentioned in various parts of the Old and New Testament. Intertwined with subtle clues indicating the aspects of this transformation, in passages previously cited, such scripture references include a subtle warning in order to illustrate the extent of one's potential to fall in a similar fashion. Among the examples of scriptures that hold special significance, St. Peter's exhortation as the chosen custodian of the revelation of Christ's son-ship is perhaps the most deliberate. By crossing over the prophetic threshold of Christ-s resurrection, (the token proof of prophetic office) as the day dawns and the day star arises in the heart of mankind, scripture is also careful to state that the truth of this revelation is not to be held exclusively by any individual.

2 Peter 1 vs. 19
We have also a more sure word of prophecy; whereunto ye do well that ye take heed, as unto a light that shineth in a dark place, until the day dawn, and the day star arises in your hearts:
20 Knowing this first, that no prophecy of the scripture is of any private interpretation.
21 For the prophecy came not in old time by the will of man; but holy men of God spake as they were moved by the will of man: but holy men of God spake as they were moved by the Holy Ghost.

2 vs. 1
BUT there were false prophets also among the people, even as there shall be false teachers among you, who privily shall bring in damnable heresies, even denying the Lord that brought them, and bring upon themselves swift destruction.

In this popular scripture reference, the day star bears a subtle connection with the warning that follows as to the eternal nature of Christ's anointing*, and the occasion for heresy as a result of any exclusive right to Christ's sacred truth. The subtle reference to the angel Lucifer raises the suspicion of an implied connection between the eternal nature of Christ's anointing and the immortality of the angels is subtly being made. Christ himself clearly draws this conclusion in two separate Gospel references, when, at the time of the resurrection, mankind is said to take on the nature of the angels. (Luke 20 vs. 34, Matt 22 vs. 28)

With this possibility thus implied, and the barrier of death itself challenged by this revealing knowledge, the alarming truth is that one's corporeal existence is crossed over to a divine nature at the time of the resurrection. To this end, those who are chosen for this purpose will enjoy a spiritual reality not unlike the spiritual existence of the angels. Subject to this eternal nature, there will be those who awaken to everlasting life and those who awaken to shame and everlasting contempt. (Dan 12 vs. 2) Thus, crossing over the barrier of this understanding is like passing into the valley of decision whereby one's spiritual fate will be decided for all time according to this newly resurrected nature and the Lord's excellent judgment. Accordingly, Jesus is careful to teach his disciples that as far as their spiritual authority is concerned, they should not rejoice in the power they have over the enemy, rather, they should rejoice that their names are written in heaven.

Luke 10 vs. 17

And the seventy returned again with joy, saying, Lord, even the devils are subject unto us through thy name.

18 And he said unto them, I beheld Satan as lightening fall from heaven.

19 Behold, I give unto you power to tread on serpents and scorpions, and over all the power of the enemy: and nothing shall by any means hurt you:

20 Notwithstanding in this rejoice not, that the spirits are subject unto you; but rather rejoice because your names are written in heaven.

By this subtle remark, Jesus himself is suggesting that not even the angels, (Lucifer or Satan as an example) are given the ability to stand in the place of moral judgment deserving of God's favor. Moral excellence itself, is therefore, not enough to merit salvation, rather, applying the founding principles of Christ's death and resurrection is the only sure way to enjoy the Lord's salvation. By drawing this surprising comparison to Satan and his fall from heaven, it seems possible that Christ is revealing how that in light of death's barrier being crossed, Satan's decisive fall from heaven is an example that even Christ's own beloved disciples need guard against.

The Angels

The disciples likewise being ministers of the Gospel, bare a remarkable kinship to the angels who are themselves ministering spirits sent forth to minister to those who are set to be heirs of salvation. (Heb 1 vs. 14) In this way, the corporeal divide that separates these two worlds is narrower by margin then one would expect. Already noted for sharing a common bond in the symbolic reference of stars, the preaching of the gospel has long carried with it an angelic fascination similar to the fascination held by the men and women of God who preach the gospel. (1 Pet 1 vs. 12) These distinct similarities are overshadowed by mankind's natural tendency to be influenced by the world of spirits. With the exception of Christ's supernatural authority to which the authority over the world of spirits is rendered, mankind has long been overtaken by the whims of this spiritual influence.

The angelic ministry, on the other hand, from the standpoint of those angels that have remained faithful, are eager to submit themselves to God's authority in the process of receiving even one sinner to repentance. (Luke 15 vs. 10) This subservience proves that the ministry of Christ's son ship must contain the potential to be on an equal scale with this angelic ministry on at least on the basis of proportion. In all actuality, the saints are even graced with the God-given authority to judge the angels themselves. (1 Cor 6 vs. 3) From the perspective of the rogue elements of this angelic nature, the effort to oppose the outpouring of this authority follows a similar but opposite attraction.

Popular folklore surrounding Lucifer as an angelic personality suggests that Lucifer was among the most intelligent and the most beautiful angels in heaven. Lucifer's growing preoccupation with his self centered tendencies moved him to attempt to exalt his throne to the heights of God's throne.(4) Since the majority of angels did not recognize Lucifer's authority, as expected, Lucifer was cast out of heaven with little support.

Unlike the sensationalism of popular folklore, Bible references are often times more enigmatic. Satan and Lucifer, commonly linked with the anointed cherub from the book of Ezekiel is often identified with a slightly human connotation In several instances, as in the book of Job, when the sons of God endeavor to present themselves before God, Satan also is among them as if he is subverting at a similar, potentially human level. (Job 1 vs. 6) Likewise, the suggestion that Lucifer the anointed cherub would need to be ordained with God's anointing suggests the possibility of a previous existence in human form. (Ez 28 vs. 16) Perhaps the prophet Isaiah in a scripture that has already been examined in this treatise presents the most startling evidence that Lucifer bears some human connection. In this passage, Lucifer's existence in human form is undeniable, when, as a spectacle, Lucifer is recognized as a man that weakened the nations. Aside from this distinct possibility, the established link between the existence of angels and some formal affiliation with the lives of their human counterparts is a subject that will shortly be explored. The probability that Lucifer represents the existence of some well-known human being remains curiously high.

The following scripture shows the credibility of a sustained and interactive relationship of Lucifer among the rest of humanity in a reference that is suspiciously human in its designation.

Isaiah 14 vs. 12

How art thou fallen from heaven, O Lucifer, son of the morning! how art thou cut down to the ground, which didst weaken the nations!

13 For thou hast said in thine heart, I will ascend into heaven, I will exalt my throne above the stars of God: I will sit also upon the mount of the congregation, in the sides of the north:

14 I will ascend above the heights of the clouds; I will be like the most High.

15 Yet thou shalt be brought down to hell, to the sides of the pit.

16 They that see thee shall narrowly look upon thee, and consider thee, saying, Is this the man that made the earth to tremble, that did shake kingdoms;

17 That made the world as a wilderness, and destroyed the cities thereof; that opened not the house of her prisoners?

18 All the kings of the nations, even all of them, lie in glory, everyone in his own house.

19 But thou art cast out of thy grave like an abominable branch, and as the raiment of those that are slain, thrust through with a sword, that go down to the stones of the pit; as a carcass trodden under feet.

Despite the viable connection with a more tangible physical reality, the notion that Lucifer exudes traces of a purely spiritual existence is also evident. The dispersion of spiritual entities, primarily orchestrated by Lucifer's original rebellion against God seldom exemplifies any peaceable existence with the world of men. The mistaken appeal of what would otherwise be considered primarily as a human quality, Lucifer's reckless pride is most likely restricted to self-centered and self serving motivations. The potential trappings of occult practice and belief at times originating with a genuine spiritual interest in the otherworldly existence of angelic creatures, also bares a direct link to Lucifer's potential snare.

The Cosmology of Man

In spite of the moral chaos that reigned over early civilization, the predestined nature of Christ's calling was well at work even from the foundations of the world. In passing through the valley of decision, the predestined purposes of this calling, largely unknown to its recipients was slowly made manifest to the sons of men. From the standpoint of the all-knowing all-seeing omnipotent God of all creation, "a thousand years are like yesterday when it is past" that falls as easily as "a watch in the night." (Psalm 90 vs. 4) From this obvious supposition, the notion of a preplanned destiny detailed for those who answer Christ's calling is clearly expounded in scripture. Subject to this predestinated nature, the details of mankind's cosmological existence seem to be implied.

God reveals this as a necessary principle in consideration of the true nature of his word.

Isaiah 46 vs. 8

Remember this, and show yourselves men: bring it again to mind, O ye transgressors.

9 Remember the former things of old: for I am God and there is none else; I am God, and there is none like me.

10 Declaring the end from the beginning, and from ancient times the things that are not yet done, saying, My counsel shall stand, and I will do all my pleasure:

The linear nature of man's limited understanding is also quickly dispelled in light of God's predestinated purposes. The nature of God's living word and it's many applications is thus made apparent from the dawn of all created nature, to the apocalyptic times of the present day. Mysteries as to the original purposes of man's existence are dispersed throughout scripture's ancient writings. Within the revelation of this mystery, the notion that mankind's former primordial state was fastened to another plain of existence becomes increasingly apparent.

The basic tenet of belief, held by New Testament scholars includes the notion that those who received God's calling were also foreknown in the heavenly realm prior to their earthly existence. (Romans 8 vs. 29) Along with this divine ordinance, the extent of God's grace, by reason of faith, to justify one's gradual journey through life would provide a sense of peace and security on the pathway to the destination of one's heavenly abode. Even Jesus' relationship with his cherished disciples seems to provoke an otherworldly response in connection with the former estate of this heavenly realm when Christ promises "you yourselves shall bare witness, because you have been with me from the beginning."

The adoption of Christ's son-ship, extended to those who are chosen to fulfill this calling, were predestinated from the foundations of the world, passing through this world, quite unaware of their former estate. Scripture maintains this belief, without lending insight into the specific nature of this former reality, save from within the reality of Christ's own existence and his ability to transcend all time in a newly resurrected glory. The essential truth of the calling of the sons of God is that one's earthly existence is destined to come full circle with one's eternal nature, previously unknown to due to the limits of one's carnal flesh.

The promise of this predestinated nature and its theological virtue is fully expounded in Paul's letter to the Ephesians.

Ephesians 1 vs. 4

According as he hath chosen us in him before the foundation of the world, that we should be holy and without blame before him in love.

5 Having predestinated us unto the adoption of children by Jesus Christ to himself, according to the good pleasure of his will.

6 To the praise of the glory of his grace, wherein he hath made us accepted in the beloved

7 In whom we have redemption through his blood, the forgiveness of sins, according to the riches of his grace;

8 Wherein he hath abounded towards us in all wisdom and prudence.

The understanding that one is predestined to be made whole by this new heavenly nature is in effect the true inheritance of the saints on their journey back to this former glory. Since the created universe in its entirety is held together with Christ as a universal bond, a common origin with the heavenly nature of the angels is also likely. The testing ground of mankind's loyalty to God is made by one's pilgrimage through the valley of the shadow of death to which the choice to return to God's service is made certain when God's covenant and law are first received. By advancing in right moral standing before God as a result of following the instruction laid out in God's eternal word, mankind is gently restored to this former glory.

The War in Heaven

All knowledge pertaining to Lucifer's fall from grace may be linked to scriptures portrayal of an epic struggle in the heavens to which Lucifer is finally vanquished by Michael, the Archangel, and cast out of the heavenly realm. Though the exact details of this epic clash can be scarcely imagined, the classical image of a seething battle reaching it's final climax, despite it's cataclysmic implications, renders the true spiritual fabric of humanities' moral existence. This spiritual reality casts it's ancient shadow over the cradle of mankind's evolving interests. The primal beginning of humanity's original debut on the world stage was a testing ground for humanity's true loyalties to emerge. Being influenced by the spiritual remnant of Lucifer's insurgence, mankind was at once caught up in the carnal influence of these ancient spiritual forces. While many chose to ignore God's help, ill-equipped to compete with this spiritual influence, the earth became filled with the violence and blood-lust accounted for in mankind's early habitation. If not for the Lord's involvement in guiding mankind through these dark periods, humanity would likely have ceased to exist.

The true necessity of this testing is laid out in the events in the heavenly realm that originally set this worldly existence in motion. Collectively, the tendency towards rebellion grew as certain of God's angels turned in Lucifer's favor, leaving the undecided to dangerously flounder in the gulf of this primordial state. A third of these angels were swept away by Satan's insurgence and thrown down from the heavenly heights to take their place on earth. To give place to these spiritually undecided the possibility that this indecision is somehow reflected in the core of mankind's ancient existence seems entirely possible. The remainder of this chapter will deal with the distinct possibility that this testing ground exists in the lives of ordinary human beings for the rejoining of this heavenly abode.

These events surrounding this dramatic fall are first recorded with the arrival of the great red dragon who bears a resemblance to the dreaded creature leviathan described earlier as emerging from the primordial waters of humanity. In a similar representation the creature with seven heads, ten horns and seven crowns upon his head is a likely symbolic representation of civilizations unbridled progression into the recourse of a self centered, economically driven society, plummeting out of control as a result of this self centered existence. In the dispensation of time this colossal creature, known only as the great red dragon draws a third of the stars of heaven and casts them to earth. The third of these stars are joined with the image of a women clothed with the sun that is in the process of giving birth. The presence of these earthbound stars is presumably represented in the birth of a male child who is destined to rule all nations with a rod of iron and is caught up to the throne of God, a likely representation of the Lord's Christ and his mission to redeem mankind.

The following is scriptures brief account of this epic struggle that supports the existence of a holy third derived from the stars of heaven and poised to rejoin their angelic counterparts in the heavenly realm.

Revelations 12 vs. 1

AND there appeared a great wonder in heaven; a woman clothed with the sun, and the moon under her feet, and upon her head a crown of twelve stars;

2 And she being with child cried, travailing in birth, and pained to be delivered.

3 And there appeared another wonder in heaven; and behold a great red dragon, having seven heads and ten horns, and seven crowns upon his heads.

4 And his tail drew the third of the stars of heaven, and did cast them to earth: and the dragon stood before the woman which was ready to be delivered, for to devour her child as soon as it was born.

5 And she brought forth a man-child, who was to rule all nations with a rod of iron: and her child was caught up unto God and his throne.

When the salvation of the world is first introduced in the Lord's Christ, represented in the man child who is destined to rule all nations with a rod of iron, with diabolical intentions of the great red dragon there to devour the child, the earth is suddenly faced with the presence of Christ's ancient foe. Scripture goes on to describe the precursor to these events, posing a slight challenge to the reader chronologically. With the saving presence of Christ formally introduced in the dawn of all creation, Christ's archrival and nemesis, Satan or Lucifer, the true enemy of corporeal nature is also cast down. Thus, the saving power of Christ's true dominion is fully engaged for the willing of the world's inhabitants in order to overcome this primal force of evil.

Revelations 12 vs. 7

And there was war in heaven: Michael and his angels fought against the dragon; and the dragon fought and his angels'

8 And prevailed not; neither was their place found any more in heaven.
9 And the great dragon was cast out, that old serpent, called the Devil, and Satan, which deceiveth the whole earth, and his angels were cast out with him.
10 And I heard a loud voice saying in heaven, Now is come salvation, and strength, and the kingdom of our God, and the power of our Christ: for the accuser of our brethren is cast down, which accused them before our God day and night.
11 And they overcame him by the blood of the Lamb, and by the word of their testimony; and they loved not their lives unto the death.

The end of the spiritual war in the heavenly realm meets the Lord's saints with a similar struggle waged on several fronts. According to historical accounts, the church throughout the ages has been faced with an ongoing spiritual warfare, which included the clash of ideologies, which were in clear violation of Christ's true faith. Within this primal struggle, the saving sacrifice of Jesus Christ's death on the cross, the saints were encouraged that they would finally emerge victorious against Satan's dark forces.

Satan eventually sends out reinforcements in the form of his own loyal followers, who take their place in the flood of humanity, who by the inherent properties of man's sinful nature attempts to carry away the woman who symbolizes the bride of Christ's virtue and his Holy church. Accordingly, scripture speaks of those individuals who were long ago marked out for condemnation and the waves of the sea who are likened to wandering stars to whom is reserved the blackness of darkness forever. (Jude 1 vs. 4-12) These same individuals are the likely candidates who made it their purpose to infiltrate the early church in order to reclaim Satan's grasp over the popular religions of the world.

Revelations 12 vs. 15

And the serpent cast out of his mouth water as a flood after the woman, that he might cause her to be carried away of the flood.

16 And the earth helped the woman, and the earth opened her mouth, and swallowed up the flood, which the dragon cast out of his mouth.
17 And the dragon was wroth with the woman, and went to make war with the remnant of her seed, which keep the commandments of God, and have the testimony of Jesus Christ.

On a spiritual front, the metaphysical hypothesis was put foreword by a distinguished church leader known as Origen of Alexandria, that suggests one possible theory surrounding the gradual demise of these fallen angels.(5) This theory entails how Lucifer's retreat into the lower region's of hell was due in part to Satan's natural aversion to aura of the Lord's divine light, whereby the minion's of the devil fell to the plain of human existence and even further into the depths of Hades itself. This theory, however, is also careful not to negate the Lord's ability to reach these rebellious demons in flight once they have declined into human form, regardless of their fallen disposition.(6)

The fallen stars of heaven that constitute a holy third that languished as a result of the whip of the dragon's tail supports the principle belief that those who are chosen by God are merely sojourning in this existing world as pilgrims on a ancient pathway back to an otherworldly realm. For those who desire to serve God, the pathway of Christ's teachings pave the way for a celestial return to this heavenly home. This journey also establishes the rewards of living a life of devoted service to God in reaching out to those in need by works of charity, as well as ministering the truth of the gospel to those who are without hope.

Angelic Worship

In order to imagine the celestial heights of the Lord's angelic hierarchy, one might likewise consider the widespread belief that this integration is determined by the proximity or remoteness to the throne of God's grace. Scripture describes how Paul had known a man in Christ who was caught up to paradise, otherwise known as the third heaven. Concurrently, Dionysius, who converted to Christianity under Paul's ministry, became an accepted authority on this angelic hierarchy, to which nine orders of angels ascend in rank in the progression of three heavenly choirs of angelic worship.(7) (Acts 17 vs. 34). The Seraphim the uppermost section of this hierarchy, was credited as the pinnacle of divine worship before God.

From the pinnacle of these majestic heights the Seraphim were known to take flight spanning the presence of God's glory while glimpsing into the countless attributes of his wisdom and goodness. In a rare glimpse into this heavenly realm the prophet Isaiah scopes out the nebulous qualities of the Lord's glorious throne room as the seraphim, each having six wings, would fly crying "holy, holy, holy, is the lord of hosts; the whole earth is full of his glory." (Is 6 vs. 1) These images provided in this divinely inspired vision exemplify the purest form of spiritual worship that any eyewitness account can render.

As the most fundamental and original form of all spirituality, worship provides an indelible connection with the spiritual fabric of all created nature. The spiritual domain accounts for an undisclosed portion of the known universe. This innate and intrinsic aspect of creation and the tendency to worship is the undisputed center of the Judeo-Christian formula. As Christ himself is careful to point out God, himself is spirit "and those who seek to worship him must do so in spirit and in truth." (John 4 vs. 23) The altruistic desire of God's perfect will is that mankind will ascend to the freedom of expression that such spiritual worship can provide; "For the father seeketh such to worship him." (John 4 vs. 23) In the journey towards taking one's place in the benefit of this worship a variety of obstacles must be avoided. The deluding nature of self unleashes the obvious pitfalls on the road to acquiring this freedom.

On the journey to this place of complete spiritual freedom and serenity involved in worshipping the one true God of all existence, mankind has frequently encountered outstanding issues that commonly distracted devotees from reaching their full potential in the area of this worship. In accordance with this innate spiritual need, since the beginning of mankind's development individuals have resorted to worshipping countless forms of idols and stumbled upon innumerable theories that allegedly connect mankind to the source of one's divine spark. From this standpoint the prophets warn that only by a conscious resolve and focus can a person hope to ascend to the reality of true intimacy with God. As Samuel the prophet warns…"do not turn aside, for then you would go after vain things which can not profit or deliver for they are nothing." (1 Sam 12 vs. 21)

Concerning this moral perversion, none is more central to the armies of darkness than the worship of angels. Based on the obscure glimpses into the cataclysmic occurrences hinted at in the book of Revelations, the seeds of this potential snare are rooted in considerable truth. Lucifer traditionally ascribed to heaven's highest order of angelic host, the Seraphim, exerted an effort to invoke the autonomous nature of creation's existence to be swept up in the deception of his rebellion. Infamous as the Lord's fallen worship leader Lucifer capitalizes on an individual's fundamental need to worship and praise the creator but motivates the devotee to pervert this worship towards one's selfish desires.

On a more fundamental basis, the underlying deception of all idol worship is the tendency to exalt self. Since the reality remains that there is only one true creator and Lord over all, the basic premise of all idol worship is to worship and serve the creature more than the creator. (Ro 1 vs. 25) Since all of creation bears a similar existence the potential snare of all idol worship is to appeal to the sense of self one encounter in varying degrees. Historically, mortal man has been elevated to divine status on a variety of occasions in early Egyptian and Roman civilizations, as well as in the oriental cultures of the Far East. Through this form of exploitation it is easy to delude oneself into enacting self-serving and self-promoting principles of belief rather than including those moral precepts that knowingly belong to God's true goodness and justice.

John's Ascending Vision

During the course of this treatise the ancient source of the deep symbols of Revelations has been explored along with the timeless significance related to Old and New Testament scripture. In view of humanity's progression into the spiritual realm, and Christ's potential to elevate the status of mankind into the glory of a new heavenly nature, the apostle John continues to ascend into the heights of his heavenly vision. Despite the many relevant layers of meaning derived out of this source of scripture, for those who care to identify the cosmological forces at work. Revelations seems to consistently draw on an underlying theme of self-discovery in light of the divine origins of mankind's existence. Many such images have already been referred to in this context like the many waters of primordial existence and the epic war in heaven to which Satan, the great dragon drew a third of the stars of heaven and cast them to earth and the rebellious Seraph known as Lucifer who was defeated by Michael the archangel and cast out of heaven.

Likewise, those symbols of God's compassionate care and attention, like the crystal sea flowing from God's throne which supplied the tree of life, bringing forth twelve manner of fruit and the leaves supplied for the healing of the nations, is also expounded with notable consistency to ancient prophecy. Through out the vivid imagery of Revelations the sense of mankind's pilgrimage, with assistance from the divine hand of God is slowly nearing it's completed route.

As John nears the conclusion of his vision, while paying his final respects to his angelic host, an epiphany of mankind's cosmological origin seems to be divulged in the angel's final exhortation. Mysteriously, the angel himself suggests a kinship or brotherhood that exists among his fellow prophets, a notion that underscores the common bond served out in these two created natures.

Revelations 22 vs. 6

And he said unto me, these sayings are faithful and true: and the Lord God of the holy prophets sent his angel to show unto his servants the things which must shortly be done.

7 Behold, I come quickly: blessed is he that keepeth the prophecy of this book.

8 And I John saw these things, and heard them. And when I had heard and seen, I fell down to worship before the feet of the angel which showed me these things.

9 Then saith he unto me, See thou do it not: for I am thy fellow servant, and of thy brethren the prophets, and of them which keep the sayings of this book.

10 And he saith unto me, Seal not the sayings of the prophecy of this book for the time is at hand.

11 He that is unjust, let him be unjust still; and he which is filthy, let him be filthy still: and he that is righteous, let him be righteous still; and he that is holy, let him be holy still.

In the last chapter of this treatise, in order to dispel the myths of satanic propaganda, certain fallacies will be identified for their potential to dissuade believers from following after the teachings that accord with godliness that were given to the saints by our Lord and Christ Jesus. The final efforts of Satan's intention to delude and mislead mankind into the snare of the fowler will be exposed so that Christ's ministry and return may be easily entreated for those who fall under this final preparation.

XII
The Lies of the Enemy

From the standpoint of modern Christianity, Satan has long been known as the father of all lies. In the context of this treatise, to the extent that this master deceiver has already infiltrated Holy Scripture, due vigilance is needed in reevaluating the time-honored acceptance of Solomon's contributions to scripture. It has already been examined how one book of the Bible, namely The Song of Solomon, effectively shaped the practice of idolatry throughout the ancient world. The ability for such licentiousness to infiltrate the accepted scriptures of the Bible validates one's inquiry into of the existence of still other myths that have infiltrated the Judeo- Christian tradition under these auspices.

The final chapter of this treatise will deal at length with dispelling the many myths made popular by these teachings, and how one may take a stand against these illusions in order to out step the enemy's long history of desensitizing and entrapping the world's population. The possibility that Solomon's wisdom has long been a safe haven for the more undecided souls of this spiritual following, and that men and women of God from both the Old and New Testament have warned of the potential entrapment behind these vain philosophies, is a disconcerting fact that has long gone unheeded.

Solomon's Philosophy

From the long and proud history of a people devoted to an all-knowing omnipotent God, Solomon's philosophy and subsequent wisdom is clearly out of step with the theological precepts that have preceded him. Especially in the book of Ecclesiastes, taking a largely existential view, Solomon is not only hedonistic, but also comes across with principally agnostic beliefs, dispelling the spiritual rewards of obedience that come from the just and merciful God of his ancestors. In the book of Ecclesiastes there is no talk of the existence of Christ's heavenly kingdom spoken of in the New Testament, nor is there the slightest notion of the lasting dominion of God's throne proclaimed in the Psalms by Solomon's father King David. (Psalm 145 vs. 13) All one is left with is the hollow sense that the good that one endeavors to do in this life is vain and pointless. Though some would take great exception to this belief, in a society currently attempting to overcome the ego of self, the impermanence of one's actions can be refreshing as well as liberating. This attitude has lead Solomon's teachings to be embraced by the majority of the known civilized world.

While the general tone of apathy evident in Ecclesiastes often goes overlooked, society has mistakenly adopted the view that to devalue self is to overcome the trappings of a self centered existence. The fallacy that the nonexistence of divine intervention will somehow render one's actions unselfish as a result of this pointless philosophy is the popular deception that has taken the entire world by storm. The tolerance of these beliefs has paved the way for the influence of still other worldly religions that continually ignore the existence of the spiritual domain of God's supreme justice.

The legacy of this existential* belief is a growing apathy, indifference, cynicism, and the notion of an autonomous self that modern civilization has come to adopt. Solomon's rendering of a vain and meaningless world is so ingrained into western culture that the belief in one's insignificance is seldom challenged. To the contrary, as will be further explored in this final chapter, there is nothing vain or meaningless about this existence, rather, the open prospect of eternal life and a restored intimacy with God the father of all creation is a noble pursuit in and of itself. Finally, to the opposite intent, this final chapter will prove that Christ himself would rather impart the discovery of one's invested role in the true spiritual value of God's everlasting kingdom.

Vanity of Vanities

From the tradition of the early Christian Church a warning of the potential to be spoiled through philosophy and vain deceit, after the tradition of men after the rudiments of the world, and not after Christ is an area of lasting concern. (Col 2 vs. 8) Although Solomon's exhortation begins by making the relevant claim that striving after worldly accomplishments is indeed a vain prospect, his exhortation does very little to differentiate the wicked from the righteous, a separation that is a firm reality in Christ's teachings. (Matt 25 vs. 23) Despite the fact that Solomon does recognize divine judgment as an inevitable reality (Ecc 12 vs. 14) his thoughts are also preoccupied with the notion that the righteous and the wicked are ultimately headed towards the same underlying fate. (Eccl 9 vs. 1-3)

Throughout scripture, vanity or even the allusion of vanity is described as a would-be snare of the enemy that should be avoided at any cost. From the standpoint of the apostle Peter, the principle custodian of the revelation of Christ's divine nature, Peter's description of these swelling words of vanity and by those who allure through the lusts of the flesh, through much wantonness seem to be tailored to Solomon's particular surmising in both The Song of Solomon and Ecclesiastes. As Peter is so careful to point out, since such so called teachers have clearly been given over to serve in corruption, a special eye of discernment is required in identifying this potential snare.

2 Peter 2 vs. 17

These are wells without water, clouds that are carried with a tempest; to whom the mist of darkness is reserved forever.

18 For when they speak great swelling words of vanity, they allure through the lusts of the flesh, through much wantonness, those that were clean escaped from them who live in error.

19 While they promise them liberty, they themselves are the servants of corruption: of whom a man is overcome, of the same is he brought in bondage.

The basic truth that Solomon is clearly brought into bondage by those things to which he is overcome is immediately made apparent in the beginning chapters of Ecclesiastes. Solomon's preoccupation with worldly wealth, although described as vain and unprofitable, is an example of the limited reality that Solomon is normally accustomed to. To the extent that Solomon's focus remains fixed on his own personal gain as an example of the very real trappings of secular society, Solomon seems quite sincere. As this platitude continues, however, for one who is considered endowed with special wisdom, the solution to this trapping is strangely omitted. Though the reader is enjoined with expectancy that the subject of divine justice will eventually be introduced in order to divulge some form of spiritual or moral lesson, this possibility remains absent to the last. There is no indication of how by being tortured for the sake of righteousness one might obtain a better resurrection, (Heb 11 vs. 35) or how one may choose to store up one's riches in heaven. (Matt 6 vs. 20) The absence of this due course suggests that Solomon chooses to focus solely on the personal direction of his own worldly wealth and pleasure.

Ecclesiastes 2 vs. 4

I made me great works; I builded me houses; I planted me vineyards;

5 I made me gardens and orchards, and I planted trees in them of all kinds of fruits;

6 I made me pools of water, to water therewith the wood that bringeth forth trees;

7 I got me servants and maidens, and had servants born in my house; also I had great possessions of great and small cattle above all that were in Jerusalem before me:

8 I gathered me also silver and gold, and the peculiar treasure of kings and of the provinces: I gat me men singers and women singers, and delights of the sons of men, as musical instruments, and that of all sorts.

9 So I was great, and increased more than all that were before me in Jerusalem: also my wisdom remained with me.

10 And whatsoever mine eyes desired I kept not from them, I withheld not my heart from any joy; for my heart rejoiced in all my labor: and this was my portion of all my labor.

11 Then I looked on all the works that my hands had wrought, and on the labor that I had labored to do: and behold, all was vanity and vexation of spirit, and there was no profit under the sun.

The worldly exploits of Solomon's brief political career, along with the vain resolve of these motivations is examined elsewhere in scripture without the drawn out commentary of Solomon's pretended search for meaning. Scripture's more ancient tradition reveals how vanity is the token proof that the house of Israel is in already in danger of backsliding into the empty promises of the world's more superficial existence. To the same extent the

Bible warns against he who is deceived that knowingly trust in vanity for vanity will be his recompense. (Job 15 vs. 31) In this fallen state, as Holy scripture points out, such individuals are incapable of impacting the world for either good or evil. The individuals who follow in this pathway are said to be in danger of being swept up into a spiritual vacuum where the entrapment of one's more brutish nature is poised to gain the upper hand.

Jeremiah 10 vs. 1
HEAR ye the word which the Lord speaketh unto you, O house of Israel:
3 For the customs of the people are vain: for one cutteth a tree out of the forrest, the work of the hands of the workman, with the axe.
4 They deck it with silver and with gold; they fasten it with nails and with hammers, that it move not.
5 They are upright as the palm tree, but speak not: they must needs be borne, because they can not go. Be not afraid of them; for they cannot do evil, neither also is it in them to do good.
7 Who would not fear thee, O King of nations? For to thee doth it appertain: for as much as among all the wise men of the nations, and in their kingdoms, there is none like unto thee.
8 But they are altogether brutish and foolish: the stock is a doctrine of vanities.
9 Silver spread into plates is brought from Tarshish, and gold from Upaz, the work of the workman, and the hands of the founder: blue and purple is their clothing: they are the work of cunning men.

Christ's preaching and teaching of the kingdom of God is quite opposite to this philosophy. Where Solomon's opinion suggests that one's great wealth and influence in the world is vain, Christ teaches that even the smallest act of obedience can have a lasting spiritual impact. To this extent Jesus speaks of a widow woman who gave two pennies as an offering. In doing so Christ assured that this women gave more than anyone else in the congregation, since in giving two pennies, she gave all the money she had. (Luke 21 vs. 1-4) This same consideration is given to the attitude behind one's actions in obeying God's moral laws in so far as those who break one of the least of God's commandments and teach others to do the same will be called least in the kingdom of God. (Matt 5 vs. 19) Thus, a clear opposition between the teachings of Christ's and the teachings of Solomon is startlingly apparent.

Popular Myths

The specific fallacies surrounding Solomon's wisdom clearly begin to show a contradicting nature in light of these newly discovered insights. Since the ability of Solomon's wisdom is a God given trait, the existence of such wisdom should not be disclaimed. (1 Ki 3 vs. 9) The nature of a lie, however, is based on the fact that essential untruths are intermingled with other facts in order to intentionally mislead the public interest. From this standpoint the existence of certain popular myths arise that are bent on weakening the resolve of God's true devotees.

"Eat drink and be merry..."

At the discovery of this vain existence, Solomon eventually shifts to the fatalistic mentality displayed in The Song of Solomon. Simply put, Solomon arrives at the logical conclusion that since one's life is so 'vain', one has nothing better to do than to enjoy the simple pleasures of life, such as: eating, drinking, and making merry. This conclusion places Solomon at the brunt of the Lord's rebuke in the saying, "let us eat drink and be merry for tomorrow we may die," (Is 22 vs. 13) which probably stemmed from an expression coined from one of the sayings from the book of Ecclesiastes. This common adage, consistent with Solomon's juvenile mentality profiled in the initial chapters of this treatise, adequately summarizes Ecclesiastes' philosophical content. The Lord quickly dismisses this mentality as an offence of iniquity that 'shall not be purged' away except by death itself. (Is 22 vs. 14)

The following passage from the book of Ecclesiastes entails this mentality adopted by Solomon as an expression of this fatalistic attitude.

Ecclesiastes 2 vs. 24

There is nothing better for a man than that he should eat and drink, and that he should make his soul enjoy good in his labor. This also I saw, that it was from the hand of God.

25 For who can eat, or who else can hasten hereunto more than I?

26 For God giveth to a man that is good in his sight wisdom and knowledge, and joy: but to the sinner he giveth travail, to gather and heap up, that he may give to him that is good before God. This also is vanity and vexation of spirit.

Regarding the practice of these natural freedoms no one would dispute the logic of one's earned ability to enjoy the fruits of one's labor. Those individuals, on the other hand, who find they are forgoing this liberty so that others may share in the same freedom, deserve the greater praise and recognition. For one so wise, Solomon's wisdom, thus far, fails to penetrate the superficial layer of selfish existence and seems content with appealing to the more selfish motivations of life. The vanity pertaining to all earthly motives seems to be the subject matter that continually dominates Solomon's speech.

To the contrary, this life should be viewed as merely a preparation for Christ's heavenly abode. The true joy of living is based on one's investment into the works of charity that secure a heavenly reward on the way to the common good of mankind. In order for one to exceed the limitations of self and reach out to the lost with an extension of the common remedy of grace, a conditioned awareness of the existence of one's predestined salvation must be maintained. (Matt 7 vs. 2) The apostle Paul goes so far to suggest that others should be esteemed better than oneself and that a man should not look merely on his own interests but on the interests of others also. (1)

"One event unto all"

Perhaps the best example of Solomon's self centered philosophy is gathered in the conclusion that the wicked and the righteous share in the same fate. The reality that the wicked and the righteous are both joined to the inevitability of death seems to be mentioned in order to equate the moral degrees of good and evil on an equal standing. This equality in death, even the subject of death itself, is rarely a popular topic in scripture except in identifying the transition from death, to the eternal life of the resurrection. Solomon's decision to emphasize the grave in order to illustrate this equal standing merely serves to reinforce the mind of death that so often keeps it's subjects in bondage. (Heb 2 vs. 15) Death as an equalizer, in this context, does nothing to inspire the righteous living that the Lord requires. Instead, by classifying these two types of lifestyles together, Solomon is dangerously close to accepting the natures of both good and evil on the same standing and without discrimination.

Ecclesiastes 9 vs. 1

FOR all this I considered in my heart even to declare all this, that the righteous, and the wise, and their works, are in the hand of God: no man knoweth either love or hatred by all that is before them.

2 All things come alike to all: there is one event to the righteous, and to the wicked; to the good and to the clean, and to the unclean; to him that sacrificeth, and to him that sacriceth not: as is the good, so is the sinner; and he that sweareth, as he that feareth an oath.

3 This is the evil among all things that are done under the sun, that there is one event unto all: yea, also the heart of the sons of men is full of evil, and madness is in the their heart while they live, and after that they go to the dead.

Solomon's pessimistic portrayal of the human condition probably includes traces of his own personal failings, to which he holds out little hope for redemption. Nevertheless, by placing good and evil on the same standing, Solomon is feeding into an indifference that is increasingly apparent among the world's population. As the love of many waxes cold the Lord's chief complaint with mankind's response is the growing indifference that fails to live up to the ideal of living a life in healthy moral standing before God and the church. Despite the obvious existence of this moral hypocrisy, the Lord encourages his true followers into attempting to live life as perfectly as possible. If this beacon of moral perfection remains visible, the promise of successfully navigating the trappings of this moral ambivalence seems far more likely.

The following scripture warns of such a trap, and recommends that the discernment between what is good and what is evil should upheld at any cost.

Isaiah 5 vs. 20

Woe unto them that call evil good, and good evil, that put darkness for light, and light for darkness; that put bitter for sweet, and sweet for bitter!

21 Woe unto them that are wise in their own eyes, and prudent in their own sight!

22 Woe unto them that are mighty to drink wine, and men of strength to mingle strong drink

23 Which justify the wicked for reward, and take away the righteousness of the righteous from him!

24 Therefore as the fire devoureth the stubble, and the flame consumeth the chaff, so their root shall be as rottenness, and their blossom shall go up as dust: because they have cast away the law of the Lord of hosts, and despised the word of the Holy one of Israel.

The absence of any notion of eternal punishment or reward exhibited in Solomon's writing is a strong indicator that Solomon did not personally endorse the belief in an after-life. According to the historical evidence formerly reviewed in this treatise, Solomon's disregard surrounding the belief in this divine existence was also shared by Zadok, Solomon's appointed high priest. (1 Ki 2 vs. 35) This essential belief was consistently passed over, due to the Sadducees central control over the mainstream Temple whose religious leadership can be traced up until the time of Christ. (2) Though the various motives pertaining to the rejection of a coming resurrection is thoroughly dealt with in the third chapter of this treatise, the likelihood that Solomon's indifference is largely based on the rejection of this divine promise sheds further light into Solomon's apparent moral apathy.

In the verses that follow, Solomon's convictions are clearly expressed as he states how the dead know not anything and that neither have they a reward. This is perhaps the most obvious contradiction to Christ's teachings, whereby Solomon's ploy to discredit Christ's heavenly kingdom is clearly at work. Solomon's existential* view, in full contradiction of the concept of an existing after-life is in gross opposition with Christ's most fundamental teachings that state that one's reward will be great in heaven when one chooses to suffer for the cause of righteousness. (Matt 5 vs. 12) Despite Solomon's recognition of a coming judgment, believers are left flat by the contradicting nature of these beliefs that clearly act as a disclaimer against any eternal form of judgment whereby the dead know not anything and the memory of them is forgotten.

Ecclesiastes 9 vs. 4

For to him that is joined to all the living there is hope: for a living dog is better than a dead lion.

5 For the living know that they shall die: but the dead know not anything, neither have they any more reward; for the memory of them is forgotten.

6 Also their love, and their hatred, and envy, is now perished; neither have they anymore a portion for ever in any thing that is done under the sun.

10 Whatsoever thy hand findeth to do, do it with thy might; for there is no work, nor device, nor knowledge, nor wisdom in the grave whither thou goest.

In the face of this untruth to stay the course of the preaching and the teaching of the kingdom of God is the essential remedy to this myth. One may recall how during the time of Christ's ministry a would-be disciple who was invited to be a follower said in reply, "Lord, suffer me first to go and bury my father." To which the Lord replied, "Let the dead bury their own dead: but go thou and preach the kingdom of God. (Luke 9 vs. 60) In short, nothing should prevent the spiritual truths of the gospel from being preached. The existence of a place of eternal condemnation and eternal reward at the right hand of the Lord's presence, as always, is a realized theological fact.

"In much wisdom there is much grief"

One of Solomon's most resourceful myths is aimed at protecting his true identity, and keeping his subjects in ignorance. The craft of this popular myth is accomplished in Solomon's saying that "in much wisdom there is much grief," and that "he who increaseth knowledge increaseth sorrow."(Ecc 1 vs. 18) From the standpoint of the early church this fallacy is quickly dispelled. The apostle Paul insists that one should study to show thyself approved unto God. (2 Tim 2 vs. 15) Elsewhere in scripture it becomes known that imperative to search the scriptures since God is the rewarded of them that diligently seek him (Heb 11 vs. 6) a search, which is likely meant to include an ongoing study of the Bible's inspired writings.

James the brother of Jesus attests to his knowledge of two types of wisdom, the altruistic wisdom that is from above, and to contrast, the wisdom that is bent towards worldly lusts and desires.

James 3 vs. 13

Who is a wise man and endued with knowledge among you? Let him show out of a good conversation his works with meekness of wisdom.

14 But if ye have bitter envying and strife in your hearts, glory not, and lie against the truth.

15 This wisdom descendeth not from above, but is earthly, sensual, devilish.

16 For where envying and strife is, there is confusion and every evil work.

17 But the wisdom that is from above is first pure then peaceable, gentle, and easy to be entreated, full of mercy and good fruits, without partiality, and without hypocrisy.

18 And the fruit of righteousness is sown in peace of them that make peace.

Clearly, therefore, the type of wisdom Solomon refers to must involve the wisdom of a more sensual quality, since the wisdom that is from above can only produce the fruits of righteousness in keeping with the joy in the spirit that comes from God alone. As for other schools of universal learning, it seems unlikely that the equitable sum of this knowledge would in some way be responsible for depressing the world's population. To the contrary, most knowledge has some practical use that defies an emotional response; save in the way the virtue of such knowledge is handled. Audaciously, Solomon does not concede to these facts, rather he ends off his ecclesiastical work by admonishing his audience of readers how that of making many books there is no end and how much study is a weariness of the flesh. (Ecc 12 vs. 12)

In reply to this obvious myth one should not back down from one's pursuit of the knowledge of Christ and his unending wisdom. King David himself explains how one may delight in the law of the Lord and meditate on it day and night. (Psalms 1 vs. 2) Lifelong learning in the study of scriptures, including both self directed studies and those conducted in a group is a practice that aught to be encouraged among all God-fearing devotees. The myth that a cap can somehow be imposed on the revelation of God's wisdom is a latent form of blasphemy that is clearly dispelled in the revelation of God's truth. Christ's anointing and wisdom is an inexhaustible spiritual resource, which is to be examined over the course of one's lifetime so that sound doctrine may be endured. (2 Tim 4 vs. 3)

"Be not overly righteous"

This particular myth may have been a useful tool for propaganda in the face of Solomon gradual turn towards idolatrous practices. When his more outspoken subjects like Asaph, the Levitical priest and temple gatekeeper were effectively challenging Solomon's values, the push for censorship and control of his subjects would have been fully endorsed by this myth. In a saying of this sort, images of bribery and debauchery are brought to mind to the estranged notion that one's efforts towards righteousness may somehow be curbed. With the prospect of evolving corruption this particular saying takes on new meaning, as Solomon says, "Be not overly righteous; neither make thyself over wise: why shouldest thou destroy thyself?" (Eccl 7 vs. 16) Living a life after Christ's wholesome principles involves the abandonment of all selfish ambitions on the part of the believer. Though the righteousness required to approach a right standing before God only comes by the sanctification of Christ's redeeming blood, Jesus clearly admonishes his disciples to be perfect. In this statement the obvious intention is to enlighten all true devotees to live a life open to the limitless potential of God's goodness. Saints throughout the ages have pushed the bounds of this ideal by a love that remains subject to the spirit of Christ's compassion and charity. In the following statement, Solomon's imposed limit on one's righteousness as though one could be overly righteous (above) takes a back seat to Christ's inspiring words regarding mankind's true spiritual potential.

Matthew 5 vs. 44

But I say unto you, Love your enemies, bless them that curse you, do good to them that hate you, and pray for them which despitefully use you and persecute you;

45 That ye may be the children of your Father which is in heaven: for he maketh his sun to rise on the evil and on the good, and sendeth rain on the just and on the unjust.

46 For if ye love them which love you, what reward have ye? Do not even the publicans the same?

47 And if ye salute your brethren only what do ye more than others? Do not even the publicans so?

48 Be ye therefore perfect, even as your father which is in heaven is perfect.

For many, the hope and pleasure of being affiliated with God's good purposes has pointed in the direction of extreme torture, persecution and even death. For these select individuals the fear of Solomon's so-called destruction as the result of being overly righteous is fleeting in comparison to the nature of Christ's virtuous life. For Christ's disciples the surmountable prospects of attaining to this right standing came into question. "Who then can be saved?" the disciples asked. To this question Jesus solemnly replies, "With men this is impossible; but with God all things are possible." (Matt 19 vs. 26) Regarding fear as an emotional response Jesus says, "Fear not them which kill the body, but are not able to kill the soul: but rather fear him which is able to destroy both soul and body in hell." (Matt 10 vs. 28) In this, Solomon's myth of being overly righteous is clearly dispelled.

Those who, despite the best encouragement, do not find themselves aspiring to the saintly heights of this moral perfection have the protection of God's grace and mercy. Even on the occasion of sin, Jesus himself acts as an advocate on one's behalf according to the virtue of his blood sacrifice on the cross. In the grand scheme of our moral standing before God, the deposition of an intense courtroom drama, with Christ holding to his role as advocate and Satan standing in the place of the accuser appropriately comes to mind.

"Godliness is gain"

The perversion of certain types of wisdom would have the potential to dampen one's spirit if they were followed after in ignorance. The bulk of prosperity teachings that exist fit into this category, are already in the vein of Solomon's self-centered preoccupation with wealth and success. The likelihood that Solomon was caught up in such a teaching due to the attraction of the more primitive self-centered beliefs of early Mesopotamia has already been explored in the fourth chapter of this treatise. Solomon's continued references to wealth and prosperity, although never actually equated with the conceit of a self-professed superior nature, perpetuates the carnal mindset that stems exclusively from worldly principles. While little is spoken to declare the rich as coming from a superior vantage point, one only needs to look at Solomon's usual stereotype as the wealthy and wise philanthropist that society so often aspires to.

One's acquired wealth is not an issue surrounding this particular myth. The fundamental deception that causes difficulty is in the belief that godliness and monetary gain increase proportionately. An encounter with this teaching provides an experience of deep insult and humiliation, since the good of one's existence may be mistakenly measured by the size of one's bank account and by the affluence of one's reputation. This popular myth stifles would-be converts who bear a natural aversion to this humiliating venture, and perpetuates a contentious rivalry in one's bid to achieve measurable success.

Without any mention of the spiritual principles of Christ's true kingdom, including the doctrine that accord's with godliness, which was most likely in keeping with the same divine principles, the edifying nature of Christ's love and commitment would be seriously dampened in the lives of believers. Fortunately the early church in light of Christ's superior goodness quickly debunked the myth of godliness existing hand and hand with monetary gain.

1 Timothy 6 vs. 3

If any man teach otherwise, and consent not to wholesome words, even the words of our Lord Jesus Christ, and to the doctrine, which is according to godliness;

4 He is proud, knowing nothing, but doting about questions and strifes of words, where of cometh envy, strife, railings, evil surmisings.
5 Perverse disputings of men of corrupt minds, and destitute of the truth, supposing that gain is godliness: from such withdraw thyself.
6 But godliness with contentment is great gain.

The high ideal of contentment successfully sweeps away the ego-ridden mentality of worldly success. The quaint attraction of being innately human and unexposed to the usual pretense involved in the pursuit of this wealth must have taken an obvious president with in the hearts and minds of early believers. The apostle Paul explains how the nature of salvation is not based on one's accomplishments lest any man should boast (Eph 2 vs. 9) rather it is based on the virtue of an indestructible life to which the faithful are akin. The natural as well as the supernatural bond that reaches through to the heart of humanity as a result of this contentment holds the only true potential to place mankind on an equal plateau of spiritual awakening.

Solomon's Authorship

King Solomon, despite his questionable moral character, has had an undisputable association with wisdom down through the ages. According to historical sources, various forms of writing including Ecclesiastes, Proverbs, and The Song of Solomon may be attributed to Solomon's authorship, while still others fall under the guise of the Apocrypha, and the Pseudepigrapha, under what is known as false authorship. An influential body of knowledge of up to eight specific texts originating out of the Judeo-Christian tradition,(3) including the writings of the Jewish historian, Eupolemus, who preserved letters exchanged between Solomon and the King of Egypt and Tyre, survives to this day.(4) Still other cultures in the tradition of modern witchcraft and Freemasonry, with books like *The Key of King Solomon*, attempt to authenticate legitimate ties to king Solomon's influence.

Solomon's religious authority is evidently certified in his authorship of at least three major writings of the accepted Bible cannon and his unshakable influence is felt in the Judeo-Christian tradition and throughout western culture. Curiously, a distinctly anti-Christian theology may be drawn from many of his most accepted teachings. While these notable contradictions could become a source of endless debate and conjecture, the true value of this discovery ought to remain in the realm of personal insight and awareness. The utmost discretion should be employed in the disclosure of these facts, since as with other Christ centered revelation the realization of this knowledge does not depend on the skill or invention of the informant, rather, it fully depends on the will of those who choose to accept the Christ-driven truth or not. Along with the body of evidence presented thus far in this treatise, there are no formal credentials attached, and so far, no substantial gain to be accumulated from the sharing.

One may, by right conclude that the combined evidence in this treatise is entirely false. One on the other hand, may see the virtue of the burden of proof thus far presented, and wonder how it went unnoticed. To this question the following explanation may be rendered.

Consider first that religion as a whole, from the beginning of time has gone through many changes. While modern society abounds with information, one's ability to process this information probably stayed unchanged since the beginning of time. What has changed in recent millenniums is that the world as a whole has emphasized a secular agenda to one's learning that has placed the world's spiritual development on a slow decline. Just centuries ago, wisdom derived from the Christian Church was carefully guarded and controlled by a mere handful of church leaders. Only within the last few centuries has the opportunity been presented that would allow authentic translations into the hands of ordinary citizens of the world.

On the theory of the swinging pendulum of conservative thinking verses liberal, a small window of opportunity may exist to take and grasp the intended spiritual truths of these more original translations before the world releases itself to the loose and augmented translations of scripture that will further degrade the world's spiritual development in an equal but opposite direction. Scripture's description of the day of Christ renders the assurance, "that day shall not come except there come a falling away first, and that man of sin be revealed, the son of perdition." (2 Thess 2 vs. 2) The possibility that just such a revelation is being rendered suggests that the time of Christ's return is eminent, and due diligence should be taken to lend credence to this likelihood.

Christ, the Beginning and the End

At the end of the spiritual struggle of life a remarkable awakening awaits where a pure spark of life may be witnessed in the world's primordial existence, and the absence of sin will becomes a sure reality. While all of creation is brought instep with God's goodness and praise, Jesus the one true Christ will remain unscathed by every dark and sinister plot, and the meek of the earth will at last be left to their promised inheritance. In the spirit of this inheritance a common thread of hope may be followed through the course of the gospels where the primal essence of this predestined nature can be witnessed firsthand. Though Christ's exhortations and preaching are included among the gospels with little interruption, the silent affirmation of a society baring the burden of civilization's slow advancement and awakening to the hope of a new unparalleled existence is evidently taking hold.

To this end the humble attributes of Christ are startlingly refreshing, the hope of one's spiritual calling is peaceable, and the affirmation of all created nature seems to give an account. The simplicity of the gospel is also in check in the realization that Christ himself was subject to the miraculous transformation that was about to occur, likely knowing down to the marrow of his bones, he gave a prophetic account of what was about to take place and made straightforward comments on the promise of the resurrection to those who would listen. The delicate nature of a mind that was fully human but also fully divine according to the divine purpose of his nature consistently showed sensitivity partial to his human side in the relationships he encountered. This, in turn, is an indication of the simple faith in humanity that inspired the massive following that was supported.

One example of Jesus' preaching that touches both the heart and minds of believers is Christ's invitation to "seek ye first the kingdom of God so that "his righteousness will be added unto you." To this nature Christ clearly sees the need of reckoning, since in and of one's self, one is ill-equipped to tap into the substance of creation that will eventually lead to a new glorious nature for Christ's faithful believers. For Jesus Christ and his followers the fact that Jesus himself was chosen for the honor of the crowning glory of all creation brings the utmost satisfaction. The mere fact that Christ stayed true to the goodness of his calling and remained obedient unto death is proof of his faithfulness. At the same token Christ was fully deserving of the honor bestowed upon him to become the substance of all things created. To this his gentle and pure existence was clearly supplanted into the delicate nature of all things that were created. (Col 1 vs. 16) To the reality of this honor, Jesus preaches contentment to the masses, according to his firsthand knowledge that all things were created with everyone's needs fully known.

Matthew 6 vs. 25

Therefore I say unto you, Take no thought for your life, what ye shall eat, or what ye shall drink; nor yet for your body, what ye shall put on. Is not the life more than meat, and the body than raiment?

26 Behold the fowls of the air: for they sow not, neither do they reap. nor gather into barns; yet your heavenly Father feedeth them. Are ye not much better than they?

28 And why take ye thought for raiment? Consider the lilies of the field, how they grow; they toil not neither do they spin:

29 And yet I say unto you, That even Solomon in all his glory was not arrayed as one of these.

30 Wherefore, if God so clothe the grass of the field, which to day is, and tomorrow is caste into the oven, shall he not much more clothe you, O ye of little faith?

31 Therefore take no thought saying, What shall we eat? or What shall we drink? or Wherewithal shall we be clothed?

32 (For after all these things do the Gentiles seek) for your heavenly Father knoweth that ye have need of these things.

33 But seek ye first the kingdom of God, and his righteousness and all these things shall be added unto you.

The righteousness of Christ is sealed up in the mystery of his resurrection, so that the nature of all things is well represented in this high calling. Though Christ's goodness is garnered in a lowliness of heart, Solomon's own glory, as favorable as it was, cannot compare to the honor that God bestowed to his only son Jesus Christ. From the platform of Christ's prolific teachings the early church was enjoined with a profound sense of value deeply connected with the intimate bounds of creation. For those who are set to awake to the same supernatural promise all worldly distraction is greatly outmatched by one's tangible participation in the coming promise of Christ's glory.

NOTES

Chapter I

The Truth About The Resurrection (Pg. 3)

1 Jn. 13 vs. 23; 19 vs. 26; 20 vs. 2; 21 vs. 7, 20-24 (**John, Jesus' beloved disciple. **)

2 Michael Grant, JESUS AN HISTORIAN'S REVIEW OF THE GOSPELS Michael Grant Publications Ltd 1977 PG 46

(**Qumran**)

3 Michael Grant, JESUS AN HISTORIAN'S REVIEW OF THE GOSPELS Michael Grant Publications Ltd 1977 pg 18

(**The Essenes and the Kingdom of God**)

4 Michael Grant, JESUS AN HISTORIAN'S REVIEW OF THE GOSPELS Michael Grant Publications Ltd 1977 pg 151

(**The Sadducees authority at the Temple**)

The Anointed Christ (Pg. 4)

5 (**The anointing of sacred articles**) (Clothes) Ex. 24 vs. 21, 20-22 (alter) Ex. 29 vs. 36 (The Tent of meeting/ The Tabernacle/ Ark of Testimony) Ex. 30 vs. 26

A Truly 'Prophetic Revelation' (Pg.11)

6 William B. Eerdman, THE EERDMAN'S BIBLE DICTIONARY Wm. B. Eerdman. Wm. B. Eerdman's Publishing Co. 1987 (See 'Satan')

The Seal Of God (Pg. 18)

7 Fleming H. Revell Company, THE GLOBAL CONCISE BIBLE DICTIONARY Global Christian Publishers 1999

(**God's Seal**)

Beyond Death's Barrier (Pg. 20)

8 Fleming H. Revell Company, THE GLOBAL CONCISE BIBLE DICTIONARY Global Christian Publishers 1999

(**The Book of Job**)

Chapter II

'Types' and 'Shadows' of The Anti-Christ (Pg. 28)

1 Fleming H. Revell Company, THE GLOBAL CONCISE BIBLE DICTIONARY Global Christian Publishers 1999

(**The ordinance of sacrifice**) pg. 482- 483

The Mystery of Lawlessness (Pg. 31)

2 James Strong, LL. D., S.T.D., THE NEW STRONG'S EXPANDED DICTIONARY OF BIBLE WORDS James Strong, LL. D., S.T.D. Thomas Nelson Publishers 2001 Global Christian Publishers 1999 (**'Satan' as a proper name**) pg. 844 7854 (5) (Satan)

William B. Eerdman, THE EERDMAN'S BIBLE DICTIONARY Wm. B. Eerdman. Wm. B. Eerdman's Publishing Co. 1987 (See 'Satan')

3 (**'Satan' as one who blocked 'the way'**)

4 (**'Satan' as the 'accuser of mankind'**)

Chapter III

The Peace Offering (Pg. 51)

1 Michael Grant, JESUS AN HISTORIAN'S REVIEW OF THE GOSPELS Michael Grant Publications Ltd 1977 pg 146-147

(**The Sadducees originating from Zadok and Solomon's priestly order**)

The Doctrine of 'Demons' (Pg. 55)

2 Wm. B. Eerdman, THE INTERNATIONAL STANDARD BIBLE ENCYCLOPEDIA Volume Three; D-E 1956 pg 70-72

James Strong, LL. D., S.T.D., THE NEW STRONG'S EXPANDED DICTIONARY OF BIBLE WORDS James Strong, LL. D., S.T.D. Thomas Nelson Publishers 2001 pg 1030 1140 (daimonion) (**Demonology and the practice of idol worship**)

3 Wm. B. Eerdman, THE INTERNATIONAL STANDARD BIBLE ENCYCLOPEDIA Volume One; A 1956 pg 375 (**Azazel**)

Idol Worship (Pg. 58)

4 Fleming H. Revell Company, THE GLOBAL CONCISE BIBLE DICTIONARY Global Christian Publishers 1999

(**'Asaph the psalmist**)

Chapter IV

Baal Worship (Pg. 64-65)

1 Fleming H. Revell Company, THE GLOBAL CONCISE BIBLE DICTIONARY Global Christian Publishers 1999 pg 69 paragraphs 1,2

(**Agricultural based Model**)

2 Abraham H. Maslow, BRITANICA CONCISE ENCYCLOPEDIA 2004 (**Maslow's Heirarchy of Needs**)

Wm. B. Eerdman, THE INTERNATIONAL STANDARD BIBLE ENCYCLOPEDIA Volume Two; B-C 1956 (Pg. 1)

3 (**self-serving tendency of worship**)

4 (**Baal's many names and the meanings**)

The 'Queen of heaven' (Ashtoreth) (Pg. 67)

William B. Eerdman, THE EERDMAN'S BIBLE DICTIONARY Wm. B. Eerdman. Wm. B. Eerdman's Publishing Co. 1987

(See Ashtoreth)

5 (**Ashtoreth's tie with Canaan and Phoenicia**)

6 (**Ashtoreth, consort to Baal**)

7 (**Ashtoreth, goddess of love and sensual pleasure**)

8 (**Ashtoreth of the 'two horns'**)

9 (**Ashtoreth, meaning of the name**)

10 (**Ashtoreth, illustration**)

'Molech' king of Shame (Pg. 69)

11 Fleming H. Revell Company, THE GLOBAL CONCISE BIBLE DICTIONARY Global Christian Publishers 1999 pg 69 paragraphs 1,2 (**Molech, meaning of the name**)

Milcom 'god of the Amorites' (Pg. 69)

Wm. B. Eerdman, THE INTERNATIONAL STANDARD BIBLE ENCYCLOPEDIA Volume One; A 1956 (See Ammonites) pg 111

James Strong, LL. D., S.T.D., THE NEW STRONG'S EXPANDED DICTIONARY OF BIBLE WORDS James Strong, LL. D., S.T.D. Thomas Nelson Publishers 2001 Global Christian Publishers 1999

pg 611 4445 (Milcom)

12 **Milcom vs. Molech, names and meanings**)

Chemosh and the 'High Places' (Pg. 71-72)

13 Fleming H. Revell Company, THE GLOBAL CONCISE BIBLE DICTIONARY Global Christian Publishers 1999 pg 274 (**The origin of 'High places'**)

14 Wm. B. Eerdman, THE INTERNATIONAL STANDARD BIBLE ENCYCLOPEDIA Volume One; A 1956 pg 317 (**Asherah, ritual worship**)

15 Wm. B. Eerdman, THE INTERNATIONAL STANDARD BIBLE ENCYCLOPEDIA Volume One; A 1956 pg 264 (**High places to Chemosh**)

Tophet and the Lake of Fire (Pg. 72-75)

16 Fleming H. Revell Company, THE GLOBAL CONCISE BIBLE DICTIONARY Global Christian Publishers 1999 pg 537 (**Tophet, high place to Molech for child sacrifice. geographic location**)

17 Wm. B. Eerdman, THE INTERNATIONAL STANDARD BIBLE ENCYCLOPEDIA Volume Four; F-G 1956 pg 157 (**Gehenna, Hell, the lake of fire**)

The Provocation (Pg. 75)

Tuvia Sagiv, PENETRATING INSIGHTS INTO THE TEMPLE MOUNT (page 2-3)

18 (**The image of Jealousy that faces North**)

19 (**Pentagonal structures**)

20 (**Strato's Tower**)

21 (**Chalcolithic Period**)

The Secret Room (Pg. 77)

Tuvia Sagiv, PENETRATING INSIGHTS INTO THE TEMPLE MOUNT (page 3)

22 (**Infrared imaging**)

23 (**Ancient stairwell, existence of**)

24 (**Possible burial site**)

Chapter IV

Weeping for Tammuz (Pg. 79)

Fleming H. Revell Company, THE GLOBAL CONCISE BIBLE DICTIONARY Global Christian Publishers 1999 pg 633

25 (**Husband to Ishtar (Tammuz)**)

26 (**Type of Worship**)

Chapter V

The 'Vineyard' (Pg. 84)

William B. Eerdman, THE EERDMAN'S BIBLE DICTIONARY Wm. B. Eerdman. Wm. B. Eerdman's Publishing company

1987 (See 'Shulamite')

1 (**Canaanite fertility rites**) James Strong, LL. D., S.T.D., THE NEW STRONG'S EXPANDED DICTIONARY OF BIBLE WORDS

James Strong, LL. D., S.T.D. Thomas Nelson Publishers 2001 Global

Christian Publishers 1999 pg 506 3041 (Jedidiah)

2 (**Jedidiah, beloved**)

Seasonal Overtones (Pg. 90)

Fleming H. Revell Company, THE GLOBAL CONCISE BIBLE DICTIONARY Global Christian Publishers 1999 pg 633

3 (**Husband to Ishtar (Tammuz)**)

4 (**Seasonal changes**)

The 'Shulamite' (Pg. 92)

William B. Eerdman, THE EERDMAN'S BIBLE DICTIONARY Wm. B. Eerdman. Wm. B. Eerdman's Publishing Co. 1987 (See 'Shulimite')

5 (**The name selomoh**) Fleming H. Revell Company, THE GLOBAL CONCISE BIBLE DICTIONARY Global Christian Publishers 1999 pg 633

6 (**Ishtar as both sister and spouse to Tammuz**)

The Primordial waters (Pg. 95)

7 Wm. B. Eerdman, THE INTERNATIONAL STANDARD BIBLE ENCYCLOPEDIA Volume Four; F-G 1956 pg 201 (**The spring of Gihon**)

Chapter V

The Song of Solomon Chapter V (Pg. 96)

8 Fleming H. Revell Company, THE GLOBAL CONCISE BIBLE DICTIONARY Global Christian Publishers 1999 pg 166 (**Defilement in the context of Idolotry**)

The Song of Solomon Chapter VI (Pg. 98)

Fleming H. Revell Company, THE GLOBAL CONCISE BIBLE DICTIONARY Global Christian Publishers 1999pg 58

9 (**The statue of Artemis of Ephesus**)

10 (**Greek fused with near eastern cults**)

11 (**Idol production modeled after Ashtoreth**)

12 Wm. B. Eerdman, THE INTERNATIONAL STANDARD BIBLE ENCYCLOPEDIA Volume One; A 1956 pg 320 (**Ashtoreth, goddess of war in Assyria**)

13 (fig 1 (a) http://www.livius.org/a/turkey/ephesus_artemis_selcuk.JPG (**Statue of Artemis with goats ascending from the hair**)

14 Michael Jordan, CULTS Prophecies,Practices, & Personalities Text copyright c Michael Jordan 1996pg 26

(**Deer sacred animal of Artemis**)

William B. Eerdman, THE EERDMAN'S BIBLE DICTIONARY Wm. B. Eerdman. Wm. B. Eerdman's Publishing Co. 1987 (See Ashtoreth)

15 (**The evening and the morning star**)

16 (**Ashtoreth depicted with a beard**)

The Song of Solomon Chapter VII (Pg. 100)

17 Fleming H. Revell Company, THE GLOBAL CONCISE BIBLE DICTIONARY Global Christian Publishers 1999pg 367 (**Mandrake as an 'Aphrodisiac', devil's apple**)

New Testament References to 'The Vineyard' (pg 103)

18 Michael Grant, JESUS AN HISTORIAN"S REVIEW OF THE GOSPELS Michael Grant Publications Ltd 1977 pg 151

(**The Sadducees authority at the Temple**)

Chapter VI

The Sons of Belial (Pg. 107)

James Strong, LL. D., S.T.D., THE NEW STRONG'S EXPANDED DICTIONARY OF BIBLE WORDS James Strong, LL. D., S.T.D. Thomas Nelson Publishers 2001 Global Christian Publishers 1999 pg 307 1100 (Belial)

1 (**Sons of 'Belial'**)

2 Fleming H. Revell Company, THE GLOBAL CONCISE BIBLE DICTIONARY Global Christian Publishers 1999 pg 85 (**Beliar, Lord of the forest**)

The Seeds of Judgment (Pg. 114)

3 Michael Grant, JESUS AN HISTORIAN"S REVIEW OF THE GOSPELS Michael Grant Publications Ltd 1977 pg 146-147

A Prophecy Fulfilled (Pg. 116)

4 Wm. B. Eerdman, THE INTERNATIONAL STANDARD BIBLE ENCYCLOPEDIA Volume One; A 1956 pg 85 (**Triangulated peace between Israel, Syria, and Judah**)

Chapter VII

The Anointing of Elijah (Pg. 126)

1 Michael Grant, JESUS AN HISTORIAN'S REVIEW OF THE

GOSPELS Michael Grant Publications Ltd 1977 pg 46
(**Qumran/ proximity to John's place of preaching**)
2 Wm. B. Eerdman,THE INTERNATIONAL STANDARD BIBLE ENCYCLOPEDIA Volume Three;D-E 1956 pg215
(**Elijah and Moses**)
James Strong, LL. D., S.T.D., THE NEW STRONG'S EXPANDED DICTIONARY OF BIBLE WORDS James Strong, LL. D., S.T.D.
Thomas Nelson Publishers 2001 Global Christian Publishers 1999
3 (**Mosheh, Moses**) pg 6374872 (Mosheh)
God Has 'Heard' (Pg. 132)
4 (**Shama. Simeon**)pg 861 8085 (Shuma)
The Valley of The Shadow of Death (Pg. 134)
5 (**Yowm.Day**) pg 551
3117 (Day)
Job's Anointing (Pg. 135)
Fleming H. Revell Company, THE GLOBAL CONCISE BIBLE DICTIONARY Global Christian Publishers 1999pg633
6 (**leviathan**)
7 James Strong, LL. D., S.T.D., THE NEW STRONG'S EXPANDED DICTIONARY OF BIBLE WORDS James Strong, LL. D., S.T.D.Thomas Nelson Publishers 2001 Global Christian Publishers 1999
(**livyathan leviathan**) pg 573 3882 (leviathan)

Chapter VIII

Eliakim son of Hilkiah (Pg. 146)
1 Fleming H. Revell Company, THE GLOBAL CONCISE BIBLE DICTIONARY Global Christian Publishers 1999
(**Hezekiah's reforms**) pg. 273
2 (**Hezekiah's tunnel**)

3 Tuvia Sagiv, PENETRATING INSIGHTS INTO THE TEMPLE MOUNT (page 3) (**Possible burial site**)
Asaph the Temple Gatekeeper (Pg. 152)
4 Wm. B. Eerdman, THE INTERNATIONAL STANDARD BIBLE ENCYCLOPEDIA Volume One; A 1956 pg 309 (**Asaph's prophetic gift**)

Chapter IX

An Ancient Landmark (Pg. 165)

Wm. B. Eerdman, THE INTERNATIONAL STANDARD BIBLE ENCYCLOPEDIA Volume One; F-G 1956 pg 201

1 (**Gihon, ancient irrigation ditch**)

2 (**Gihon, ancient spring sacred in Jerusalem**)

3 (**Gihon, Solomon drinking at his coronation**)

James Strong, LL. D., S.T.D., THE NEW STRONG'S EXPANDED DICTIONARY OF BIBLE WORDS James Strong, LL. D., S.T.D. Thomas Nelson Publishers 2001 Global Christian Publishers 1999

4 (**Shiloah, Shiloah**) pg 231

7975 (Shiloah)

The Spring Of 'Gihon' (Pg. 167)

5 William B. Eerdman, THE EERDMAN'S BIBLE DICTIONARY

Wm. B. Eerdman. Wm. B. Eerdman's Publishing Co. 1987

(See 'Map')

New Testament Accounts (Pg. 171)

Wm. B. Eerdman, THE INTERNATIONAL STANDARD BIBLE ENCYCLOPEDIA Volume One; B-C 1956 pg 91

6 (**The pool of Bethesda**)

Chapter X

Diana of Ephesus (Pg. 180)

1 Fleming H. Revell Company, THE GLOBAL CONCISE BIBLE DICTIONARY Global Christian Publishers 1999pg 58 (**Popularity and spread of the worship of Artemis 600 B.C.**)

2 Michael Jordan, CULTS Prophecies,Practices, & Personalities Text copyright c Michael Jordan 1996pg 26 (**Artemis of Ephesus, one of the seven ancient wonders**)

3 Fleming H. Revell Company, THE GLOBAL CONCISE BIBLE DICTIONARY Global Christian Publishers 1999pg 58 (**Artemis of Ephesus modeled after Ashtoreth**)

4 Fleming H. Revell Company, THE GLOBAL CONCISE BIBLE DICTIONARY Global Christian Publishers 1999pg 58 (**Photo of idol, Artemis of Ephesus**)

5 (fig 1 (a) http://www.livius.org/a/turkey/ephesus_artemis_selcuk.JPG (**Statue of Artemis with goats ascending from the hair**)

Michael Jordan, CULTS Prophecies,Practices, & Personalities Text copyright c Michael Jordan 1996pg 26

6 (**Most famous Ephesus Temple, Built around 600 B.C.**)

7 (**Roman Sanctuary of Dianna on the Aventine**)

Developments at Asia Minor (Pg. 182-184)

8 Wm. B. Eerdman, THE INTERNATIONAL STANDARD BIBLE ENCYCLOPEDIA Volume One; A 1956 (See Asia Minor) pg 325 (**The foothold of Jewish dispersion to Asia minor 546 B.C.**)

Michael Jordan, CULTS Prophecies, Practices, & Personalities Text copyright c Michael Jordan 1996

9 (**Onset of the Cybeline cult at 800 B.C.**) pg 20

10 (**Meteorite as a sacred icon to Cybele at Phrygia**) pg 21

11 (**Mithraism, initiation similar to Cybeline cult**) pg 31

12 Philip Carrington Archbishop of Quebec, THE EARLY CHRISTIAN CHURCH VOLUME II THE SECOND CHRISTIAN CENTURY Cambridge At The University Press 1957 pg 175

(**Melito and Old Testament books reviewed by Rabbis at Jamnia**)

13 Philip Carrington Archbishop of Quebec, THE EARLY CHRISTIAN CHURCH VOLUME I THE FIRST CHRISTIAN CENTURY Cambridge At The University Press 1957 pg 428

(**Rabbi Akiba speaking in Jamnia in favor of including Cant.**

Philip Carrington Archbishop of Quebec, THE EARLY CHRISTIAN CHURCH VOLUME II THE SECOND CHRISTIAN CENTURY Cambridge At The University Press 1957

14 (**Melito's writings second century fragment**) pg 178

15 (**Constantine, not initially Baptized**) pg 480

16 (**Constantine, presiding at the council of Nicea**)"

17 (**The venerable day of the sun**) " Father Michael Collins & Matthew A. Price, THE STORY OF CHRISTIANITY Oxford University Press 1999

18 (**Fall of Rome to the Goths in 410 A.D.**) pg 70

19 (**Fall of Constantinople to the Turks in 1453**) pg 76

Succession into the Modern age (Pg. 184)

Michael Jordan, CULTS Prophecies,Practices, & Personalities Text copyright c Michael Jordan 1996

20 (**Order of St. John**) pg 42

21 (**The rank of 'Knight'**) "
22 (**Accumulation of corporate wealth**) "
23 (**Edward II, confiscating the wealth**) "
Development of the Freemasons (Pg. 185)
Michael Jordan, CULTS Prophecies,Practices, & Personalities Text copyright c Michael Jordan 1996
24 (**Templar knights dispanded in 1312 A.D.**) pg 43
25 (**Rosicrucian link to alchemy**) "
26 (**Origins via Christian Rosenkreutz**) "
27 (**Gaining in popularity**) "
28 (**Sir Thomas Dunkerly**) "
Development of the Freemasons (Pg. 185)
rapidnet.com (Freemasonry Christian or Antichristian)
29 (**The English constitution of Freemasonry**) pg 1
Masonic Preoccupation with with 'Lucifer' (Pg. 186)
Freemasonry watch.org/site Quotations Written by High Level Masons Praising Lucifer, The Taxil Hoax Canard Refuted
30 (**Frequent references to Lucifer by high level Masons**) pg 4
31 (**Writing samples dedicated to Lucifer**) pg 4
rapidnet.com Freemasonry Proven to Worship Lucifer
32 (**Symbolism, Tradition of (Carl Claudy)**) pg 2
33 (**Phoenix, (William Schnoebelen Satan's door revisited**) pg 4
34 (**Seal of Solomon**) pg 2
freemasonry watch.org/site Quotations Written by High Level Masons Praising Lucifer, The Taxil Hoax Canard Refuted
35 (**Sovereign Grand Commander Albert Pike 33 degree Letter to Italian Grand Master Guiseppie Mazzini 33 degree 15th August 1871, Archives British Museum London**) pg 9
The 'Hellfire' Clubs' (Pg. 188)
Michael Jordan, CULTS Prophecies,Practices, & Personalities Text copyright c Michael Jordan 1996
36 (**Sir Francis Dashwood**) pg 88
37 (**Venus worship**) "
The 'Wiccan' Religion (Pg. 189)
Michael Jordan, CULTS Prophecies,Practices, & Personalities Text copyright c Michael Jordan 1996
38 (**Gerald Gardner's connection to the Rosicrucians**)pg 52
39 (**Wiccan rejection of Satan**) "

40 (**Wiccan beliefs**) "
universalclass.com inc. OCULTOPEDIA SPIRITUAL STUDIES
41 (**King Solomon** pg 1
The Bible's Teaching on 'Witchcraft' (Pg. 191)
Michael Jordan, CULTS Prophecies,Practices, & Personalities Text copyright c Michael Jordan 1996
42 (**Basic Tenet of Wicca**) pg 52
43 (**Fraudulent Mediums Act**) "
The Hermetic Order of the Golden Dawn (Pg. 194)
Michael Jordan, CULTS Prophecies,Practices, & Personalities Text copyright c Michael Jordan 1996
44 (**Hermetic Order of the Golden Dawn**) pg 90
45 (**Crowley's aversion to Christianity as a youth**) pg 46
46 (**Satanic affiliation**)pg 90
47 (**Crowley's Basic tenet of Satanism (Aleister Crowley Liber Al vel Legis**) "
freemasonry watch.org/site Quotations Written by High Level Masons Praising Lucifer, The Taxil Hoax Canard Refuted
48 (**Hymn to Lucifer**) pg 10
Michael Jordan, CULTS Prophecies,Practices, & Personalities Text copyright c Michael Jordan 1996
49 (**Crowley's death /addiction to heroin**) pg 91

Chapter XI

The 'Morning' Star (Pg. 204)
Fleming H. Revell Company, THE GLOBAL CONCISE BIBLE DICTIONARY Global Christian Publishers 1999
1 (**Leviathan**) pg 350
2 (**Lucifer 'The morning star'**) pg 359
3 James Strong, LL. D., S.T.D., THE NEW STRONG'S EXPANDED DICTIONARY OF BIBLE WORDS James Strong, LL. D., S.T.D. Thomas Nelson Publishers 2001 Global Christian Publishers 1999 (**'Lucifer 'meaning of the name'**) pg. 428
1966 (Lucifer)
The 'Angels' (Pg. 208) encyclopedia.thefreedictionary.com/Fallen%20 angel (Fallen Angel)

4 (**Traditional folklore surrounding 'Lucifer'**) pg 2

The War in Heaven (Pg. 212) encyclopedia.thefreedictionary.com/Fallen%20 angel

(Fallen Angel)

5 (**Theory of Origen Of Alexandria** pg 2

6 (**Fallen angels taking human form**) pg 2

Angelic Worship (Pg. 216) sarahsarchangels.com/archangels/9orders.html

(The Nine orders of Angels)

7 (**Three Choirs of heavenly worship**) pg 1

Chapter XII

Popular Myths (Pg. 225)

1 THE HOLY BIBLE New International Version Zondervan Publishing Houseext copyright 1989,pg 1336

2 Michael Grant, JESUS AN HISTORIAN"S REVIEW OF THE GOSPELS Michael Grant Publications Ltd 1977 pg 151

(**The Sadducees authority at the Temple**)

Solomon's Authorship (Pg. 234)

www.brainyencyclopedia.com Brainy Encyclopedia (Later Legend)

3 (**approximately 'eight' books attributed to Solomon**) pg 3

4 (**letters Solomon/ Egypt / Tyre / Eupolemus**) pg 3

Illustrations

Solomon's Temple (artist's rendition) www.usm.maine.edu/~maps/exhibit1/theme3.html pg 80

(model lay-out) www.templemount.org/solomon.html pg 80

Engedi garden habitat (artist's rendition) www.antiquemapsandprints.com/SCANSB/b-1882.jpg pg 81

High place to Molech (photo) www.angelfire.com/oh5/bibhom/molech.html pg 81

Ishtar of Assyria (photo) www.mingyuen.edu.hk/history/1baby/17nimrud/06nimrud-genie-2.htm

pg 81

Artemis of Ephesus (photo (fig 1a)) www.livius.org/a/turkey/ephesus/ephesus_artemis_selcuk.JPG pg 105

(photo (fig 1b)) www.senkrontours.com/st58details.asp pg 106
Spring of Gihon (photo) http://alpha.furman.edu/~mcknight/jer9B.htm pg 199
Hezekiah's Tunnel (photo) http://cc.cumberlandcollege.edu/acad/rel/hbible/HebrewBible/images/HTbig.gif pg 199
Ephesus (photo) www.trikeit.co.uk/be_lon/photos.html pg 200
Phoenix (artist's rendition) www.cs.toronto.edu/~cosmin/pngtech/8bpp.html pg 200
Seal of Solomon (photo (stone))
www.4dw.net/royalark/Ethiopia/orders.htm pg 201
Map of Asia Minor www.jesuschristsavior.net/Land.jpeg pg 202

Glossary of Terms

ANOINTING. The spiritual choosing of God of an individual or thing symbolized by the act of anointing with oil as a ceremonial rite of individuals and or articles purposed for the process of worship.

ANTI-CHRIST. An existing force and state of being that may be traced to the original source of God's anointing and favour, unnaturally used to oppose and conceal the truth.

CHALCOLITHIC PERIOD. The period between the late fifth and late fourth millennia BCE (approximately 4300-3300 BCE) designated by the advancement in the technologies of metal.

CHRIST. The anointed savior designated by God for fulfilling the unique purposes of his will for the salvation of mankind.

CHRIST'S SONSHIP. Jesus Christ, God's only Son, born of God, and declared to be God's son according to the spirit of holiness by the resurrection from the dead. (Rom. 1 vs. 4) By virtue of a miraculous transformation that transcends time.

DEFILEMENT. The spiritual consequence and stigmatizing quality produced by sin and, or the act of becoming ceremonially unclean as a result.

DOCTRINE OF DEMONS. The ritual practice of idol worship recognizing and theorizing over the spiritual sanctification of animals for demonic influence.

ESSENCES. A community of Jewish ascetics known to exist in the second century BCE neighbouring the Dead sea who traditionally followed a strict code of religious conduct.

EXISTENTIALISM. The philosophical belief in the exclusive power of self-determination.

GENERATIVITY. The ability and propensity to pass on knowledge and wisdom.

MASLOW'S HIERARCHY OF NEEDS. The theory of Abraham Maslow formulated on the evidence that human beings are motivated by unsatisfied needs at varying degrees and levels.

OBLIGATIONS OF KINGLY RULE. The legal and moral obligations stipulated for kingly rule according to Hebrew law laid out in Deuteronomy. (Deut. 17 vs. 14-19)

PEACE OFFERING. A conditional offering of thanksgiving and free will often involving a vow.

PREEMINENCE. The state of being placed first in priority as well as chronologically first in power of influence as a result of the transforming power of God's spirit and Christ's resurrection.

PROPHET. God's anointed servants, subject to a supernatural protection based on God's divine purpose, with a revealed awareness of Christ's ministry and resurrection.

THE PROVOCATION. The method and practice whereby individuals made a deliberate effort to provoke God by various forms of disobedience in an attempt to make God go far from the Temple. (Ez. 8 vs. 6)

RESURRECTION. The transformation and reanimation of a living being into a new heavenly nature that bestows a new plain of existence, to which Jesus Christ is identified as a living example.

ROCK OF THE ANTI-CHRIST. The imitation of Christ's pre-eminent nature in the form of Satan's original attempts to oppose men's forthcoming salvation, beginning with the serpent in the Garden of Eden.

SADDUCEES. A group of religious authorities known to exist at the time of Christ who probably descended from Zadok, (Solomon's appointed high priest) and consistently rejected the notion of a coming resurrection and, or afterlife

SANCTIFICATION. The appointment of God's anointing and favour provided to facilitate safe passage in the attainment of the resurrection of the righteous.

SANHEDRIN. The high court of the Jewish authority comprised of a group known as the Sadducees, (probably descended from Zadok, the high priest appointed by Solomon) and known to exist at the time of Christ.

SEAL OF GOD. The spiritual sign that the miraculous nature of God's divine wisdom has been revealed to an individual.

SELF-ACTUALIZATION. The ability and fulfillment of one's spiritual self.

SIN OFFERING. A mandatory offering made for the atonement of sin fulfilled by Christ's sacrificial death on the cross.

TYPES AND SHADOWS. An ordinance of active duty towards God that by it's nature fittingly symbolizes a character or personality written about in scripture.

WORD OF PROPHECY. The generative design of God's word, which includes a rite of passage whereby Christ is identified as the Son of God through the revelation of his transformed glory and resurrection.

Printed in the United States
68551LVS00003B/67-81

9 781424 121786